Stanley W[illegible] days after the assassination of Maha[illegible]rs to Rama*, his novel about that fateful event, was filmed in [illegible] and translated into nine languages but has been banned in India for more than a quarter of a century. Wolpert is the author of fourteen books, including *A New History of India*, now in its third edition; *Jinnah of Pakistan* a life of the founder of Pakistan; *Tilak and Gokhale*; and a life of Zulfikar Ali Bhutto called *Zulfi Bhutto of Pakistan*. He teaches at the University of California, Los Angeles.

AN INTRODUCTION TO INDIA

Stanley Wolpert

PENGUIN BOOKS

Penguin Books India (P) Ltd., 11 Community Centre, Panchsheel Park, New Delhi 110017, India
Penguin Books Ltd., 80 Strand, London WC2R 0RL, UK
Penguin Putnam Inc., 375 Hudson Street, New York, NY 10014, USA
Penguin Books Australia Ltd., 250 Camberwell Road, Camberwell, Victoria 3124, Australia
Penguin Books Canada Ltd., 10 Alcorn Avenue, Suite 300, Toronto, Ontario M4V 3B2, Canada
Penguin Books (NZ) Ltd., Cnr Rosedale and Airborne Roads, Albany, Auckland, New Zealand

First published in the US by the University of California Press 1991
Published in India by Viking 1991
Published in Penguin Books 1994

10 9 8 7 6

Made and Printed in India by Swapna Printing Works Pvt. Ltd.

for my son

A D A M

Compassionate Artist

Contents

FOUR
Society
117

FIVE
Arts and Sciences
157

SIX
Polity and Foreign Policy
199

Preface

All of us, who wear cotton cloth, use the decimal system, enjoy the taste of chicken, play chess or roll dice, and seek peace of mind or tranquility through meditation, are indebted to India. Surprisingly few Americans, however, have much more than a superficial understanding of India's great, deep-rooted Civilization, or of the causes of her complex modern problems and recurring conflicts. In this book I have tried to unveil India's ancient–modern profile and body politic, stripping away enough, I hope, to reveal her remarkable beauty, but without hiding her scars, painful wounds, or deep erosions and natural damage wrought by Time.

My own lifelong romance with India began more than four decades ago, when I first visited the bustling ports of Bombay and Calcutta in the immediate aftermath of the British withdrawal and Partition, the dawn of India's independent incarnation. I have since returned many times, for the last decade at least once a year. For thirty-two years I have taught Indian history at UCLA, and remain a student of that fascinating subcontinent we call South Asia. For richer and poorer, then, in sickness and in health, I have merged my own brief existence with India's timeless tide, seeking to fathom that unique "River" as I move along, without drowning in its swift currents or bottomless depths.

Most of what I know about India I have learned from wise gurus and kind friends, all of whom I thank for the wisdom they have shared with me, absolving them, however, of any responsibility for my own errors of understanding or analysis. My karmic debts are so many that I may forget to acknowledge some of my most important teachers, so to those unnamed guides

I apologize. To W. Norman Brown, who taught me my first Sanskrit shlokas, my special thanks. To Holden Furber, who taught me more critically to examine all sources of History, equal thanks.

To A. L. Basham, Stella Kramrisch, Ernest Bender, Norman Palmer, Hester Lambert, Sir Cyril Henry Philips, Shiela Gujral, Raghavan Iyer, Justice R. S. Narula, Madhu and Gopi Mehta, Piloo and Vina Mody, Bish Pandey, Z. H. Zaidi, Neemai Sadan Bose, Chhote Bharany, M. N. Das, B. R. Nanda, Dr. Karan Singh, Prakash Kaul, Krishna Rasgotra, Ravi and Shiela Kalia, Patwant Singh, Surjit Mansingh, Pratapaditya Pal, Indira Nalin, Prakash Tandon, Shankar Bajpai, Keval Singh, Milon and Anita Banerji, Rajni Kothari, Bhiku Parekh, Nirad C. Chaudhuri, Jerry and Joyce Hundel, Ved Mehta, B. B. Misra, S. Chandrasekhar, Dr. and Mrs. A. S. Marwah, Firoze and Silloo Dordi, Tapan Raychaudhuri, Rita Dar, Inder Singh, and R. K. Narayan, C. R. Gharekhan, and P. N. Chopra, I am deeply indebted for many gifts of erudition.

So many Indian families have "adopted" us that I always feel At Home when visiting India. I thank our dear friends, Madhukar Shah and Tunni, their Royal Parents and beautiful children, all of whom have been more than kind to Dorothy and myself, and to Daniel and Debra, as well as Adam and Joy, whenever we barge in on them in Delhi. Through Madhukar I came to know his kind uncles, Raja Dinesh Singh and Dr. Nagendra Singh, and their gracious Maharanis. Justice Dr. Nagendra Singh's sudden death two years ago deprived the World Court as well as India of one of its greatest jurists. Pama and Sunanda Patwardhan remain our first and dearest friends, our Pune neighbors at least one incarnation ago, although now they live in Madras. Pama's eldest brother, Rao Sahib Patwardhan, epitomized India's strength and wisdom, a valued member of Jawaharlal Nehru's Congress Working Committee and a patron to Vinoba Bhave, Mahatma Gandhi's foremost disciple. Our dearest Bombay friends are Bala and Bhanu Sar Desai, whose lovely daughters, like themselves, personify modern India at its best. My Indian Brother, Vishnu A. Narain of Patna, died just a few years ago, before I could visit his home in that ancient Mauryan capital, and for me he will always remain the exemplar of India's gentle sweetness and silent suffering strength.

I first reached India just a few days after Mahatma Gandhi was assassinated, and on my first day ashore took the *darshan* of watching one-seventh of his ashes sprinkled on the waters off Bombay from Malabar Hill. A decade later, on my thirtieth birthday, I walked with Vinobaji, and shortly before and after that met with Prime Minister Jawaharlal Nehru and his daughter. I had the good fortune of meeting Mr. Nehru several more times before his death, and have always admired him as one of India's wisest and noblest leaders, and a brilliant master of the English language. Vinoba Bhave, of course, was India's "Walking Saint," and his stooped, spare, barefoot skeleton has always reminded me of India's most impoverished peasantry and the harshness of their daily struggle, and the uplifting power of their faith. Over the ensuing decades I have been privileged to meet with, interview, and come to know many other great leaders of modern India, and more of her unsung yet equally heroic children. From Lord Louis Mountbatten, I relearned that one needn't have been born in India to fall under her ineffable spell.

From Madame Vijaya Lakshmi Pandit, one of India's most brilliant and beautiful daughters, I learned much about Mahatma Gandhi's persuasive powers, as well as those of her brother Jawaharlal. From Prime Ministers Indira Gandhi and Morarji Desai I learned of the pitfalls and evanescence of power. From gentle Jaya Prakash Narayan, spiritual Father of the Janata movement, I learned the singular strength of weakness and the potency of Principle. From my wise old friend, Foreign Minister Inder K. Gujral, I have learned the supreme virtue of patience and goodwill. Thanks to my young friend Minister Maneka Gandhi, I have come to admire the selfless idealism and courage of India's youthful leadership. Each time I hear my friend Ravi Shankar play his sitar, I relearn the magic of Indian music at its best. Whenever I meet with my friends Khushwant Singh or R. K. Narayan, or read one of their many fine books, I better appreciate the genius of Indian literature and the charms of its modern masters. From my dear Indian students, too many of them to name, I have learned optimism and hope for a better future. I thank all of them for those priceless gifts.

India is my attempt to repay, in small measure, these karmic debts I have acquired in forty-two years. I have tried in this book to distill the essence of all I have learned and believe to be true about India and her Civilization.

I am most grateful to the University of California Press for so beautifully producing *India*. My special thanks and appreciation to Stan Holwitz, who lured me Home, and to Shirley Warren and Rebecca Frazier, artist

Cheryl Carrington, and Cathy Hertz, my splendid India-hand copy editor. I thank my dear friend, Dr. Sy Greenstone, for his beautiful photographs of India.

Finally, to the co-Author of my life in all of its good works, dear Dorothy, thanks again for never giving up on this one, and much Love.

S. W.

Los Angeles
April 1990

Postscript:

Grandlove and thanks to dearest Daniel and Debra for our first grandchild, Samuel Elliot Wolpert, born on May 21, 1990.

S. W.

June 1990

The Environment

Thou art the ruler of the minds of all people,
Thou Dispenser of India's destiny.
Thy name rouses the hearts
Of the Punjab . . . Gujrat, and Maratha,
Of Dravid, Orissa, and Bengal.
It echoes in the hills of the Vindhyas and Himalayas,
Mingles in the music of Jumna and Ganges,
And is chanted by the waves of the Indian sea.

—from Rabindranath Tagore's *Jana Gana Mana*
("The Mind of the Multitude of the People"),
India's National Anthem

India is the world's most ancient civilization, yet one of its youngest nations. Much of the paradox found everywhere in India is a product of her inextricable antiquity and youth. Stability and dynamism, wisdom and folly, abstention and greed, patience and passion compete without end within the universe that is India. Everything is there, usually in magnified form. No extreme of lavish wealth or wretched poverty, no joy or misery, no beauty or horror is too wonderful, or too dreadful, for India. Nor is the passage to India ever an easy one for Western minds. Superficial similarities of language and outward appearances only compound confusion. For nothing is "obviously true" of India as a whole. Every generalization that follows could be disproved with evidence to the contrary from India itself. Nor is anything "Indian" ever quite as simple as it seems. Each reality is but a facet of India's infinity of experience, a thread drawn from the seamless sari of her history, a glimpse behind the many veils of her maya-world of illusion.

Persians first used "India" for the land that was East of their ancient empire, through which a mighty "River"—the *Indus*—flowed. The country beyond that River Indus came to be known as "India." The people who lived there were Indians. In their own earliest works, however, Indians referred to their land as *Bharata*, which may have been the name of their greatest ancient warrior or tribal chief. India's longer Epic is called *Mahabharata*, "Great Bharata," and is the story of warring tribal cousins, whose struggle for power on the plains of Delhi probably occurred around 1000 B.C. Modern India's Republic officially adopted *Bharat* as its alternate name, when the Constitution of India was enacted on January 26, 1950.

In many ways India is more truly a state of mind than a national body, even as Indic Civilization has endured for more than 4,000 years as an empire of ideas rather than territorial boundaries. Often nebulous and self-defeating, conflicted and fragmented, the rambling bullock-cart continent called India is at once the oldest and most sorrowful as well as the happiest and most beautiful civilization on earth. Her very weakness at times has been her greatest strength, since for sheer endurance India is unique. Bowing low before the onslaught of armies and elements, India has survived every invasion, every natural disaster, every mortal disease and epidemic, the double helix of her genetic code transmitting its unmistakable imprint down four millennia to no less than three-quarters of a billion modern bearers. Indians have demonstrated greater cultural stamina than any other people on earth, with the possible exception of the Chinese. Old as she is, India continues to grow and flourish, transmuting her ancient forms into innovative modernity, adapting her past to suit the present, overcoming Death itself by creating such ingenious concepts as reincarnation, yet welcoming individual extinction as the ultimate goal of Salvation through "Release"—*Mokṣha*.

Indic Civilization has enriched every art and science known to us. Thanks to India, we reckon from zero to ten with misnamed "Arabic" numerals and use a decimal system without which our modern computer age would hardly be possible. Ancient Indians were the first humans to spin and weave cotton into cloth that continues to provide our most comfortable summer attire. Indians taught us to domesticate and eat chicken, to play chess, to gamble with dice, to love mangoes and elephants, to stand on our heads for good health, to believe in the coexistence of contradiction, and to appreciate the beauty and universal possibility of nonviolence. India is the birthplace of Buddhism as well as Hinduism, motherland of Ṣikhs and Jains, the abode of more rishis, sadhus, mahatmas, and maharishis and their many cults than is any other place on earth. India is a learning laboratory for linguists, a museum for ethnographers and anthropologists, a treasure trove for archaeologists, a nightmare for epidemiologists. The average Indian bazaar is more crowded and colorful than most museums the world over. A modern Indian city street is filled with more vitality, color, sound, and smells than any theater or carnival on earth. India pulsates, vibrates, scintillates with such a plethora of human, animal, botanical, insect, and divine life that no camera or recording device, no canvas, pen, or cassette can fully capture the rich design of daily, "ordinary" existence. Each of her hundreds of thousands of urban and millions of daily village dramas is enacted free of charge before audiences that never pause to note the beauty or poignant tragedy unfolding itself on countless stages under India's tear-filled sky.

Indians are among the world's most sensual yet most austere people. Sex is worshiped as religious ritual in this land that invented monasticism. Copulation in every imaginable form has been carved into stone, immortalized on countless facades and inside the sacred "womb house" of Hindu temples for almost 2,000 years. Yet to celibate sadhus such erotic art is viewed only as a test of their unwavering powers of yogic concentration. Shiva, India's oldest divinity, is still worshiped mostly in phallic form, symbol of his mighty erect lingam, with which he "seduced" the wives of many thousands of Brahman sages in the Epic Pine Forest. The same Shiva is also "Great God" of yogic abstinence, whose powers of concentration were such that he could sit without moving for thousands of years on the skin of the tiger he stripped with a flick of his smallest fingernail. Another most popular Hindu deity, Krishna, might indeed be called the Father of his country, since he supposedly married no fewer than 16,000 adoring milkmaids, who bore, mythology has it, 160,000 of his divine children! The Mother Goddess is worshiped throughout India by many names, in both benevolent and malevolent forms, but her most popular symbol remains a smooth round perforated stone, called *yoni*. The Mother is India's soil incarnate, consort of every male divinity, whose powers are inert without the stimulus of her inspiring, beautiful body. That divine "Power," called *Shakti*, is a unique attribute of the female, whose sexual inspiration and creative energy is prerequisite to life. Without her Mother Goddesses, India would never come alive, but thanks to their fecundity her soil teems with children, taught early in life to worship the Mother and divine sexual fire.

Nature is always nearby in India. Sacred cows and lumbering water buffalo often reside in the most spacious front rooms of town houses, and seem to know quite well precisely where to turn off the street and clamber up a few stairs to the parlor room they call home. Birds and lizards of many varieties make their nests in the beams or rafters and on the walls or ceilings of urban dwellings, cheering their human neighbors with morning and evening raga-chirps, or performing the vital service of keeping houses they inhabit free of dangerous stinging insects. Households blessed with a cobra family in residence rarely complain, since those regal hooded snakes are considered good luck for childbearing women, and rarely attack humans unless startled or threatened. Every Indian child learns early in life never to reach under a tablecloth or into any dark closet, or as a rule anywhere in the house that might have insufficient light to reveal the coiled body of a sleeping cobra. Night guards, who patrol evey Indian town, always pound the pavement with their stout lathis and usually shout or sing as well to warn snakes of every variety of their approach, doubtless warning thieves and other criminals in the process while keeping innocents trying to fall asleep wide awake!

Forest-dwelling yogis learned long before the first Indian cities were built, of course, that their surest defense against being poisoned or devoured by most crawling, flying, or prowling jungle creatures was to sit so perfectly still that they appeared to be the natural flora, or an outcrop of stone. Some of India's loveliest ancient seals and stone and bronze statues depict snakes or leaf-covered vines wrapped around human arms, legs, or torsos in what must have been quite a familiar sight for many millennia. Not that such equipoise was ever easy to attain. Nor has the danger of poisonous snakes been eradicated. Quite the contrary. As population pressures continue to encroach upon dwindling jungle or hitherto untilled land, India's reptiles appear to be retaliating. Annual estimates of deaths from snakebite are well over 100,000, much lower than the toll from India's most modern predators, the automobile, bus, truck, and train, whose lethal powers have now escalated to the point where India can claim the sorry distinction of being one of the world's most hazardous nations in which to drive or ride.

Most Indians, however, continue to walk from their village huts to fields they till nearby, and if ever they ride it is usually on a wooden bullock or buffalo cart, whose prototype was built in the third millennium B.C. Such carts are almost as common in big cities as in villages, but the modern urban incarnation generally wears pneumatic rubber tires on its bulky wheels, much to the relief of those who ride. India now produces millions of its own bicycles, the most efficient inexpensive mode of urban middle-class and student transport, and a growing number of motor-scooters, motor-bikes, and automobiles, built in collaboration with Ford, and several British, Italian, Japanese, and Czech multinationals. Three-quarters of the more than half-million Indian villages, the most remote of which are still without permanent land links to neighboring towns or cities, are currently receiving satellite-transmitted broadcasts from New Delhi, thanks to U.S. space technology and cooperation. The most advanced tools of scientific technology are thus tuning India's most remote primal cells of diverse village traditions into the mainstream of national goals and aspirations, accelerating the process of modernized change and integration by generations overnight. Even as India's villagers are now brought to American homes by TV news reports, although usually only when dread disaster has struck, or to Washington and New York thanks to the genius and beauty of a Festival of India or new production of the *Mahabharata*, the modern world daily intrudes its seductive images of affluence and power into village air, jolting Indian minds from their bullock-cart ruts of antiquity onto swifter, more dangerous highways.

The River

India and the River mirror each other, bubbling with life, always changing, ever the same. Much like India, the River is impossible to grasp in her entirety, most elusive when she appears simplest, deceptively deep even when her surface shines clear. Refreshing cradle of life, the River nonetheless often proves dangerous, especially to strangers. Like India, the River is beautiful but polluted, timelessly enduring yet transient.

India's most fertile Northern plains, still the major centers of South Asia's population, are all gifts of great rivers. The Indus, since mid-August 1947 the main artery of Pakistan, is westernmost of the great Northern riverine systems, and was the cradle of Indic Civilization. Born in mountain abodes of eternal snow and ice, the Indus, like her sister-rivers to the east, flows abundantly all year long. Indus water rich in mineral sediment annually journeys some 2,000 miles from Tibet to the Arabian Sea, bearing enough fresh water to cover the State of California a foot deep. Small wonder the Greco-Persians called the Indus a "Lion." For thousands of years, fierce Indus floods roared down Himalayan valleys to bury the hapless inhabitants of towns and villages erected too close to its banks. Stronger, more devastating at flood tide than the Nile, the raging Indus remained a terror to its valley folk until relatively recent barrages of concrete and vast storage-tank lakes conspired to tame and divert its floodwaters. Following the Partition of British India in 1947, India and neighboring Pakistan argued bitterly over what each nation considered its fair share of precious Indus Valley canal waters, without which fecund soil on both sides of the new border would soon turn into desert wasteland. International mediation resolved that vital conflict in 1960, yet each nation periodically accuses the other of siphoning off more water than it merits according to solemn treaty.

"Five Rivers"—Persian *Punjab*—flow like fingers of a giant open hand into the Indus, merging with that main artery as it races toward the sea. The land of those five great rivers is still called "Punjab" in both Pakistan and India, although since the fateful 1947 Partition only four of the original five flow through the former state, while a mere two fructify the latter. India's Punjab was further divided in 1966, losing its lower eastern half to the Hindu-majority State of Haryana, following years of bitter conflict with Punjabi-majority Sikhs. Despite its much-diminished size, however, thanks in good measure to its fertile soil and abundant resources of hydroelectric power, India's Punjab emerged in the 1970s as the wealthiest of India's twenty-five States. The hard-working Sikh majority of that most industrially advanced and agriculturally rich Punjab resented sharing their abundance with India's much poorer population elsewhere throughout the republic, insisting on greater autonomy, including control over the lion's share of their state finances. New Delhi's refusal to grant such demands only added fuel to Punjabi Sikh agitation for still greater independence. A small group of Sikh extremists called for total national separation from the Indian Union, urging creation of a Sikh "Land of the Pure"—*Khalistan*. *Pakistan*, also meaning "Land of the Pure," had, after all, been created as a national homeland for most of South Asia's Muslim minority in 1947, so why not grant a similar nation-state to India's Sikhs? India's central government refused to entertain the demand, arguing that with barely 2 percent of the total Indian population, only half of whom lived in Punjab, the Sikhs could never support an independent nation.

"Mother" Ganga (Ganges) is India's most sacred river. Ganga is worshiped as a Goddess, and Hindu temples line her northern left bank as she emerges bubbly white and icy cold from the solid rock of Himalayan Rishikesh, racing down past sacred Hardwar, goal of countless Brahman pilgrims, to expand in girth and drop her sediment as she slows to a more matronly pace en route toward Kanpur and Allahabad, home of the Nehrus, independent India's "First Family." At Allahabad the Ganga merges with her sister goddess Yamuna (Jumna), who joins her after sluggishly meandering past Old Delhi's Red Fort (Lal Qila) and Agra, reflecting the ivory minaret profile of the Taj Mahal beneath her swarthy rippling veil. At thrice holy Allahabad, a third goddess river, Saraswati, invisibly merges with sisters Ganga and Yamuna, all wending their watery way to Varanasi (Benares), holiest of holy cities of Hindu India. Believed by some to be the "oldest" city on earth, Varanasi is more certainly the most sacred place for any devout Hindu to die. Varanasi's crowded temples raise their ornate spires of stone like worshiping joined hands and arms stretched in supplication toward the sky as their well-worn "steps" (*ghats*) descend below the greenish-brown slime of the river, which has absorbed more ashes of Hindu bodies than any other stretch of water on earth. The pungent smell of sandalwood, compounded with that of charred flesh and marigolds, wafts over Varanasi waters, borne on winds vibrant with mantra-prayers, punctuated by the tinkling of Brahman bells and muffled whimpers from scavenger dogs that hover around smouldering pyres, while carrion hawks and kites circle slowly overhead. Ganga water at Varanasi is said to have "magic powers," and ailing Hindus from every corner of the subcontinent journey to those bustling ghats for an immersion believed by many sufficient as a cure for any ailment. Devout Hindus not only wash themselves in the bubbling green of Varanasi water but also drink it, and carry bottles and brass lothas of the precious fluid home with them for future use, or to share with relatives too weak to have made the pilgrimage themselves. Visitors are advised to exercise greater caution, however, at Varanasi than almost anywhere else in India. Its reputed healing powers have attracted so many lepers and others afflicted with disease that outbreaks of bubonic plague have been reported there in recent years.

Many other mighty rivers drain the Himalayan foothills to join Mother Ganga's stately, ever-widening flow toward the east. The greatest of those life-generating arteries are the rivers Ghogra and Gandak, of Epic fame, which merge with Ganga herself near the ancient Mauryan capital of Patna. Here, too, River Son moves up to join Ganga from the south, draining rugged highlands of Bihar and Chota Nagpur, whose dark mountains hold the richest stores of Indian iron and coal. East of Patna, Mother Ganga flows another 300 miles to Bengal, where she blends her deep waters with the powerful flow of divine Brahma's "son"—*Brahmaputra*. This great young riverine hero rises in Tibet close to the source of Indus, racing almost a thousand miles east before veering south and slashing his foamy way through glacial ice east of Lhasa, down India's *Arunachal* ("Dawn's") State, through troubled Assam and *Meghalaya* ("Abode of Clouds"), bordering crowded *Bangladesh* ("Nation of Bengal"), where it finally joins the mainstream of Ganga's flow, pouring through 10,000 rivulet mouths into the Bay of Bengal.

The Islamic Republic of Bangladesh, born in 1971, constituted the eastern half of British Indian Bengal until it became East Pakistan in 1947, following Partition. Although only the size of New York State, Bangladesh, with a population of over 100 million, is one of the most crowded and impoverished nations of the world. Millions of desperate Bangladeshi Muslims have fled across India's borders to cultivate some land for themselves in the virtually unpopulated rugged jungles of Meghalaya, Assam, and their neighboring eastern states of Mizoram, Manipur, and Nagaland. The indigenous tribal peoples of these states bordering Bangladesh fiercely resent what in several states has become a massive Muslim "invasion" of their lands. Joining forces to organize a "Seven (States) United Liberation Army," these northeastern Indian Mizo, Manipur, Naga, and Assamese tribals recently launched a violent movement to try to terrify Bangladeshi immigrants into returning to their Muslim homeland.

Unlike the great Northern rivers, none of those that cross Central and Southern India are perennially fed by snow or ice. All depend entirely on scant springs and the bounty of monsoon rains, which fall for one-third of the year at most. The South is, therefore, generally drier and less populous than the Northern riverine plains. Unlike China's great canals that link its northern and southern rivers, India has as yet never attempted to tap its perennial waterways for southern fructification. Much of central India's desert wasteland might then be brought to life, and the mostly barren Southern states of Maharashtra and Andhra could also be remarkably enriched. Not that so monumental an engineering project could be easily accomplished, although like China, India has sufficient cheap and—for much of each year—mostly idle peasant labor, to make what would otherwise be an impossible task, a potential reality.

Three major rivers drain central India, flowing from east to west, the Mahi, the Narmada, and the Tapti, all emptying into the Gulf of Cambay. Surat, the port city north of Bombay at the mouth of the Tapti, was where British merchants first established themselves in modest trade with Agra's Great Mughals early in the seventeenth century. Bombay was no more than a series of tiny villages at the time, as were Calcutta and Madras. None of those great port cities, India's major bustling metropolises of the last century, existed prior to the advent of British rule. The western Ghats ("Steps") form a mountainous spine down peninsular India south of Bombay, leaving but a narrow and very well-watered rich littoral shelf, whose lower half is the spicy Malabar Coast, facing the Arabian Sea. All the rest of Southern India's great river systems flow from west to east. The Mahanadi, literally the "Great River," is the vital artery of Orissa, even as its longer southern neighbor, the Godavari, is for Andhra. Mightiest of all the great southern rivers is the Tungabhadra-Krishna, which rises in the mountains of Mysore and meanders more than 1,000 miles across the heart of India's Southern peninsula before pouring itself into the Bay of Bengal north of Madras. Farther south still, below the former Indo-French capital of Pondicherry, is the long but lazy River Kaveri.

From the dawn of Civilization, Indians have settled along their riverbanks, using the rich flow of such water not simply to sustain life but also to assure ample surplus for all those artisans, craftsmen, bureaucrats, and armies removed from direct dependence on the soil, thanks to the River's bounty. Fresh water and fertile sediment conspired to nurture ever-growing populations, North and South, but wherever her great rivers flowed, wide and deep islands of local culture emerged and consolidated. Variations of language and social custom evolved over millennia and centuries around those riverine nuclei of civilized life. Long before the dawn of the Christian era, most Indians of the North spoke one or another dialect or popular language of the Indo-Aryan branch of the great Indo-European language family, whose classical language is Sanskrit, and whose most popular regional form is the central Gangetic plain's Hindi, modern India's national language.

By the Christian era, however, throughout the southern third of India's subcontinent, south of the River Godaveri, at least, India's populace spoke one of four major variants of the Dravidian language family, quite distinct from Indo-Aryan, and virtually unique to South India as well as northern Sri Lanka, the neighboring southern island formerly called "Ceylon."

Tamil, the classical Dravidian language, is still the mother-tongue for more than 50 million South Indians in the state recently renamed *Tamil Nadu* ("Land of the Tamils"), which in British Indian times had been Madras. Deep roots of cultural identity, fostered by a rich body of ancient Tamil literature, including Epic poetry, devotional songs, and religious philosophy, have given birth to periodic passionate political outcries for separate "Dravidistan" nationhood since before the dawn of Indian Independence in 1947. The redrawing of India's provincial boundaries a decade later, however, was designed from New Delhi primarily to placate Dravidian demands, carving out Tamil Nadu for the Tamils, the State of Andhra for Telugu-speakers, Karnataka (former Mysore) for the Kanarese, and a Malabar State called *Kerala* for Dravidians who speak primarily Malayalam. Passionate anti-Hindi sentiment in the South led for several decades to annual burnings of India's flag and Constitution, but "Dravidistan" extremist agitation tapered off during Mrs. Gandhi's last years in power, owing to her generous economic policy toward the South, and in some measure because of the shifting focus of Tamil extremism to Sri Lanka. The northern third of that island nation, where Hindu Tamils predominate over the otherwise majority of Sri Lanka's Sinhalese Buddhists, received much more than mere moral support from Tamil Nadu neighbors, many of whom sent money, arms, and helped train growing cadres of "Tamil Tigers" demanding a separate *Eelam* Tamil nation since the mid-1970s.

Indians of all ages, regions, and languages love their rivers. Before dawn Hindus go to the nearest river to bathe and pray, ritually washing themselves with water drawn in brass pots or clay dishes, holding their nostrils as they immerse their heads and bodies, bobbing up and down like happy porpoises or frolicking elephants. Every morning washerfolk (*dhobiwale*) flock to India's rivers with heavy bundles of dirty cloth, beating their wash against smooth stones before spreading colorful saris and white dhotis out in the sun to dry along riverbanks. Religious festivals lure tens of millions to sacred river cities to dance and pray in tune with the ancient rhythms of the Hindu lunar calendar, often crushing, even at times killing themselves to reach the water at the precise instant astrologically reputed to be most auspicious for good health or long life! The River, like India, waits patiently, mutely watching, accepting folly and wisdom alike. Her bounty, now pure, now polluted, both gives and takes life from her countless children, much the way Mother Ganga was reputed in Epic lore to have "drowned" each of her sons as soon as he was born, until her distracted husband, King Santanu, begged her to desist from what he viewed as so barbaric a practice. Ganga agreed and let their last son live, but as punishment for being pressured to do so, abandoned her poor husband, who never fully appreciated how perfectly divine a wife he had.

Heat

Heat is the most palpable, all-pervasive element of India's environment. Heat is to India what fog and rain are to England, what hazy sunshine and smog are to southern California. From March through early November most of India is hot, much of it sizzling. Indians worship several gods of heat: Vishnu and Surya as sun-gods, Agni as god of fire. Coping with intense heat has probably taught Indians more of their philosophy than they like to admit. They may, indeed, have been the first people to make a virtue of necessity, but would not be the last. A general lack of "action-mindedness" long and often noted by foreign visitors as a common quality among Indians was perhaps India's first line of defense against heatstroke or sunstroke. Rudyard Kipling to the contrary notwithstanding, even Englishmen acclimatized to India's "noonday sun" rarely stepped outside in it, unless they were up in Simla's salubrious heights or those of some less renowned British hill station. Most Indians, of course, developed natural pigmentation to ward off the worst effects of heat, yet death from sunstroke remains common in India.

Intense heat may have inspired India's ancient *rishi*s ("wise-men") to practice yoga meditation, thereby keeping themselves as "cool" as possible in what would otherwise have been a life-jeopardizing environment. We now recognize that yoga has many useful applications. but slowing the body's metabolism by sitting still and controlling one's breath if not actually reducing the heartbeat is surely one of the best ways to diminish wear and tear. Divine yogis, such as Lord Shiva, used the single-pointed laserlike heat of their meditation to vaporize demons and other intruders on their peace by focusing a third-eye of fire on troublesome objects. Heat is also credited with creation, but the self-generating *tapas* ("heat") that ancient hymns of India celebrate for sowing "seeds" of life was more closely related to erotic passion than solar energy.

Wherever India's heat is coupled with riverine waters or ample monsoon rains, the abundance of agricultural yields has been uniquely supportive of life. Population densities of well over 1,000 per square miles are thus found in most of the eastern Ganga's plain as well as Bengal, and along the narrow Malabar coast, where two—and often three—crops of rice are grown annually. Irrigation canals in the North have greatly expanded double and triple cropping, moreover, allowing India today to support more than double the population she had at the birth of her Republic in 1950, although at much the same bare margin of rough grain caloric subsistence for most peasants. Owing to expanded irrigation works, the use of chemical fertilizers, newly developed high-yielding seeds, and mechanized agriculture, the growing urban middle class and wealthiest segment of India's population enjoy a richer, more varied diet than had hitherto been possible. Average overall Indian yields of most crops remain, however, much lower than outputs in Japan, China, Canada, the United States, and most western European nations. The general enervating impact of heat may help account for such poor overall productivity.

South of Delhi an arc of primarily barren desert encompassing most of Rajasthan may be found within a radius of more than 300 miles, and from Allahabad a similar half-circle to the south would cover most of Madhya Pradesh, India's rugged, barren "Middle Province." Hindu *Rajput*s ("Sons of Kings"), whose royal families dominated these central desert domains for more than a thousand years, appear to have invaded India from Central Asia early in the Christian era, although their astrologers trace their royal lineage to divinities of Sun and Moon. A golden sunburst remains the symbol of the Maharaja of Mewar, whose enchanting capital at Udaipur is built around a lovely artificial lake, nestled in a natural fortress of hills, and was never conquered even by the mightiest of Great Mughals. The brilliantly beautiful colors worn by Rajasthani peasants, whose scarlet and saffron turbans and mirror-shimmering skirts and vests are among the brightest costumes in all of India, seem designed to offset the drab grays and mauves of nature's garb, even as the peacocks and green parrots of Rajasthan are among India's loveliest birds. Rajasthani bands of wandering musicians, dancers, and fortunetellers, known to history as "Gypsies" because they stopped for so many years in Egypt en route to Roumania, have added color to most of the world by now. Romani, the Gypsy language, is closest to Rajasthani, a modern Indo-Aryan tongue descended from Sanskrit and related to Hindi. With so little moisture and such intense heat, Rajasthan has never been able to support its population more than marginally and remains one of India's poorest states with the nation's lowest literacy rate, especially among women. Poverty has never diminished the artistry or high spirits of Rajasthan's populace.

If India ever learns to harness its solar energy economically, the desert states of Rajasthan and Madhya Pradesh could become valuable centers of power generation and transmission. Even as oil reserves have catapulted Arabia to affluence, solar power might launch Central India into an age of rich growth and development, especially were it used to help tap Mother Ganga's perennial flow. India's major liability might then become her greatest asset.

Monsoon Rains

India's rainy "season"—*monsoon*—usually starts early in June and ends late in September. When the monsoon is on time, giant rain-fattened turbanlike clouds roll toward the elephant trunk profile of the peninsula's western littoral the first week in June. Without monsoon rains the entire Southern peninsula would be as dry as the desert of Rajasthan and Madhya Pradesh. As June's summer sun heats India's land mass more quickly than it does the surrounding waters of the Indian Ocean, continental air rises and moisture-laden ocean air blows toward the land from the southwest. Everywhere in India the monsoon is welcomed with joyous song and dance. Ancient Brahmans kept a weather eye on the dark clouds that annually gathered to the southwest, noting precisely when they reached the coast and rose over the western Ghat mountains to drop their bounty of life-giving rain. The Soma altar was thus designed and slowly constructed each year to be ready to light a few days before the monsoon started, so that it would seem as if Brahmanic mantras and sacrificial offerings brought the rain. Peasants timed their ploughing and sowing accordingly. If the rains came too early, of course,

Brahmans lost credibility, and precious water was wasted on furrows devoid of seed. If the rains came late then crows and other scavengers reaped the only harvest, leaving Brahmans to chant and offer up Soma and *ghi* (ghee; clarified butter) to sacrificial fires in vain, while the prospect of grim famine loomed blacker than clouds on every horizon.

India's still predominantly agricultural economy has often been called a "gamble in rains," since the monsoon third of every year is when tanks and reservoirs, as well as most rivers and irrigation canals throughout the land, are given fresh sustenance that must last them until the next monsoon begins. Bumper harvests in recent years have finally given India sufficient surplus stocks of grain to avert the sort of famine disasters that decimated the land in the last decade of the nineteenth century and as recently as the terrible Bengal Famine of 1943, which claimed over 3 million lives. Monsoon failures sometimes come in two or three successive years, however, and no amount of government storage can provide adequate buffers against catastrophe of that order of magnitude. India's more than half a billion peasant population remains pathetically vulnerable to whims of nature and winds of change.

The Malabar Coast, south of Goa, with its bounty of about 100 inches of rain during those turbulent monsoon months, has India's most beautiful beaches, palm-fringed and dotted with lagoons, surrounded by banana and mango groves, pepper trees, and cloves, with tea and coffee plantations thriving at higher elevations on the Ghats. It was these lush and lovely beaches that Portuguese merchant seamen in the vanguard of western Europe's many waves of imperial assault upon India first sighted. Hardly surprising that they found India too enticing, too enriching, to leave alone. Her natural fruits were too delicious, the beauties of her women too intoxicating, and the allure of India's wealthy variety of produce, finer arts, and ingenious crafts all conspired to seduce visitors from afar. Malabar, the modern state of Kerala, is the one region of India in which matriarchy survived until modern times, reflecting perhaps the earliest pattern of Dravidian society, where the Mother dominated and determined all important aspects of life and behavior. Male-dominated Indo-Aryan tribes and clans invaded India much later from the northwest, establishing their patriarchal patterns of marriage and inheritance over the northern river valleys, extending them gradually to the rest of the subcontinent.

Monsoon rain clouds rise so rapidly over the western Ghats that they lose most of their moisture before blowing east across the heartland of the Southern peninsula. The western half of that landmass is the Deccan ("Southland"), most of which is now part of the State of Maharashtra, literally "Great Country," whose capital is Bombay. The serrated lava-trap of the dry and dusty Deccan gives it much the same appearance as the "badlands" of the American Southwest. Most Marathi-speaking peoples of Maharashtra are as tough and undemonstrative as the soil they labor so hard to till. The old Deccan capital of Pune (Poona), approximately ninety miles east of Bombay, was for centuries a bastion of indigenous Maratha power and of traditional Hindu learning as well as a cradle of modern India's Nationalist movement. It remains an important center of higher education and has recently become one of India's major modern industrial and chemical centers, and home of the Indian Officers' basic training National Defense Academy. The region that produced so many generations of British "Poona Colonels" thus continues to train their Indian incarnations in somewhat altered leadership molds, yet with much the same meticulous interest in snappy swagger sticks, waxed mustaches and boots, buckles and belts that shine thanks to ample spit, polish, and elbow grease.

Andhra, the eastern half of the upper peninsula, named for one of India's most ancient dynasties, was carved out of the predominantly Telugu-speaking districts of the Dravidian South. Hyderabad, the capital of Andhra, was hereditary domain of the Muslim Nizams of that city of slums, palaces, and mosques since the early eighteenth century. Although the Nizams were long fabled for their fortune in jewels, elephants, and "motorcars," most of Andhra's population remain penurious peasants and fisherfolk, who supplement a marginal living netted from grudging seas with cotton spinning and weaving. Much like Maharashtra, Andhra receives precious little monsoon rain, but its littoral on the Bay of Bengal provides fertile rice land, where several of the major peninsular rivers deposit sediment as they pour into the sea. The State of Orissa just north of Andhra along the coast is also quite depressed and often falls victim to natural disasters, including hurricanes born in the Bay of Bengal. Some of Hindu India's greatest temple architecture and art is found there, however, at Bhubaneshwar and the beautiful coastal village of Puri.

South of Maharashtra and Andhra are the two most populous and wealthy Dravidian states, Karnataka and Tamil Nadu States. Bangalore, capital of Kanarese-speaking Karnataka, is one of India's fastest-growing urban industrial and electronic centers and also the home of South India's Air Academy. Formerly famed for its quiet and pleasant English gardens, Bangalore is rapidly becoming more famous for its traffic jams and smog. Not too distant Mysore, however, tranquil home of the ex-Maharaja for whom an entire kingdom was once named, retains much of its storybook princely charm, with a sumptuous summer palace on a suburban hill that has recently been converted into a hotel. The once seemingly inexhaustible Kolar gold fields of Karnataka helped cover the domes of its Maharaja's many palaces and the shining towers of South India's Hindu temples with laminated layers of never-fading magnificence. The icons, doors, and sacred vessels of solid gold stored in South Indian temples, mosques, and palaces alone would probably suffice to sustain India's economy for years. Most of the vast hoard of jewels and precious metals accumulated in the North has long since been looted by foreign invaders, primarily Persian, Turkish, Mongol, Afghan, and British. The South, however, thanks to the deep desert wasteland and rugged Vindhya and Satpura mountain belts that block easy access from the Northern plains to the Deccan, has remained relatively unplundered. Hindu temples continue to receive generous donations, never reported, rarely counted by their Brahman guardians who have always enjoyed tax-free autonomy over the lands and wealth within their often high and ample walls, where the gods themselves are believed to reside in appropriate splendor and comfort. Could the frozen assets of those gods somehow be invested on behalf of the submarginal millions of India's most impoverished population, the "miraculous" goal of Mahatma Gandhi's dream of the "Uplift of All" (*Sarvodaya*) might, indeed, be achieved within a single generation. However, this is as likely as "manna" dropping in the laps of India's landless during the next monsoon.

A narrower arm of India's southwest monsoon whips around the southern tip of Tamil Nadu, up the Bay of Bengal to the mouths of the Ganga and her fertile delta. Those winds sometimes come up the bay's natural funnel with hurricane force, lashing tidal waves of terror and destruction, which periodically drown from 10,000 to half a million Bengali lives in a single day. Population pressures continue to drive the poorest peasants to the most vulnerable sea-level islands that are often without effective communication links to the mainland; hence their inhabitants receive no advance warning of such impending catastrophe, despite modern satellite monitoring of monsoon winds. The well-watered riverine plains of Bengal are thus doubly drenched by monsoon rains that rise against Burmese, Himalayan, and Bhutanese mountain walls, dropping as much as 800 inches of rain on some Assamese hill stations, which rarely see sun or sky for weeks on end.

Deflected by the world's highest mountains, monsoon clouds veer west up the Ganga valley to Bihar, the Ruhr of India, and to Uttar Pradesh (U.P.), its rural heartland, then on to New Delhi itself, which receives some 85 percent of its annual 25 inches of rain during the monsoon third of each year. Modern India's global capital, whose huge plain, much like Los Angeles, continues to attract as a giant magnet more and more millions, would be a desert wasteland without its monsoon quota. Thousands of tanks and plaster-lined wells are filled during the rains, allowing Delhi's populace to reap rich orange, tangerine, sugarcane, and sesame crops, as well as vital vegetables and wheat. The site of at least seven and possibly as many as ten capitals of India, since the dawn of her Civilization, Delhi's plain is replete with sandstone ruins of antiquity that attest both to the evanescence of power and the persistence of imperial ambitions. No other patch of Indian soil has witnessed so much pageantry or pain, heard so many pretentious promises, or hosted as much tyranny and treachery. To the monsoon, however, Delhi is almost the end of the windy line, where clouds are relieved of all but the last of their burdensome moisture before the demise of September.

Mountain Walls

A valance of mighty mountains hangs over South Asia, India's shield against the icy blasts of Siberian frost and the biting yellow sands of Central Asia. India's Northern mountain wall is called *Himalaya*—"Abode of Snow," an awesome arc of stone and ice some 1,500 miles long and 200 miles in width, capped by no less than fifty peaks over five miles high. The Himalayas are the world's youngest and tallest mountains. They appear to have sprung up about 60 million years ago, when the far more ancient granite of India's pre-Cambrian shifting peninsula rammed itself against the then submerged edge of southern Tibet. South India seems to have broken away from East Africa as earth's crust cooled, and fused itself, following continental drift north, to Asia's littoral, snapping the Himalayas aloft to spectacular heights in that passionate embrace. The much tougher old rock of the drifting peninsula buckled up as well when that continental fusion occurred, but the resulting Vindhya and Satpura ranges of Central India rose merely from 3,000 to 5,000 feet above sea level.

Hindu Epic myth has its own explanation of Vindhya's humble stature compared to Himalayan Mt. Kailasa (or Mt. Meru), the abode of India's gods. There was supposedly a time when Vindhya grew so "big with pride" that he blocked the very sun's rays from reaching Kailasa's pantheon of divine inhabitants. Several gods shivered with rage, and deputed a messenger, the Brahman sage Agastya, to deal with the upstart. Vindhya was Agastya's student, and when his guru approached he bowed low, as a proper Hindu student should. "Stay that way, Vindhya, till I return!" Agastya ordered. But the old Brahman never went back to his Northern home, spending his remaining years in the deep South. Thus brash Vindhya was tricked into behaving with proper deference to the gods. Agastya may have been one of the first Aryans to forge across the Central mountain ranges to "colonize" or what Aryans came to call "civilize" the "wilds" of India's Southern domain, whose indigenous Dravidians considered themselves more advanced than any Northerners. Indo-Aryans, in any event, like their Greco-Roman cousins, put their gods atop the highest mountains, whether named "Olympus" or "Kailasa." The Himalayas have in consequence long enjoyed a place of special reverence among Indians.

Without her Himalayan wall, North India would have none of her fertile plains, for the beds of detritus and rich sediment that fill the Indus Valley and Punjab and extend many thousands of feet below the fertile surface of Ganga's vast plain are gifts of Himalayan stone ground to sand by rushing waters of melted Himalayan snow. Mineral wealth of every variety, including vast quantities of gold, have poured down from "Father Himalaya's" silvery walls, and gave credence to many fabled tales of India reported by Herodotus and other Western patriarchs of history. Herodotus wrote of India's "gold-digging ants," who filled their bags with golden "dust" and ran so "swiftly" that only "she-camels" who had recently "dropped their young" could catch them! Thanks to Herodotus' proclivity to report everything he heard, however, we do get our earliest written corroboration of Indian cotton, or, as he recounted it, "trees" in India bearing "wool." He also noted "many tribes" in that most remote and "wealthiest" of Persian imperial satraps, each of whom spoke "different languages." Several centuries later,

Alexander the Great found the Punjab divided into at least as many principalities as there were rivers, and in some measure it was thanks not only to the different languages, but to the indifference of neighboring Indian monarchs to the security of one another's domain that the mighty Macedonian conqueror marched across all of them, defeating each, one at a time. Were it not for his own army's "rebellion," which was in fact a "sit-down strike" on the banks of the Beas River, Alexander might have become India's first true Emperor.

Similar Indian disinterest in political unification, or perhaps it is rather Indian "suspicion" and "mistrust" of neighboring "strangers," no matter how close they may actually be compared to other foreigners, has left India vulnerable to conquest throughout her long history. To this day, in fact, bonds of "National" unity are much less powerful for the overwhelming majority of Indians than those of familial, caste, local and provincial, or linguistic-regional ties. In an era of Global History, however, that "weakness" may turn into one of the greatest strengths Indians have, since it usually predisposes them to feel very much at home wherever they wander, as long as they have intimate members of their own family or caste or local community somewhere close at hand. What it may portend for India's national integrity and security is another matter. There has, at any rate, never been any single simple "Indian mind" or "Indian response" to external threats or challenges or, for that matter, to internal policies threatening change.

The Northern mountains serve as a watershed and natural boundary separating India from China. In most respects Indic and Sinitic Civilizations are as remote as are either of these two grandparents of all other Asian cultures from Western Civilization. Pan-Asian movements based on the unifying force of nonviolent Buddhism or the strength of sentimental ties generated by more recent anti-Western national struggles against imperial powers have never long managed to overcome deeper cultural differences and political conflicts that continue to divide India from China. In recent decades those differences have led to brief violent skirmishes and unending cartographic disputes over their common border. As these two most populous nations on earth continue to modernize and develop, moreover, their natural competition for control of the rich resources and peoples who inhabit the major intermontane Himalayan basins of Kashmir, Nepal, Sikkim, Bhutan, and India's northeasternmost State of Arunachal Pradesh seems destined to intensify.

India's northernmost State of Jammu and Kashmir remains a thorn in her relations with Pakistan, the most incendiary legacy of a deep-rooted Hindu–Muslim conflict that led to the 1947 Partition of South Asia, but has not, unfortunately, been dissolved by that traumatic upheaval. The de facto battlefield partition of Kashmir has, for example, never really been accepted by or satisfied either neighboring nation, and Pakistan's close ties with China are often viewed from New Delhi as posing a potential "pincer's threat" against the Kashmiri "jewel" in the "crown" of the Indian Union. Most Kashmiris in the coveted Vale are Muslims, and many of the indigenous folk who live in the state's more remote northeastern wing of Ladakh are Sino-Tibetan in ethnicity as well as language. The state, however, is secured by New Delhi with India's most powerful permanent military force based in and around Srinagar, and along the never fully quiescent border with Pakistan's Azad ("Free") Kashmir territory. The natural beauty and placidity of Srinagar's Lake Dal with its sumptuous houseboat accommodations and heavenly backdrops of snow-white mountains are rarely disturbed by such geopolitical problems. China's determination to maintain a road across Ladakh's *Aksai Chin* ("White Stone") alkaline desert, however, led to the first exchange of fire between Asia's two competing "superpowers" in the late 1950s, bringing an end to what had hitherto been an era of "Indo-Chinese Brotherhood."

The Hindu Kingdom of Nepal spans most of the central arc between Tibet and India's U.P. and Bihar States. From his Kathmandu capital, the "God" (*Deva*) King of Nepal and his ministers maintain their buffer state independence as a remarkably sturdy "root between two stones." Nepal's Hindu royal family, which claims descent from the Sun through Udaipur's line, and their Brahman ministers, rule over a predominantly Tibeto-Mongol populace of hearty martial Gurkhas and peasant Newars. They look more Chinese than Indian, as does the pagoda-style architecture found everywhere in the valley, although their Nepali language is derived primarily from Sanskrit. Mother India has retained much closer diplomatic as well as cultural ties to Nepal, while China from the far side of Everest's peak has remained more aloof, perhaps thus inadvertently attracting Nepal's rulers by giving them a greater sense of political and economic independence. At least eighteen yak passes link Nepal to Tibet, however, two of which are major arteries of trade that could easily become military highways should

Beijing so desire. Until quite recently, Nepal has deliberately kept itself a backward hermit kingdom, sensing, no doubt, that the isolation it thereby enjoyed was the surest defense of its much cherished freedoms. Modernity with all its latest forms of terrorist violence and stress as well as technological comfort and pleasure is rapidly encroaching, however, as each jet load from New Delhi, Lucknow, and Patna flies over Himalayan foothills into Kathmandu.

The largest natural pass from India to Tibet wends its way through "thimble-sized" Sikkim, second tiniest of India's states, less than 3,000 square miles with under half a million people, some of them indigenous Lepchas, but most Nepalese and Tibetan in origin. Wedged between the Kingdoms of Nepal and Bhutan, Sikkim's royal house retained quasi-independent status until 1975, when the State of Sikkim was fully integrated into India's Union. The vital trade route from Sikkim's mile-high capital of Gangtok to Tibetan Gyangtse has made that strategic state too important to modern India's first line of Northern defense to leave it in the hands of a royal house whose allegiance to New Delhi had never been enthusiastic. With an elected Congress government, however, all the difficulties of representative rule in any pluralistic tribal society have come to Sikkim, bringing long intervals of autocratic "Governor's rule"—New Delhi martial law—to the Himalayan thimble that must obviously be prepared to withstand any sting of advancing Chinese needles. Thanks to American high-altitude armor and radar equipment, flown to India in response to the Chinese invasion of 1962, Sikkim and its mighty mountains, whose highest peak is Kanchenjunga, now bristle with modern weapons of war and Indian soldiers trained to use them.

The "Dragon" Kingdom of *Bhutan* ("End of Tibet"), east of Sikkim, is the last of the world's Mahayana Buddhist monarchies, which once included China as well as Tibet and Sikkim. Slightly larger than Switzerland, Bhutan, with its more than a million people, mostly Tibetan in origin, is now closely linked to India by modern roads as well as the most advanced units of the Indian Army. Indian engineers have been careful to build no highways north of Bhutan's midsection, however, hardly wishing to expedite the possible advance of any Chinese force south from Tibet. Under Indian tutelage and foreign policy direction, Bhutan has changed quite rapidly and continues to take lengthy strides toward modernity, with the economic potential of its enormous hydroelectric power and rich resources of Sal and Teak forests, as well as incalculable mineral wealth, ripe for development by joint Indo-Bhutanese enterprise.

"Dawn's Province," *Arunachal Pradesh*, is the eastern anchor of India's Northern tier wall of glacial ice, bristling with modern martial power. Bordering Burma as well as China and Tibet, Arunachal is much like Kashmir, at least in strategic terms, not in communal configuration. With its mostly Tibeto-Burman Buddhist populace, however, Arunachal has much the same feelings of "foreignness" from most of India as do its immediate neighboring states among the now turbulent northeastern "Seven." Few, if any, Bangladeshi immigrants have ventured as far north as Arunachal, nor is it very likely that they would survive the frost of that glacial province's winter months. Ethnic, linguistic, and religious proximity to Burma and Tibet, as well as China, however, keep this region spinning with centrifugal alienation from New Delhi. To the youthful Himalayas and their ancient indigenous peoples, however, politics and diplomacy are generally far less worrisome than tectonic quakes, avalanches, floods, frost, and famine. Faced with so many daily challenges to survival, these sturdy, usually cheerful mountain folk worry more about the earth opening beneath their feet, or the sky falling, than distant thunder out of Delhi or Beijing.

Father Himalaya's ice palaces were the goal of Hindu kings and heroes, like Yuddhistira of Epic fame, eldest of the noble Pandavas, who persisted in climbing the empyreal heights until Lord Indra himself opened the golden gates to welcome him to his heavenly respite. Yuddhistira's faithful dog alone had persevered with him to the end of that arduous trail, and when Indra tried to dissuade the valiant monarch from bringing his dog into the palace of the gods, the good king replied, "The dog and I are together!" His loyalty was then rewarded, the dog transformed into divine *Dharma*, god of "Religion" or "Law," and Yuddhistira, to this day revered as *Dharma-Raja*, "King of Religion or Law," was invited by Indra, King of the Gods, to join Kailasa's pantheon.

Historic Prologue

> *India is the farthest part of the inhabited world towards the east, . . . in this part . . . all animals, both quadrupeds and birds, are much larger than they are in other countries, with the exception of horses . . . there is abundance of gold there, partly dug, partly brought down by the rivers. . . . And certain wild trees there bear wool instead of fruit, that in beauty and quality excels that of sheep, and the Indians make their clothing from these trees.*
>
> —Herodotus, *The Histories* III: 106 (trans. Henry Cary)

The ineffable fascination of modern India is a product of the complexity of its many ages of coexistent reality. Nothing is ever totally forgotten in this land of reincarnation. Traditionally, Indians view history as an endless series of cycles, each dawning in a golden age and ending with darkness. Since by such traditional reckoning we are now nearing the middle of the "Dark Age" (*Kala Yuga*), most Indians are hardly shocked at the tragic procession of wars, terrors, and fatal traumas that plague our modern world. They generally believe that deterioration is destined to continue for many more thousands of years before things start turning again toward an era of sweetness and light.

Mahatma Gandhi called his ideal golden age of righteousness *Ram Rajya*, the "Reign of Rama." According to Epic lore, King Rama ruled over Ayodhya as an earthly emanation of Lord Vishnu; hence whatever he did was deemed divine. Several hundred miles east of Delhi, the city of Ayodhya flourishes on the banks of the river Ghogra in U.P. It is a city of Hindu temples and millions of pilgrims visit it to this day, raising their voices to Rama and his divine wife, Sita. Countless mantras of "Sita-Ram" and "Ram-Ram" echo from that hallowed spot, believed to have been the site of Rama's ancient capital and his birthplace. After the thirteenth century of the Christian era, Muslim armies swept over Ayodhya, soon erecting their own city, Faizabad, beside it, building many mosques from the bricks and stones of desecrated Hindu temples, which iconoclastic Muslims view as sacrilegious. Following India's Independence and the birth of Muslim Pakistan in 1947, devotees of Rama attacked those mosques, partially tearing one down, claiming it had been built over the very site of Rama's birthplace. Muslims, fired by such vandalism, responded with rioting. Ensuing bloodshed brought out the Indian Army, units of which still remain entrenched inside Babri Mosque, whose gates are now locked to Hindus and Muslims alike. Outside those gates, however, worshipers of Rama sit day and night, singing, chanting mantras, and collecting signatures on petitions to government to "restore Rama's birthplace" to its proper historic condition. They claim to be in no rush, of course, since all believe that *Ram Rajya* will return—if only after another few thousand years. By the late 1980s, however, Hindu–Muslim rioting over that still hotly disputed single mosque-temple had already claimed hundreds of lives in Bihar as well as U.P.

India's history is shrouded in myth; yet much of Indian mythology, if not all of it, has roots in historic reality. Those roots are so deeply buried, or have for so long been burned or destroyed by floods, that we may never be able to trace them to what we call historic truth. It is as yet impossible, for example, to identify the original King Rama, whose virtuous life and prosperous reign probably gave birth to the many fables of his supernatural prowess. There seems good reason to believe, however, that such a king did reign, probably somewhere between the rivers Ghogra and Ganga in the fertile plain east of Delhi between about 1000 and 700 B.C. He may even have had a lovely wife named Sita and a loyal younger brother named Lakshman. Until the requisite verifying coins or epigraphic proof carved on stone or gold plate preserved from that era may be discovered, we must rest content with the Epic tales we know, discounting most of those stories as myth, but treasuring whatever gems remain as possible history. Ours is a slow, often frustrating process, for not only time, but both river floods and monsoon rains have conspired to obfuscate ancient India's early millennia. Still, progress is made. Glimmers of light, patches of color, the faintest echoes of real people reach out to us across that dark gulf of the past. Everywhere we look in India we can see the rebirth of ancient forms, arts, crafts, customs, and institutions—the living archive of ethnohistory that daily presents itself for inspection in village hovels, timeless tools and carts, pots painted with ancient folk art, cloth woven to antiquity's traditional patterns.

History is alive throughout India. Wherever we turn we find its myriad artifacts and vibrant evidence: palaces, temples, mosques, Victorian railroad stations, Buddhist stupas, Mauryan pillars; each century has its unique testaments, often standing incongruously close to ruins of another era, sometimes juxtaposed one atop another, much like the ruins of Rome, or Bath. Paradoxically, in some respects the earliest epoch of Indian history was more "modern" than many much later eras, almost as if to validate traditional cyclical theories.

Pre-Aryan Urbanization

More than 4,000 years ago people living along the river Indus and throughout most of what is now Pakistan enjoyed a highly sophisticated, urban, commercial civilization. Thanks to careful excavations at more than fifty sites around the Indus Valley, most important of which were undertaken at the twin "capitals" of Mohenjo-daro and Harappa, we can confidently date this civilization to at least 2300–1700 B.C. The grid patterns of urban planning and the remarkably advanced sewer and septic-tank drainage, as well as hypocaustically regulated baths characteristic of Indus cities attest to the precocity of the builders, rulers, and bureaucrats of Indus Civilization. Its arts were equally advanced, displaying technological as well as creative ingenuity, both of which are embodied in one beautiful bronze "dancing girl" cast by the lost wax process, and in many remarkable seals, whose pictographs remain undeciphered, but whose gods and animals look quite at home in modern India. One seated figure in yogic position appears to be

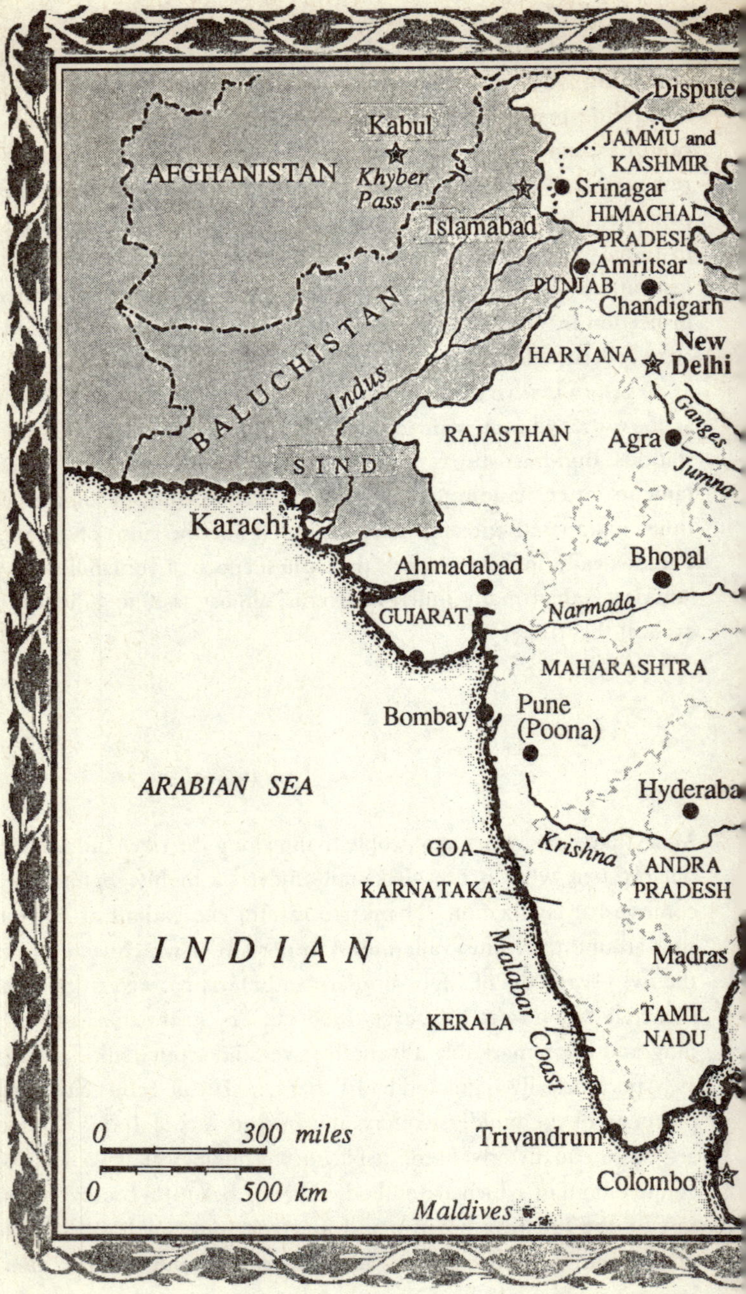

Kabul
AFGHANISTAN
Khyber Pass
Islamabad
Disputed
JAMMU and KASHMIR
Srinagar
HIMACHAL PRADESH
Amritsar
PUNJAB
Chandigarh
BALUCHISTAN
Indus
HARYANA
New Delhi
Ganges
RAJASTHAN
Agra
Jumna
SIND
Karachi
Ahmadabad
Bhopal
GUJARAT
Narmada
MAHARASHTRA
Bombay
Pune (Poona)
ARABIAN SEA
Hyderabad
GOA
Krishna
ANDRA PRADESH
KARNATAKA
INDIAN
Malabar Coast
Madras
KERALA
TAMIL NADU
0 300 miles
0 500 km
Trivandrum
Colombo
Maldives

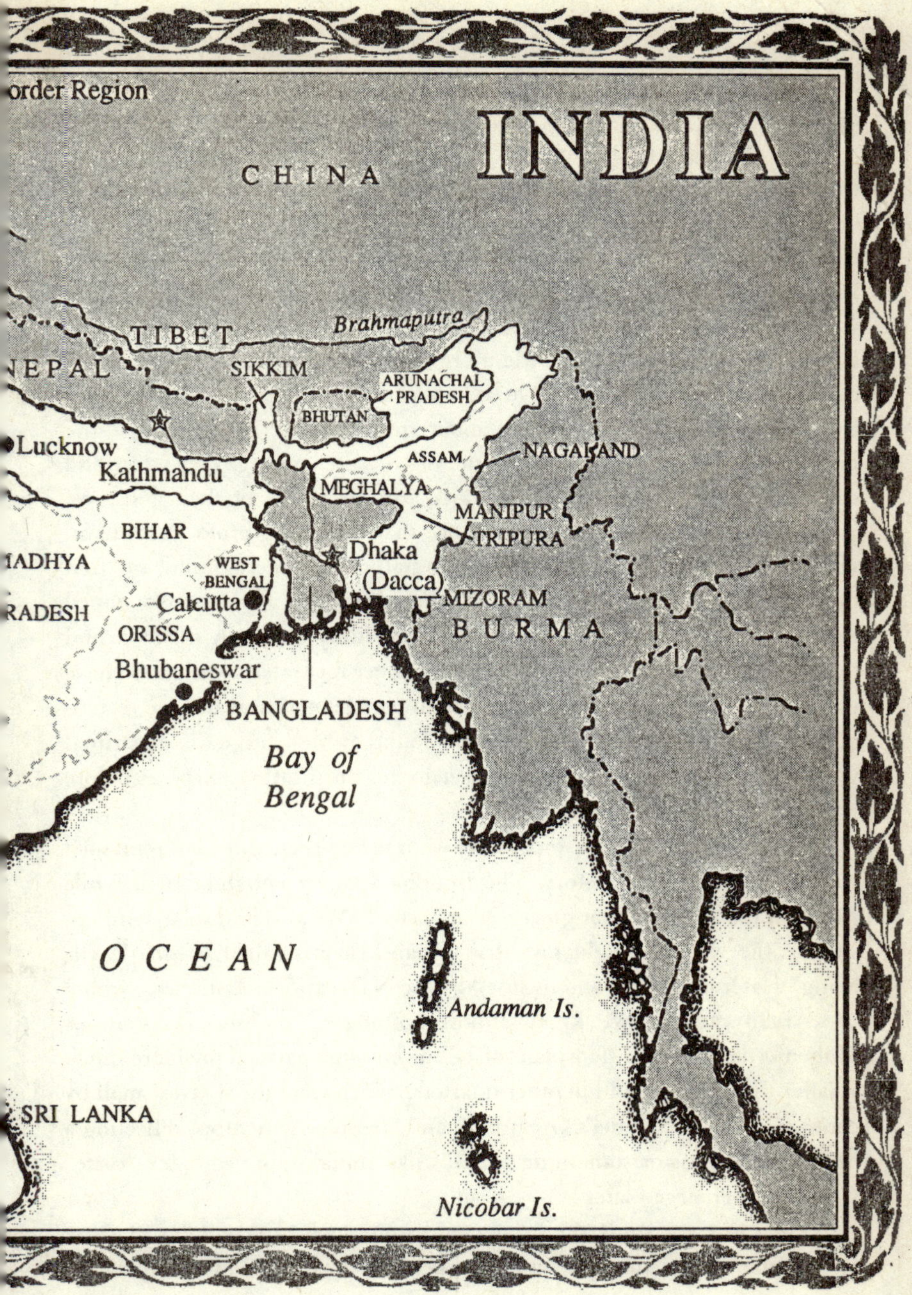

order Region
INDIA
CHINA
Brahmaputra
TIBET
NEPAL
SIKKIM
ARUNACHAL PRADESH
BHUTAN
Lucknow
Kathmandu
ASSAM
NAGALAND
MEGHALYA
MANIPUR
TRIPURA
BIHAR
ADHYA
RADESH
WEST BENGAL
Calcutta
Dhaka (Dacca)
MIZORAM
BURMA
ORISSA
Bhubaneswar
BANGLADESH
Bay of Bengal
OCEAN
Andaman Is.
SRI LANKA
Nicobar Is.

Shiva as "Lord of Beasts," and several humped bulls look alive, or at least as if they were modeled from zebus still walking the streets of any Punjabi town.

Viewed from the air, modern Pakistani homes built close to Harappa, the Northern "capital" of India's first major incarnation, are not only made of bricks burned to much the same hue of salmon, but appear to have been constructed with floorplans similar to those of their most ancient ancestors. Practical-minded Scottish engineers used so many of the bricks they found scattered around ancient Harappa as a bed for their Punjabi railroad in the late nineteenth century that little more than bare floorplans and sewerage drains remain of what must have been solid two-story homes in the ancient city that seems to have supported about 40,000 people. Who exactly those people were, however, remains a mystery—as is the language they wrote and spoke, the precise nature of their polity, and the names of their gods. We assume from various shreds of evidence that they were proto-Dravidians, possibly using a language that was a grandfather of modern Tamil, and that they were ruled by a king, who was worshiped as a god. They also worshiped the male phallus, it appears, symbolizing a fertility god such as Shiva, and the Mother Goddess. They had special reverence for water, which must have played a central role in their ritual. Hindu temples continue to have rectangular tanks, much like the "great bath" found at Mohenjo-daro, and ritual washing is important to Hindus, especially for purification purposes before approaching the icon of any god.

Certain plants, like the pipal tree, were sacred then and have remained so throughout Indian history. The Buddha attained enlightenment while seated in the shade of that great tree at Sarnath. We also find solar symbols, such as the wheel of light rays that in Sanskrit was called *su-asti* ("well-being"), later corrupted and misused by the Nazis as *Swastika*, their symbol of "Aryan purity." We know almost nothing of the social system of Mohenjo-daro, yet the floorplans of houses in some parts of town are much smaller than those found in other quarters, which were themselves small by comparison to the citadel's Great Bath and "temple" structures, reflecting a hierarchy of class or something perhaps like India's more complex "caste" system that emerged later.

The more we study the bronze and stone tools and remains of these remarkable Indus sites, the more it appears that earliest Indic Civilization contained many of the cells of the later Indian socioreligious organism. The seals themselves were obviously used to identify produce, shipped to Mesopotamia along the Makran coast, since several have been found at Sumerian digs and elsewhere. Indus exports probably included cotton cloth, a fragment of which was found at Mohenjo-daro, which still remains India's premier commercial product and export. Indian cotton cloth is now in demand, however, not only throughout Africa and Southeast Asia but also in some of the finest shops of Rome, Paris, London, New York, and Beverly Hills.

Indus Valley planners obviously understood enough secrets of water control to allow their cities to flourish for almost a thousand years, yet not without periodic rebuilding. Mohenjo-daro seems to have been rebuilt no less than ten times and was probably abandoned after the last great flood forced its surviving inhabitants to flee. We obviously don't know what happened in those dark final hours that caught so many Indus residents off guard, their outstretched skeletal remains alone mutely attesting to the panic that must have suddenly seized them. Perhaps earthquake tremors preceded the flood, or possibly triggered it. Tectonic shock might, in fact, have ruptured a major Indus dam, releasing its trapped waters. The coast has fallen since Indus Valley times, immersing the three lowest layers of Mohenjo-daro totally under water, eluding all attempts to shed historic light on their remains. Whatever cataclysmic events caused the fall of Indus urban Civilization, they appear to have come shortly before tribes of wandering pastoral Aryans reached India's western borders, somewhere between 1600 and 1500 B.C. With mighty Indus walls shattered by earth's rumbling surface and most pre-Aryan defenders drowned or forced to abandon her citadels, fleeing south for their lives, the new arrivals found scant resistance as they moved their flocks of goats and kine over the River and through the rubble that had once been a flourishing civilization.

Aryan Conquests and Emerging Synthesis

Devout Hindus believe the Aryans have always lived in India, at least since before the first Ice Age, when they migrated south from the North Pole. Historical scholarship and comparative linguistic studies of the past century and a half give us better reason to hypothesize, however, that Indo-Aryans were the easternmost wing of the once cohesive Indo-European-speaking tribes, whose great dispersion from pastureland somewhere between the Caspian and Black Seas probably occurred around 2000 B.C. That monumental Indo-European dispersion impelled some tribes west to England and Ireland, others to Germany, Greece, and Rome, still others east to Iran, from which Indo-Iranian wing the Indo-Aryan tribes broke away about 1500 B.C., migrating over snow-capped *Hindu Kush* ("Killers of Indians") mountains, down Khyber and Bolan Passes, into the Indus Valley.

All that we know about the early Aryans was preserved through oral tradition by their priestly bards, Brahmans, whose heirs painstakingly memorized thousands of Sanskrit poetic hymns considered sacred, eventually recording their scripture in "Books of Knowledge" called *Vedas*, most important of which is the *Rig*. Vedic prayers were addressed to no less than thirty-three named gods, to whom Kings (*Raja*s) and Warriors (*Kshatriya*s) as well as *Brahman*s and Commoners (*Vaishya*s) appealed for long life, good fortune, heroic sons, and rain. India's early Aryan tribals were hearty, lusty, life-affirming, drinking, gambling, fighting people, who resembled their Homeric cousins much more than they would their Gangetic Valley descendants. Their most important god, Indra, was a young hero, who wielded his *vajra* ("weapon") much the way his Icelandic cousin Thor hurled thunderbolts, using it daily to "pierce" the dark outer "covering" of the cosmic Demon, thereby releasing the sun, waters, and lowing cows.

The Vedas report nothing about the pre-Indian history of the Aryans, nor do they say anything specific concerning the Aryan conquests or Indus Valley Civilization, exept for a few references to "dark" (*dasa*) peoples, who lived in "fortified cities" (*pur*), and had to be "subdued." Indra's daily defeat of demon Vritra may, nonetheless, allegorically reflect the conquest by Aryan forces of light over the demon darkness of pre-Aryan "shells" (fortresses), possibly even King Indra's piercing of pre-Aryan dams, thus releasing their waters. The Vedas, however, were not compiled as histories but as hymnals; hence their disinterest in temporal matters, even such earth-shaking events as may have occurred less than a century before those chants were first "heard" by the Rishis. For Rishis and Mahatmas, however, and those Hindus who revere them, this world of rebirth (*samsara*) and pain is, after all, more "illusion" than real. Why bother with names, dates, or even the most dramatic of historic events? The difficulty of firmly establishing dates throughout Indian history is in part attributable to at least such widespread belief in their insignificance by many of India's best and brightest philosophic minds.

What seems clear, however, is that between about 1500 and 1000 B.C., Aryan tribes conquered the remaining pre-Aryan *dasa*s throughout the Indus Valley and Punjab, moving as far east as the plains of Delhi. When they first reached India, the Aryans were still pastoral nomads; hence no trace has been found of their villages or huts. By the end of this half millennium, however, no doubt because of much they learned about urban civilization from the *dasa*s they enslaved, Aryan cities began to rise on those plains around Delhi, whose first capital was named for Lord Indra (*Indraprastha*).

The Aryans brought the horse as well as cows to India. Aryan Rajas rode to war in horse-drawn chariots, which helped them defeat all who confronted them, as did their well-aimed arrows and hafted axes. Nomadic wandering across the Iranian plateau had toughened them into fierce warriors, and like Indra himself, they must have taken heart from draughts of "divine" Soma, swallowed before doing battle. That nectar of the gods apparently grew wild in the hills of northwestern India, and whether narcotic or psychedelic in nature, the effects of its "juice" was such that it "settled in every joint" and was worshiped in Vedic hymns as a deity second only to Indra in power. The most important ritual of Vedic Aryan faith was, in fact, building the annual Soma altar, whose fires were lit just before the monsoon started. Soma libations were deemed essential prerequisites to rain. Cows were used as early Aryan currency, paid to Brahmans who chanted mantras as they poured out Soma juice and clarified butter (*ghi*). Agni, the god of fire, smacked his hot lips and soared toward the sky as he tasted the divine offerings, passing them up to many solar divinities, whose presiding judge-on-high was Varuna.

By about 1000 B.C., iron was discovered in such accessible profusion on the Barabar hills near the Ganga around modern Patna that it could be "peeled" off for use in weapons as well as for axes and ploughs. An era of rapid change was thus launched, as the Aryan expansion eastward accelerated, owing to the conquest of hitherto impenetrable Gangetic Sal forests with iron tools and weapons. As pastoral nomadism was replaced by iron plough agriculture, tribal villages were incorporated into territorial kingdoms. India's two great Epics reflect the courtly life and martial conflicts of this era of rapid change and cultural syncretism evolving from the early integration of Aryan and pre-Aryan cultures.

The longer Epic, *Mahabharata* ("Great Bharata") is the story of a monumental struggle for territorial power around the plains of Delhi among rival Aryan cousins. The five "good" Pandava brothers are pitted in long, often treacherous battle against their 100 "evil" cousins, who initially conspire to oust them from their rightful capital by winning a game with loaded dice. Aryans loved to gamble almost as much as they enjoyed Soma. Even noble Yuddhistira, incarnate "King of Religion or Law" (*Dharma*), eldest of the Pandavas, could never resist a challenge at craps, and kept losing roll after roll, until his kingdom and entire fortune were gone, finally sacrificing even the lovely polyandrous wife of all five brothers, Draupadi. Several times the length of *Iliad* and *Odyssey* combined, *Mahabharata* is uniquely rich in ancient Indian legend, lore, character, and custom. Its heroes are all Kshatriyas, but they wander for years in North India's jungles after losing their court, prior to returning home to fight and win the epic eighteen-day battle that ends the fabulous tale. Shortly before the battle is joined, however, a brief religiophilosophic dialogue was inserted in the earlier epic. Called *Bhagavad Gita* ("Song of the Blessed Lord"), it has since become more important to Hinduism than the rest of the rambling work. Reflecting as it does post-Christian era concepts rather than ideas current in 1000 B.C., the message of the *Gita* will be considered later.

The setting of the shorter Epic, *Ramayana* ("The Story of Rama"), is about 300 miles east of Delhi at Ayodhya, and probably reflects Aryan court life several centuries later than that depicted in the *Mahabharata*. As they advanced to the east and south, Aryans came into contact with and conquered many different peoples, some quite primitive jungle folk. The *Ramayana* may be read as an allegory of what Aryans see as the conquest of "uncivilized demons" who inhabited Southern forests and disturbed the meditations of sadhus seeking enlightenment through yogic concentration. Prince Rama and his perfect wife Sita were also obliged to leave their capital and palace to wander in treacherous jungles for many years, and while so doing beautiful Sita was abducted to the island of Lanka by its demon-king Ravana, darkly as villainous as Rama was virtuous. Subsequent additions to the Epic core turn Prince Rama into an earthly emanation (*avatara*) of solar god Vishnu, sent down to save the world from Ravana's terror and torture. The original story might, however, truly indicate how perilous life in North India was from the tenth to the eighth century B.C., when respectable people could hardly venture beyond their palace walls without risking abduction, robbery, or rape. Earlier episodes of courtly intrigue at Ayodhya among the doting old king's three wives also reflect the sordid politics of harem rule, so common to subsequent eras of Indian history.

Enlisting the aid of jungle birds and beasts, especially monkeys, whose General, Hanuman, is still worshiped as a Hindu deity, Rama finally finds his poor bride and saves her after defeating Ravana in prolonged single combat. The traditionally low and suspect status of Indian women was then made painfully clear, however, since even all-virtuous Rama refused to take his bride back until she first proved her chastity through ordeal by fire. Agni himself emerges golden from the flames as Sita approaches and escorts her to Rama. They fly home together in Rama's "private plane" to inaugurate the era of Ram Rajya. Many years later, nonetheless, courtly tongues started wagging and male chauvinist questions were asked about how it was possible for Sita to live so long in Ravana's palace without once allowing that tall, dark, and handsome demon-king to lay a finger on her beautiful body. King Rama not only listened to such scurrilous gossip, but believed it, once again calling on Sita to "prove" herself. This time, in despair, she cried out to her Mother, Earth's Goddess, for "Sita" means "furrow." At her supplication, the earth opened, and up came Mother Goddess on her throne of gold, taking her lovely daughter up onto her lap, away from such foolishly doubting men.

While Aryan Epics reflect an exalted status of Kshatriyas in this era from about 1000 until 700 B.C., duller "commentaries" on the Vedas were composed by Brahman priests, who exalted themselves and their rituals in prose *Brahmana*s. Every detail of each ritual sacrifice was elaborated in these handbooks of priestly lore which helped inflate Brahmanic pretentions as well as the cost of ceremonies that soon required as many as sixteen or seventeen Brahmans to carry them out. Rajas and Vaishyas paid the lavish price in cows, Soma, ghi, and other nectar consumed by the flames. Brahmans prospered and emerged by the end of this era as nothing less than "gods on earth," whose sacred feet supposedly never touched common dirt, thanks to Brahmanic powers of levitation. Perhaps because of their status as currency, cows were now also worshiped, as were the mantras chanted by Brahmans; sacred utterances such as "*Om*" came to symbolize the universe, for example. "Sound" itself, *Vach*, was deified, as was demiurge *Brahma*, and a new specially mighty impersonal absolute called *Brahman*.

Rama's defeat of Ravana, however, symbolizing the Aryan conquest of non-Aryan demons in Gangetic forests and farther south, permitted patient sadhus to continue silent yogic meditation in those jungles. Soma sacrifices in the Gangetic valley were more often than not ill-timed to "bring" monsoon rains, and the pretentions as well as inflated costs of Brahmanic ritual started seeming more and more hollow to kings and commoners alike. For where was the Raja who never lost a war, despite all the cows he paid his Brahmans? Or the wealthy merchant who never died? Or the pious prince who never fell ill? Why waste so many valued creatures and resources on "magic" that didn't work? Some Kshatriya princes started asking radically different questions, seeking inner paths to salvation that had nothing to do with ritual sacrifices or the costly and elaborate Brahmanic establishment.

Pre-Aryan wisdom distilled from the "heat" of silent yogic meditation provided Aryan conquerors with new mystic keys to understanding and salvation. After some seven centuries of Aryan and pre-Aryan intercourse, a synthesis of what seems to have been the finest fruit of both systems emerged in scripture called *Vedanta* ("End of the Vedas"), starting by about 800 B.C. The texts of this last stage in Vedic intellectual evolution were compiled in the woods around eastern U.P. and Bihar, mostly by Kshatriyas, and are known as *Upanishads*, meaning "to sit down in front of" in Sanskrit, since that was how these ideas were conveyed, esoterically, by a single guru to his student in forest clearings. Upanishadic dialogues, often brilliant, introduced new concepts that were to become axiomatic to the subsequently emerging Hindu synthesis. The "laws of action" (*karma*) and pessimistic ideas of "reincarnation" (*samsara*) and the material world as "illusion" (*maya*) bubbled up to Vedantic light from pre-Aryan antiquity, or so it would seem, for ideologically Upanishadic thought was as far removed from robust Aryan optimism and nature-worship as Bihar is from the North-West Frontier. The ultimate goal was now "release" (*moksha*) of one's "Soul" (*Atman*) from this veil of material sorrow and pain, and from any imperative of rebirth. Historically, Aryan conquerors by this time appear to have fallen under the spell of deeper pre-Aryan profundity and quiet wisdom. Upanishadic texts, however, continued to pay lip service to Brahmans and their rituals, hence were accepted as Vedic scripture, despite their radical doctrines. Brahmans have long been ingenious assimilators and synthesizers.

Several centuries later, a more revolutionary Kshatriya Prince named Siddhartha Gautama (c. 563–483 B.C.), worshiped the world over as the Buddha, taught his own system of salvation that thoroughly rejected Brahmanic Vedic authority. The Buddha shared, however, the same eastern Gangetic environment that spawned earlier Upanishadic ideas, many of which he accepted. From what we know of Gautama's early life, and unfortunately none of our sources dates from less than a century after he died, he was born to a royal house in the foothills of Nepal, fled its ease and comfort in his late twenties, wandered for some years in the woods of Bihar, and attained "Enlightenment" (*Buddha*-hood) after deepest meditation under a tree. He devoted the remaining half century of his life to teaching his four "Noble Truths" and won so many converts and disciples that he founded a monastic order. His patron ruled the mightiest mid-Gangetic Kingdom, called *Magadha*, and granted the Buddha so many tax-free mountains from which Buddhist monks carved out their austere stone dwelling chambers, *Vihara*s, that soon the entire region was renamed Bihar.

One of the reasons Raja Bimbisara found the Buddha's rational doctrines so attractive was that he was sick of watching his favorite goats sacrificed on Brahman altars. Merchants of Magadha also responded warmly to the Buddha's nonviolent teaching, obviously feeling more in tune with the moderate pessimism he preached without fee of any kind than they did toward increasingly greedy and militant Brahman demands. The Buddha himself rejected all Brahmanic pretentions to sacrosanct powers by virtue of birth alone, insisting that "only those who behave as a Brahman *should* are worthy of receiving the respect of a Brahman." Many centuries later, the Brahmanic establishment was again to prove its unique adaptability and diplomatic skills by bringing the Buddha under the infinitely expandable umbrella of Hinduism, as an avatar of Vishnu.

Mahavira (c. 540–468 B.C.), the "great hero" founder of Jainism, was also a prince turned sage, seeking enlightenment in similar sylvan glades. The extreme severity and austerity of Mahavira's doctrine rendered it less palatable, and less universal in appeal than was Buddhism, but several key concepts of Jainism would prove of seminal import to Mahatma Gandhi, as they have to many devout Hindus. Indeed, the religion of Jainism is widely viewed by Hindus as a "sect" of Hinduism rather than a separate religion, and has remained to the present most influential in the wealthy western State of Gujarat, and among Bombay's banking and mercantile community. Jain doctrine will be considered in the next section, but like Buddhism, followers of Mahavira could choose the much steeper monastic path toward salvation or the easier low road of lay discipleship and support. Most Jains have opted for the latter.

By the end of the sixth century B.C. there were at least a dozen princely states in North India, all named in Buddhist or Jain sources of a slightly later period. These principalities generally fought their immediate neighbors over land or trade or both, unless ruling families were allied through marriage or regional alliances were reached for mutual benefit or united attack upon some third or fourth party. As a rule, Brahmanic Aryan and later Hindu Rajas and Maharajas liked to prove how powerful they were by turning loose a white stallion at the outer reaches of their domain, letting him roam free for a full year, to be followed by a troop of cavalry, who staked claim to all lands within the footloose stallion's range in the name of their Raja. Naturally, a king whose territory was thus usurped would usually respond by trying to kill or capture the stallion and horsemen who followed its trail. So ancient India's countless miniwars began and continued, until both sides were exhausted, or one surrendered, or enlightened monarchs converted to nonviolent Buddhism or Jainism, or monsoon rains began.

Ancient Imperial Unification and Its Limits

North India was still divided when Alexander the Great and his Macedonian army crossed the Indus in 326 B.C. A few years later, although Alexander died while marching home, North India was imperially unified, owing in great measure to Alexander's catalytic inspiration. Alexander's dream of world unity seems to have been transmitted to a "young stripling" named Chandragupta, whom he met shortly before his own recalcitrant army forced him to abandon India before completing her conquest.

In 324 B.C. Chandragupta Maurya founded the first dynasty to unite Gangetic and Indus Valleys under its sway. Chandragupta remained in power for some 20 years, and his Mauryan heirs governed most of India for another 120, the total life span of India's first imperial dynasty thus matching that of its last foreign rulers. Without British railroads, a telegraph system, or other weapons of modern technology, the Mauryan achievement was by far the more impressive. How was it done? First of all, Alexander showed in less than two years of victorious campaigning across the Punjab just how vulnerable those petty Aryan rajas were, how vainly narrow their vision.

None of them rallied to his neighbor's support. Each was hung separately. Chandragupta's base of power was in Magadha, his capital at Pataliputra, modern Patna; hence once he'd consolidated his grip over smaller Gangetic neighbors he could cross the Punjab with ease, for Alexander had removed its major martial obstacles.

Like Alexander, Chandragupta appears to have had a wise old teacher. Most of our primary source information about Mauryan polity comes from the *Artha Shastra*, "Textbook of Material Matters," attributed to a Brahman named Chanakya, and also called *Kautilya*, India's Machiavelli. Trusting no one, the *Artha Shastra* advises its "Prince" to train and test his own army of spies to check on the loyalty of his wives and closest ministers as well as generals and lesser bureaucrats. It should come as no surprise to anyone familiar with Kipling's *Kim* to learn that India may have invented the institution of spying, or at least developed it into a fine art, much as it elaborated upon imperial bureaucracy to the ceaseless frustration of everyone but its bureaucrats. For almost half a century after the British left, Indians continued to blame "British rule" for much of their bureaucratic red tape. Actually, the British probably learned from Indians about bureaucratic procrastination, officiousness, paranoia, and all the other contagious diseases of any complex administration. Chanakya's work remained the standard text for several Indian Empires, Guptan as well as Mauryan, almost a timeless tribute to human treachery, venality, and the corrosive pettiness of power. There was even an elaborate "Circle" (*Mandala*) theory of foreign policy that Chanakya developed, teaching every Indian monarch that the king ruling the circle of his immediate neighbor was his "Enemy," while just beyond lived his "Friend."

Megasthenes, first Greek Ambassador to the court of Chandragupta, published a personal memoir, *Indiḳa*, based on his tenure at Pataliputra, but regrettably only fragments of that invaluable primary source have survived. Those tantalizing bits throw light on the size and complexity of the Mauryan capital, whose fortified wooden walls were many miles long, surrounded by a wide moat. The Emperor's harem included a number of Greek women "guards," and just to "avoid assassination," Megasthenes reports, Chandragupta slept in a different bedroom every night. Had Megasthenes caught Chanakya's proclivity to expect the worst of people? Or were daily—and nightly—problems of India's first Emperor much the same as those of many subsequent "Universal Monarchs"? Elsewhere Megasthenes wrote that Indians "never lie" and showed "no interest" in litigation, but his contacts were obviously limited, as are the surviving fragments of his report.

Chandragupta's grandson, Ashoka (reigned [r.] 269–232 B.C.), was the wisest Mauryan as well as the greatest monarch of his day, and one of the most remarkable Emperors of World History; that is, if we can believe the enlightened messages carved onto numerous pillars Ashoka erected around his domain to keep his subjects informed of his imperial policies. For the first nine years, however, he simply followed Chanakya's handbook in realpolitik, conquering the kingdom of Kalinga, present State of Orissa, to his south. That war proved so costly in human life, causing the slaughter of hundreds of thousands, that Emperor Ashoka decided after winning it to follow paths of war no more. He turned instead to the Buddha's Law of Righteousness (*Dharma*), advocating love and nonviolence (*ahimsa*) as the worthiest ideals for empires as well as monastic orders. His faith in the Buddha's message of righteousness was posted North and South, to the distant borders of Ashoka's realm, where it would be read aloud to subjects of high or low birth, thus helping propagate goodness and moderation in all things. From this era of "Buddhist Imperial Rule," India becomes mostly vegetarian in her eating habits, at least, if not long able to banish war and violence from state policy.

Owing to Ashoka's hosting of the Third Great Council of Buddhism at Pataliputra around 250 B.C., that message of universal love spread beyond India's borders, to Burma and Sri Lanka initially, thence throughout Southeast Asia. Traditionally, Indian monarchs relished the hunt, and at least once a year ventured atop their lead elephant upon the mass slaughter of all that moved and roared within the contracting drum-beating net of their servants. Ashoka turned those yearly hunts into "pilgrimages of Dharma," going forth instead to plant seeds of love for the Law in the hearts of all who saw and heard him. Many of India's great tree-lined highways were first constructed at this time, and Ashoka's personally appointed "Overseers of the Law" ventured more often than he could to remote corners of his realm, reiterating imperial policies. India's diverse peoples and tribes thus received their first infusions of what we would now call national ideology and culture.

Mauryan imperial rule survived Ashoka's death by several decades, but rebellion contracted its southern outposts, while invasions soon spread from the northwest across the Punjab. None of Ashoka's sons or grandsons inherited his great ability to inspire and rule. Brahmanic discontent with what had virtually become a Buddhist state, moreover, spread with each fire lit to consecrate a Vedic altar, until a Brahman general led the coup that ended the Mauryan dynasty in 184 B.C. Was the message of love simply too fragile to overcome human power, lust, and greed? Had India's bastions of empire been lulled into a false sense of security, left too weak to defend themselves, by believing philosophic ideals that were never meant for administering any state?

The Mauryan collapse heralded a return to political fragmentation that would last for 500 years. Ashoka's ideals of nonviolence and unification both proved historic exceptions rather than rules of Indian history; yet once they were articulated, and even briefly tested in action, they would never be forgotten. Indian poets and saints, if not monarchs or aspiring political leaders, would often seek to inspire others to return to that "golden age" of Ashokan Dharma. It was in some respects a second Ram Rajya, only now there were pillars of polished sandstone still standing with inscriptions to attest to the reality of that enlightened age. And the famous four lion capital of Ashoka's pillar, now permanently preserved in the museum at Sarnath, which has become the symbol of India's government, reminds us with the sweet smiles of its lions' faces that even Emperors of the World, like kings of the jungle, could learn to advocate goodness, kindness, and justice for all.

Greco-Bactrian legatees of Alexander's frontier provinces were the first invaders to pour over the passes and recapture the Indus Valley. They were followed by Persians from the west and Scythians from the north, fierce mounted horsemen out of Central Asia, barbarians, whose only advantage over civilized India was their skill in martial arts. Like the Aryans, they conquered and were themselves seduced and conquered by the rich beauty and wisdom of India. The greatest of their monarchs soon became Buddhists, and it was along the "diamond path" of Central Asia's silk route that China learned the wisdom of the Buddha by the first century of the Christian era. North-West India's Gandharan bridge to East Asia and Persia was to emerge as the ancient world's most vital artery of cultural exchange as well as trade. Buddhism journeyed east over those passes at the top of the world, evolving into a religion with many schools and countless gods, among them a compassionate "Savior" (*Bodhisattva*) resembling Jesus in some respects. Buddhist monks had for some time been venturing West as well, and their reverential gesture of piety, open hands pressed together, would soon become as common among Christians as it remains among Hindus, who use it with "*Namaste!*" as their regular greeting. Might the concept of divine grace and and a blessed Savior also have originated on Indian soil? Judas Thomas the Apostle was said to have spent his last years in India, and his "tomb" is worshiped by South Indian Christians, who call themselves "Syrian Christians." Whatever the historic accuracy of such speculation or enduring myth may be, the Greco-Bactrian-Persian bridge proved a busy two-way cultural highroad for several centuries both before and after the dawn of the Christian era.

The Hindu synthesis emerged with the second great imperial unification of North India, the golden age of the Guptan Dynasty (c. A.D. 320–550). Chandra Gupta I asserted his power from the gateway passes of the North-West Frontier to the Bay of Bengal, choosing Pataliputra as the capital of India's classical Hindu Empire. The new blood and new ideas that had poured into India during the previous five centuries of fragmentation obviously sufficed to keep fresh barbarians at a distance, and the Guptan line grew only stronger for fully a century in power. The peak of Guptan glory was reached in the reign of Chandra Gupta II, "Whose Effulgence Matched the Brightness of the Sun," from A.D. 375 to 415. Kalidasa, the Shakespeare of India, lived and wrote his great Sanskrit plays and poems at Chandra Gupta's court. The most beautiful and world renowned of Kalidasa's dramas is *Shakuntala*, named for its forest-nymph heroine who captures the heart of her sporting king, and bears his son, Bharata, after they marry by self-choice "love-rite." Kalidasa's genius at depicting characters with all the universal foibles and weaknesses of human flesh, and his brilliance at portraying unique details of Indian court life and Guptan mores, provide the best insights into daily life during India's golden era. The contrast between the forest retreat of Shakuntala's saintly stepfather and sylvan friends and the courtly world of King Dusyanta and his jester reflect polar settings of Indian society and its continuing romantic search for escape from the bustle of urban demands to the idyllic delights of nature. For all its luxurious urbanity, Guptan India never lost its ideal of the simple life in a jungle clearing, even as modern India has retained the same Gandhian goal of retreat to a self-sustaining village ashram.

With the emergence of Hinduism and its prolific pantheon of new gods, temple homes began to be built in every city of Guptan India, and at every sacred riverbank or mountaintop, wherever the gods might require shelter. The greatest and sturdiest of those stone temples have survived the ravages of time and invading armies, as have the contemporaneous paintings and monumental sculptures of the caves at Ajanta, Ellora, and Elephanta. Classical Indian arts were all religiously inspired, eloquently echoing the undying faith of generations of artists, artisans, and patrons, who expended their lives and fortunes in such labors of devotion to the divine. The beautiful forms, motifs, and symbols that animate India's universe of divine art were to be repeated, refined, and regionally altered, yet basically preserved in their classical molds to modern times. Such visual continuity has helped reinforce pillars of tradition provided by Scripture and Epic literature that extended the white umbrella of Hinduism to every remote corner of a subcontinent, whose regional variations remained vivid, but whose overarching integration was bolstered by each interlude of Empire.

Buddhist pilgrims from China have left several firsthand reports of their travels in Guptan and post-Guptan India, further beacons of historic light into this era of classical integration. Those Chinese pilgrims noted the Hindu dynasty's tolerance of Buddhist ideas, a product no doubt of the Buddha's integration within the Vaishnava fold, yet also reflecting deeper currents of Indian patience with and toleration of differences. The "caste" system had by now evolved its own techniques for coping with pluralism, permitting Indian society to maintain its tenuously integrated continuity without threatening the manners, habits, or "purity" of diverse segments of that delicately balanced Hindu system. By leaving local customs and mores alone, interfering as little as possible with the private, familial habits of people in disparate provinces and limiting imperial rule to the collection of taxes and overall maintenance of security against foreign invasions, Guptan monarchs assured their prosperous tenure for almost two centuries. Much of the secret of their success was the "weakness" of their rule, its minimally intrusive nature. Imperial Indian power has been greatest when it was least bothersome, could remain untested, and was thus impervious to rebellion or displacement. Often true of British rule, the same might also be said of independent contemporary New Delhi's power.

Islamic Conquests

Adherents to the militant brotherhood of *Islam* ("Submission" to the will of Allah) slashed their sharp scimitars through the body politic of South Asia, starting in Sind in A.D. 711. The faith founded by Prophet Muhammad in the sands of Arabia a century earlier thus reached India's shore the same year as it did the Iberian Peninsula, borne with zealous fervor by its galloping legions of true believers in God Almighty and His awesome Last Judgment. Muslim armies were to continue their assault on Indian soil for the next thousand years, during the last 500 of which Muslim monarchs would rule most of India. Not since the Aryan invasions had so powerful, persistent, unyielding a challenge been launched against Indic Civilization and its basic beliefs and values. In many ways, the Islamic impact was more divisive, its legacy more deeply threatening to Indian Civilization, than Aryan rule ever was, for the Aryan–pre-Aryan synthesis gave birth to Hinduism. The only major offspring of Hinduism and Islam has been the Sikh community, which may prove almost as disruptive a challenge to Indian unity as Islam has been.

The Arab conquest of Sind came by sea. The desert sands of that lower Indus province of modern Pakistan proved no springboard, however, for conquering the rest of the subcontinent. Sind remained an isolated Muslim outpost in South Asia for almost three centuries before emerging as a portent of India's "Muslim era." The true dawn of that era came when Mahmud of Ghazni, "Sword of Islam," led his first band of Afghan raiders down the Khyber Pass in A.D. 997 on what would for the next quarter century be an annual hunt. Mahmud's game were Hindus and their temples, whose icons offended his sensibilities as much as their gold and jewels roused his greed. The rapacious Ghaznavid raids were followed by those of their successors to Afghan power, Ghors, whose bloody "holy wars" (*jihads*) against Hindu India left an equally bitter legacy of communal hatred in the hearts and minds of India's populace. Those early centuries of fierce Muslim assaults upon "infidel" Indians confirmed Hindus in their views of Muslim "foreigners" as polluting "Untouchables," although far more predatory. The gulf of mistrust, fear, and hatred that was soon to divide India's population from its martial Muslim rulers subsequently served to undermine all attempts to reunify the subcontinent, whose political fragmentation since 1947 reflects in part the historic incompatibility of those early centuries of Muslim–Hindu intercourse.

After 1206, Muslim Sultans of Perso-Afghan-Turkish descent made the rust-colored plains of Delhi their home for three and a quarter centuries. No fewer than thirty-five Muslim Sultans sat on thrones of five successive dynasties at Delhi, ruling over a kingdom aptly called "despotism tempered by assassination." Once Muslim rulers settled permanently on Indian soil, however, they encouraged doctrinal accommodation toward Hindu subjects, no longer given just the extreme options of Islam or "death." Like Christians and Jews, Hindus were permitted to retain their own faith at the price of paying a special head tax for "Peoples of the Book," those whose partially revealed Scripture raised them above "infidel" status. Not that Brahmans enjoyed paying for the privilege of remaining second-class subjects in their own land! Still, it was better than forced conversion or death.

Over time the process of cultural accommodation and synthesis, linguistic, artistic, genetic, rubbed off many sharp edges of doctrinal difference between Hindus and Muslims. Most of the Muslims, who represented close to one-fourth the total population of India by the late nineteenth century, were descendants of converts or Hindu mothers. After centuries of residence in India, the "Brotherhood" of Islamic faithful acquired some of the features of Hinduism's "caste" system, particularly with regard to marriage, Sheikhs and Sayyids, Afghans and Muslims, of Persian or Turkish ancestry preferring mates from within their "own" communities. In some circles Muslim eating habits became more restrictive. No "strangers" have ever remained totally aloof from the impact of India. Islamic iconoclastic fervor was also tempered by time and the impossibility of destroying every statue on every Hindu temple in the land. Muslims were soon sated by gestures of symbolic destruction of gods and goddesses, most of whose images, if they date from pre-Muslim times, have a broken nose, arm, or other fractured feature, hacked from their stone body by some angry Muslim sword.

Islam's final wave came out of Central Asia, led by a direct descendant of Ghengiz Khan and Tamerlane named Babur, "the Tiger," founder of the great Mughal Empire. From 1526 to 1530 Babur defeated every Sultanate and Hindu Rajput army that took the field to challenge his relentless march. Born to fight and rule, Babur turned Delhi and Agra into twin capitals of the Empire he bequeathed to his heirs, Great Mughals who ruled India for more than two centuries. The Mughal Empire was the strongest dynasty in all of Indian History, nominally retaining the throne of Delhi until 1858, although for most of its last century the Mughals ruled as puppets of British, Maratha, or Afghan power.

As had been true of the Mauryan and Guptan dynasties, the third Mughal Emperor proved to be the greatest monarch of his line. Akbar, "the Great," reigned almost half a century (1556–1605), the high point of Mughal "national," enlightened rule, although not of territorial sovereignty. Akbar was the first Muslim monarch to initiate a general policy of religious toleration toward Hindus, wooing the Rajputs through marriages that forged potent "national" alliances, seated on his throne of inlaid marble as quasi-divine monarch of *all* Indians. Some orthodox Mullahs considered Akbar a traitor to Islam, raising battle cries of "Jihad" against him. The Emperor's elephant corps stamped out such rebellions with ease. Several of Akbar's leading advisers were Hindus, the head of his imperial revenue department had been born a Brahman, his military commander, a Rajput prince. Akbar chose his leading lieutenants personally, rewarding them lavishly with lands, whose revenues, generally about one-third of all crops, sufficed to support from 500 to 50,000 cavalry troops and their horses, always ready to gallop at the emperor's call. The system proved effective in securing the borders, expanding them over the Hindu Kush to incorporate most of what is now Afghanistan within the Delhi-Agra-Fatehpur Sikri imperium. Fatehpur was Akbar's own new capital, created to celebrate the birth of his son and heir, although an inadequate water supply forced its abandonment after little more than a decade. Its haunting sandstone shell survives on the Jaipur road west of Agra, a tribute to Akbar's eclectic ingenuity, its ghostly ruins all that remain of his dream of uniting Hindus and Muslims within a single polity.

Persian poetry and arts added sophistication and colorful beauty to the Mughal court and its urbane culture during the effulgence of its seventeenth-century golden age. Persian became the official language of the Mughal Empire, rather than Babur's cruder native Barlas Turkish tongue, and was to remain so until English deposed it in 1835. Like their Persian neighbors, Indian monarchs have generally loved beauty, luxury, sensuality, pageantry, and the trappings of power. The Great Mughals pandered to such indigenous tastes, importing the best Persian artists and craftsmen to their sumptuous palaces, adding pearl mosques and peacock thrones encrusted with jewels to marble, fountained halls, engraved with Persian poetry, such as "If there be Paradise on earth, it is here, it is here, it is here!" Shah Jahan ("Emperor of the World") was the most extravagant of Mughal spenders. His profound remorse, or guilty conscience, following the death of his beloved wife, Mumtaz, resulted in the construction of the Taj Mahal, which provides breathtaking proof of the magnificence of Mughal art at its apogee. Little wonder that centuries later, a different sort of extravagant empire would dub its early film-makers "moguls."

The fatal weakness of later Mughal monarchs was not their spendthrift waste, however, but their return to narrow-minded Islamic orthodoxy. India's starving millions could at least derive vicarious pleasure from viewing the Red Fort at Agra or the Taj Mahal, but what joy or satisfaction could Hindu masses feel from Emperor Aurangzeb's (r. 1658–1707) reimposition of the hated head tax on non-Muslims? Or what pleasure could they take from his ban on alcoholic beverages? Or on repairs to Hindu temples? The "prayer-monger" *Padishah* ("Emperor") conquered more real estate than any of his ancestors, yet Aurangzeb did so only after wading to his throne through the blood of his brothers, and stirring up a storm of Hindu hatred throughout the Deccan, Rajasthan, and the Dravidian South. He also unified the Sikhs of the Punjab as no Mughal before or after him did, by torturing and beheading the ninth Guru, for refusing to convert to Islam. The first Guru, Nanak (1469–1538), had founded the Sikh faith, a peaceful blend of his own inherited Hinduism and Islam, which he learned from his dear Muslim friend. Following Aurangzeb's harsh persecution, however, Sikhs fused themselves into an "Army of the Pure" (*Khalsa*), changing their names from passive "Disciples" (*Sikh*s) to martial "Lions" (*Singh*s). Militant Sikhism was thus forged in the furnace of Mughal antipathy, the swords of that mightiest of Punjabi warrior communities initially sharpened against Muslims. After mid-1984, however, when Mrs. Gandhi ordered the Indian Army to "liberate" Amritsar's Golden Temple, Hindu–Sikh antipathy became modern India's most volatile internal problem.

Maratha opposition to Mughal rule was led by Shivaji (1627–1680), father of the Maratha confederacy, and spread from its Poona (Pune) base within half a century of his death to the environs of Delhi, Calcutta, and Madras. As the founder of Indian guerrilla warfare, Shivaji was reviled by Mughal generals as a "mountain rat," but his shrewd tenacity in battle was matched only by his Hindu faith in his motherland. Shivaji made *Sva-raj* ("Self-rule" or "Freedom") his mantra, launching the first major Hindu revolt against Muslim monarchs and their armies. His successors were so inspired by his fierce "national religious" passion that Pune would remain one of the key cradles of Indian Nationalism in the late nineteenth century. Brahman *Peshwa*s ("Prime Ministers") of Pune administered the Maratha confederacy under nominal control of Shivaji's heirs. The singularly astute Peshwas remained a unique secular and religious dynasty ruling the Deccan for almost a century, until the British defeated their last incumbent in battle in 1818.

After Aurangzeb's death in 1707, Mughal power started its slow decline. Court feuds and factional in-fighting at the center coincided with growing provincial autonomy and the emergence of several regional limbs more robust than the Delhi-Agra head. The Nizam was the first powerful minister to abandon Delhi and carve out his own southern kingdom in Hyderabad early in the eighteenth century. Nawabs of Oudh and Bengal, formerly mere deputies of the Great Mughal, became virtual kings in their own wealthy Gangetic domains by midcentury. Simultaneously, Afghanistan became a powerful threat from the west, under its own Amirs, who embarked on a series of bloody plundering raids into the Indus Valley, wresting the Punjab as well as the North-West Frontier from Delhi together with the peacock throne.

As the Great Mughal thus diminished in status, potent new forces appeared along India's coast, trading quietly, inconspicuously, at first. They came by sea from the West, and for most of the early eighteenth century were so busy fighting one another that they seemed uninterested in or incapable of challenging any Indian rulers, local or regional, not to speak of the awesome might of that empire, whose twin capitals were remote from the tiny British and French "factory" towns that dotted the Southern peninsular trunk of the slumbering elephant that was India.

Westernization and Modernization

Western Europeans were lured to India in the late fifteenth century by the pungent scent of spices and the prospect of enormous profits to be reaped from direct access to their source in the "Indies," around the southern Cape of Africa. Spices were needed to make European meats palatable in that prerefrigeration era of history and to mull wines and ales. Arab and Venetian middle men grew wealthy on the most lucrative spice trade and, after the Turks seized Constantinople in 1453, they, too, threatened to become spice-dealing barons. Prince Henry the Navigator of Portugal invested heavily in his Lisbon school of cartography and navigation for half a century before that Portuguese national commitment finally bore fruit. Admiral Vasco da Gama led a tiny fleet of three cannon-bearing caravellas across the Indian Ocean to weigh anchor at the port of Calicut on India's Malabar Coast in 1498. The spices he carried to Lisbon a year later brought enough to pay for the entire fleet and all its expenses no less than thirty times over. For devout Portuguese Catholics at Lisbon's Court, short-circuiting Arab and Turkish Muslims was almost as delicious an incentive for expanding that direct trade with India as were its rich profits to Iberian merchants. A new age in East-West relations that would ultimately affect the nature of life throughout India had begun.

For most of the sixteenth century, with the aid of Papal mandates and sea-faring cannon, Portugal enjoyed its lucrative monopoly over the Indian Ocean spice trade. The Arabs, who had previously controlled the spice trade from India to Ormuz and Aden, never mounted cannon on their dhows, which were swiftly driven away by Portuguese fire. After 1580, Spain's King Phillip absorbed Portugal and its vast profits through a marriage that brought Iberia unity and world power. Eight years later, however, Queen Elizabeth's English buccaneers helped cyclonic winds blow Spain's "invincible armada" to the bottom of the North Sea. The Indian Ocean trade was thus opened suddenly, it must have seemed miraculously, to Dutch and British sea merchants, who initially joined forces in a Protestant "crusade" against the Catholic monopoly over Eastern seas and spices. As the seventeenth century was about to dawn, on December 31, 1600, Elizabeth I granted her royal charter to a company of twenty-five London "adventurers" led by Thomas Smythe, permitting them to export precious bullion and monopolize England's Eastern trade for fifteen years. It was the first of many incarnations of Britain's East India Company, humble merchants who would in two centuries replace the Mughal Empire with their own Raj.

The British learned much from their Portuguese precursors in India. They learned to fortify "factory" warehouses, erected at strategic ports around India's coast, and to hire and train Indian sepoys (*sipahi*, originally "police") to guard their forts, soon expanding those police guards into Company armies. They learned to serve the Great Mughal, who really needed nothing from the West but naval protection for his annual pilgrim ship to Makka, replacing the Portuguese escort flotilla after Captain Best defeated it on the high seas off Surat in 1612. Their astute mixture of nonproselytizing and emphasis on profitable trade gave the British an advantage over their Portuguese competitors at Agra's Court, where Jesuit Fathers were constantly conspiring to convert young princes as well as Great Mughals. British merchants sought permission only to engage in "quiet trade," and learned from Portuguese errors as well as positive experience by initially banning all missionaries from British East India Company vessels or forts.

From their Dutch "friends" the British learned that Europeans in search of profits could be more treacherous than Indians, falling back on Surat and Malabar as their major bases of trade only after a Dutch massacre of British merchants at Amboina in 1623. The Dutch also developed a specie drain-minimizing triangular trade in the Indian Ocean, using cotton cloth they bought for gold along the Coromandal coast to purchase far more valuable cargoes of spice than they could have secured by selling the same gold directly tc Spice Islanders. It wasn't long, however, before the Dutch decided simply to buy Indian weavers instead of their produce, shipping thousands of South Indian slaves to the Islands to cultivate spices on Dutch Company-owned plantations. From the "wise Dutch," British Company officials thus learned before century's end to multiply their profits by exploiting India's cheap labor as much as her rich natural resources. It was, however, the ingenious French who taught suppliant British merchants how to move from the porch and backyard of India's mansion through its heavy gates into the great treasure-filled quarters of the imperial palace.

Joseph François Dupleix, Governor of the French Company at Pondicherry in the early eighteenth century, was the first European to perceive that the Mughal Empire's disintegration was western Europe's golden opportunity. The "Nabob Game" Dupleix devised and inadvertently taught his English contemporary in South India, Robert Clive, to play, turned the key that opened every door to India's all but undefended imperial palace. Dupleix understood the dynamics of India's post-Aurangzeb internal distintegration, and took full advantage of it with his command of modern European muskets and techniques of close-order drill, which he used to scatter the Nawab of Arcot's huge, undisciplined army outside Madras in 1746. The French had seized that British Company fort on the coast north of Pondicherry after learning that France and Britain were at war over Austria's succession. Clive, an insignificant Company scribe at the time, was among those captured, but he was soon released by the French. Dupleix had bigger fish to fry, buying up his choice of disaffected claimants to various South Indian thrones of Mughal provincial power that fell vacant in the 1740s. Dupleix's Nawabs were enthroned by French political "advisers," who remained at their sides, leaving enough Indian Sepoys trained in modern martial tactics under "green beret" command just beyond the palace gates to help keep the puppet Nawabs in line. If any Nawab tried to assert his independence he was never heard from again, while a new prince of the same family would immediately be found to sit more docilely on the throne. Had Dupleix been permitted to complete his game, he might have become the power behind every Indian throne, but the early stages of the process proved expensive, and Versailles soon lost confidence in their brilliant but arrogant servant who never bothered to write home or explain why his business had evolved into so costly an enterprise. The man who could have been India's king was, therefore, recalled, leaving clever Bob Clive to play and win his own Nabob Game in Bengal.

Clive's victory in the "Mango-Grove," called "Plassey" in 1757, was achieved more by subverting the new young Nawab of Bengal's army, through the treachery of his jealous old uncle, Mir Jafar, than by any superior strength of British arms. Clive's agents had contacted and paid Muslim Mir Jafar handsomely with gold squeezed from Hindu bankers of Calcutta in return for the ambitious Mir's promise to keep his powerful cavalry in rein throughout the June battle of Plassey. When the fighting ended in British victory, therefore, Clive installed Mir Jafar on the throne of Murshidabad, sent the former Nawab's headless corpse downriver, and returned to Calcutta himself with a king's ransom. The decade that followed was one of shameless British plunder of Bengal, for the nominal Nawab was enthroned up North, but English birds of "prey and plunder," as Edmund Burke later called them, flew by every British clipper into Calcutta's crowded harbor, extorting as much as they could squeeze from timid and terrified "natives," whose gentle passivity left them helpless victims to this new breed of foreign vulture. When monsoon failure followed before the end of the 1760s, Bengal's dusky fields turned white with the bleached bones of a third of its dead peasant population.

Britain's Parliament took some notice of the Company's corruption in

Bengal only after the Honourable Company reported its bankrupt inability to pay the government a promised annual tax of £400,000 for trading in India, which had seemed small enough to the Commons in view of the conspicuous wealth displayed by returned Nabobs like Clive in London-town. Thus began a series of Parliamentary inquiries, each of which imposed more controls inhibiting Company servants in Bengal, Bombay, and Madras from doing whatever they pleased, requiring periodic review of Company books and officials by Home Government committees and ministers, as well as the annual day of India debate in both Houses of Parliament. First the government of Lord North, and later that led by William Pitt, passed acts designed to control, regulate, and Anglicize the administration of the Company's remote, wanton, unwieldy outposts in the "Orient."

Warren Hastings, the Company's first Governor-General (1773–1784) of Bengal, ruled India more like a Nawab than an Englishman, hanging those he disliked, extorting funds from rich royal widows as well as from lying Rajas, and selling British troops to serve as mercenaries for native allies. His primary loyalty was to his mercantile Company, not to the Crown of Great Britain, which tried its best to restrain him by sending out several advisers as his councillors. Hastings ignored them, however, and finally fought a duel with the most troublesome, Philip Francis, driving him home, where Francis pressed for Hastings's impeachment. Although Hastings saved and integrated British India, just when Cornwallis lost Britain's first Empire in America, it was Lord Cornwallis who went as the Crown's most trusted Governor-General and Commander-in-Chief to India while Warren Hastings was being tried for "high crimes." Before leaving Calcutta in 1793, Cornwallis signed a code of forty-eight regulations that would become the backbone of the British Indian Empire, which soon displaced old Mughals with its breed of new Civil Servants.

Many new ideas as well as techniques and institutions—which in sum we call "modernity"—came to India as a consequence of Western rule. Private ownership of land throughout Bengal was one of the first and most important of these, introduced by Cornwallis's Regulation Code. Zamindars who had hitherto been appointed by Mughal Emperors to collect the imperial (or Nawab's) share of each harvest, and held their positions of authority only as intermediaries between monarch and peasant as long as their ruler desired, now became Landlords (*Zamindars*). They were given solemn deeds to property in return for which they promised annually to pay to the

Company Raj a permanently fixed sum of revenue that would never be changed and which collectively was a bit more than the total required to administer the entire region. India's soil would thus pay for the new government.

As a good Landlord himself, Cornwallis firmly believed that only by giving Bengal's Zamindars a permanent stake in the system would they keep their property as fruitful and well cared for as possible and remain loyal to the British Raj. He was proved right about the latter at least in 1857–1858, when Zamindari loyalty saved Calcutta during the Indian War ("Sepoy Mutiny"). But these were not the original Zamindars, who had by then lost their lands through foreclosure. They had used their deeds to secure loans they could not repay in years of monsoon failure, and they learned to their amazed anguish that British justice defended private property and its documents more than traditions or the tattered honor of an outdated aristocracy. Absentee moneylenders, mostly Hindu, residing in Calcutta, the Tagores, Roys, and Sens, thus replaced Mughal Zamindars as new Landlords of Bengal, becoming bankers and leaders of an early nineteenth-century Hindu renaissance and social revolution as well. Once set in motion the pace of change accelerated.

The growing use of English in Bengal, Bombay, and Madras—indeed, wherever British Company officials or merchants ventured—proved an equally revolutionary agent of change. One of the Company's best and brightest young servants, Mountstuart Elphinstone, rightly predicted early in the nineteenth century that by introducing English education to India, he and his colleagues in the Company Raj were "paving the highroad" for their "return home." By opening doors and windows to Western learning, science, and literature, the poetry of revolution and freedom as well as gospels of loyalty and reverence for authority, the English handed keys to young Indian minds that soon echoed the cries of Milton, Burke, Mill, Morley, and Gladstone. Pandora's box could never be closed. As Thomas Babbington Macaulay, the Company's first Law Member and Britain's leading champion favoring English education for Indians, put it before the House of Commons in 1833:

> It may be that the public mind of India may expand under our system till it has outgrown that system; that by good government we may educate our subjects into a capacity for better government; that, hav-

> ing become instructed in European knowledge, they may, in some future age, demand European institutions. Whether such a day will ever come I know not. . . . Whenever it comes, it will be the proudest day in English history.

Few Englishmen were as enlightened or liberal as Macaulay, however, and most servants of the Raj tried to keep the lid of Indian aspirations and hopes clamped down as tightly as possible, for as long as superior British power permitted.

Strong winds of Evangelicalism blew from London's Clapham Sect of "Saints" to the Company's presidency ports of Calcutta, Bombay, and Madras after 1813, when the ban on missionary travel to and settlement in India was lifted. The Church of England appointed its first Bishop of Calcutta, and he sailed east with three archdeacons, and the first wave of Methodist, Baptist, and Scottish Church missionaries as well, all of whom were eager to help bring India's "benighted heathen up" to Christ. Few Hindus or Muslims appreciated being told to "repent" on their knees to keep from "burning in Hellfire" as their unbaptized ancestors were doing, but many Indians attended mission schools and were helped at mission hospitals. Indeed, to this day some of India's finest private schools are run by missionaries, American and Australian as well as British, as are several of India's best hospitals. The total number of Indian converts to Christianity would always remain far below one percent of the population, and most of those converted came from the "outcaste" bottom rungs of Hinduism's ladder or the most impoverished ranks of Muslims—"rice Christians," as they were called. More recently, Billy Graham and his Mission have had greater success with East India's Naga and Mizo tribals, who had no previous roots in either of India's great religious traditions. Motivated by their zeal to teach Indians to read the Bible, British Missionaries pioneered the study of many modern Indian languages, compiling the first bilingual dictionaries as well as grammars in Marathi, Bengali, Hindi, Tamil, and Telugu. The inadvertent benefits to Indian secular learning and international communication of Christian missionary labors thus proved to be of considerable utility and value.

The Industrial Revolution, born in Manchester's midland factories and mills in the last quarter of the eighteenth century, triggered almost as many changes in Indian society and economic life as it did in Great Britain itself. Manchester manufacturers' faith in laissez-faire and their lobby's power in

Parliament put an end to the Company's monopoly privileges after 1813, opening India to rapacious armies of free merchants, seeking new and bigger markets for their prolifically produced goods. Cotton cloth manufactured in Manchester mills was sold up a thousand rivers throughout Bengal for half or one-quarter the price of hand-woven "Dacca," launching a revolution of sorts in British India's economy by putting millions of Indian spinners, weavers, and other handicraftsmen out of work in a matter of decades. British India's Company Raj imposed no inhibiting duties on British imports. While Britain was quickly transforming itself into a more urbanized, industrialized "modern" society, India thus fell backward in time, so to speak, losing most of its artisan manufacturing capabilities, forcing millions of unemployed craftsmen to return to the soil to scratch meager livelihoods directly from crowded land. By the end of the nineteenth century, India was, in fact, less urbanized than it had been at the beginning, with over 90 percent of its much larger population dependent upon the land alone for support.

Technological innovations introduced in India by the new British Mughals did, nonetheless, stimulate positive, enduring changes, whose legacies continue to help modernize Indian life. The "penny" post and telegraph systems, introduced in imitation of British models during the second and third quarters of the nineteenth century, were perhaps the most important unifiers in recent Indian history. What better way to inculcate the concept of British India as a "single state" than to charge no more for delivering a letter or parcel a thousand miles away than in one's own neighborhood? And how could anyone learn important news, whether of a personal, business, or public nature, faster than by the magic of silver wire transmission? The Post & Telegraph Service, integrated into a single system by British India's Crown Raj after 1858, inadvertently stimulated nascent "National" unification of distant, often disparate, provincial Indian consciousness. Communicating with one another, Indians of Bengal and Bombay, Madras and Punjab soon realized that they shared the same fears and aspirations, the same dreams and despairs. Soon the brightest among them realized that it was time to come together, meet regularly to discuss those problems and plans, thus perhaps helping themselves and one another to find sensible, or at any rate plausible, solutions.

The railroad provided the ideal means to facilitate such face-to-face meetings. Britain charged India heavily for every mile of steel rail hammered into her soil, shipping all rolling stock as well as track thousands of miles from Birmingham's mighty mills to Bombay and Calcutta in British bottoms, guaranteeing handsome profits to every interested British party along the way. Still, in historic retrospect, whatever the price, however exorbitant it may have seemed, nothing has proved a better bargain or more useful to India's economic growth and development as well as national unity. The fifty thousand or so miles of railway infrastructure planted on Indian soil by British imperial enterprise has been a modernizing network for independent India, her steel frame grid accelerating change.

Indians employed in all of the institutions introduced or adopted by the British Raj became, whether they liked it or not, agents of Westernization—and, as a rule, of "Modernity." The Army, largest of such institutions, was no exception, although purposely kept as "traditional" as possible during most of the era of Company Raj, since British officers soon learned that change often translated into mutiny. Even so innocuous a matter as trying to simplify headdress and ordering sepoys of the Madras Army to shave their beards had led to revolt in 1806. Thereafter, laissez-faire became the first rule of military life as well as commercial enterprise. Brahmans and other high-caste Hindus of the huge Bengal Army were permitted to cook their own food, wear their turbans any way they wished, and keep their scraggly beards, as long as they fought hard and stayed "true to their salt." By the middle of the nineteenth century the Company had armed and trained almost a third of a million Indians to fight and subdue other Indians, all of whom were either integrated into the regulation provinces of the British Raj or became "subsidiary ally" princely states, namely, Nabob-puppets.

The only region that eluded such integration was Afghanistan. British troops marched twice over those North-West Frontier passes, each time subduing Kabul and "liberating" its palace, but never defeating or pacifying the fiercely independent Pathan tribals of that hermit kingdom, who wiped out a British Indian Army in the disastrous First Anglo-Afghan War, and the British Resident of Kabul with most of his escort during the Second. But even such mighty warriors as the Gurkhas of Nepal and the Sikhs of the Punjab were firmly brought into line before midcentury, although the cost in Bengal Brahman and Kshatriya lives lost was high. The Sikhs paid dearly for their soil with the blood of their bravest warriors, taking the highest toll of British Indian lives since the First Afghan War, but by 1849 the entire Punjab was "painted red" as regular British domain. It came none too soon, for in less than a decade the Sikhs would be called upon by British commanders to help them recapture Delhi.

By the mid-1850s British power was so great, the engines of British industry moved with such speed and self-confidence that it seemed as though nothing and no one could slow them down. Arrogant Company rulers saw no reason to continue any pretense of Nabob Game politics, and emerged from the shadows behind most of their puppets' thrones to stand in the glare of full sovereign power before Indians of every class. Ex-Nawab's pensions were discontinued without notice, princely territories proclaimed to have "lapsed" to British hegemony, other states including that of Britain's first major Indian ally, the land of King Rama himself, Oudh (now U.P.), annexed outright. The Great Company, which had once been so true to its contracts at least and its word as well proved faithless as a prostitute. Lands that had enjoyed tax-free status since the dawn of the Mughal Empire were usurped by beardless British Collectors riding at the head of troops of Indian sepoys.

The ancient aristocracy all across the Gangetic plain and Central India seethed with frustration and hatred. Then the high-caste Hindus and devout Muslims who filled the ranks of Bengal's Sepoy Army feared that their British Christian officers were trying to convert or turn them into Untouchables or infidels, when new Enfield rifles with greased cartridges were issued in 1857. British Colonels and Brigadiers ordered their men to "bite off the tips" of those cartridges, which the Hindus believed to be greased with cow fat, Muslims with pig fat, each an anathema. Every sepoy who refused to obey those "sacrilegious" orders was stripped of martial insignia, sent home to simmer and spread the fever of his anger to his entire village or town in North India's heartland. By May 1857, when the torch of Mutiny ignited the cantonment at Meerut, north of Delhi, all of Oudh and Delhi itself were dry tinder awaiting Revolt. Within the month the last of the Mughals was restored to his throne, and Lucknow and Kanpur (Cawnpore) were in flames. The Indian War had begun, and would rage as a bitter racial conflagration for more than a year.

Britain's victory in 1858 was the victory of Western modernity over India's aristocratic and traditional religious longings for a return to the past. It was not simply the decayed and dying Great Mughal Empire that they wanted to restore in all its glory, but a past symbolized by Shivaji Maharaj, who hated all Mughals as well, the Maratha Confederacy, and King Rama himself, a golden age of Hindu myth when Gods walked on earth miraculously to save their devout suppliants from demon darkness. It was all of those incompatible eras and dreams divided by centuries or millennia, each with its clamoring band of dedicated loyalists clutching tattered banners of faded fortune, Mughals in Delhi, Marathas in Cawnpore, the Nawab of Oudh's courtiers in Lucknow—less than a day's march from one another but a march never made. For they were all divided by unbridgeable gulfs of belief, by doctrines that taught them to hate or mistrust one another, by cries of terror and ancient fields of battle soaked with the blood of ancestors who never learned that to be free of foreign rule "Indians" had first of all to think of themselves as Indians, not as Brahmans, or Rajputs, or Afghans, or Mughals. That, too, was part of modernity.

The British were also divided in many respects. Their Presidency Armies of Bengal, Bombay, and Madras each had its own separate command, and there were Yorkshire lads and Westminster boys, and men of Gloucester and Orange. There were Scotsmen and Welshmen, Manchester manufacturers and Leadenhall merchants. But they were all British. Once the gauntlet had been thrown down and the sky blazed with mutiny, regional differences faded, local dialects paled to insignificance before the enormity of the challenge by "faithless natives" that welded them into a single bullet, which each of them bit with tenacity. The new Enfield rifles helped them win, firing faster and surer than the older sepoy muskets. The telegraph gave them a vital assist, flashing its warning word of "mutiny" from Agra to Calcutta, before that silver lifeline could be cut. Then Calcutta flagged down a British fleet of fresh troops headed toward China's Opium War, just as they were sailing across the Bay of Bengal, and London never hesitated to send more troops and more rifles and more, until the job that needed doing was done. Until the war was won.

For India by midcentury had become more than a mere mercantile company's monopoly outpost. It was an empire ten times the size of Great Britain, a continent teeming with uncounted millions of people, whose needs for British manufactured products were incalculable. She was a world of "lost and benighted souls," all of whom needed "saving." She was a virgin field of infinite capability for absorbing the time and talents of the younger sons of Britain's finest families, who really had no better prospects for employment back home. India was the sort of distant challenge that dreams and myths are made of, and soon she would become the brightest jewel in the crown of Britain's Empire. No price was too high then for Britain to win her back, especially since all costs of the Mutiny would be recharged directly to India's soil, added to her annual revenues over the next decade. The Company, however, had to pay in part as well, for the War cost too many British lives for the merchant proprietors of Leadenhall Street's John Company to weather it unscathed. The Commons and Crown made the Company Britain's scapegoat. On November 1, 1858 Viceroy Lord Canning read aloud in Allahabad the Proclamation of Queen Victoria announcing her British Crown's (Parliament's) direct assumption of full responsibility for India's administration and Her Majesty's solemn desire that all the princes and peoples of India "should enjoy that prosperity and that social advancement which can only be secured by internal peace and good government. . . . In their prosperity will be our strength; in their contentment our security, and in their gratitude our best reward."

Young India's Revolutions and Reforms

For India, however, the immediate aftermath of that horrible war brought neither prosperity nor contentment, certainly no gratitude. There was initially only the acid taste of bitter defeat, the stench of death and more dying as countless bodies of "Nigger Pandeys" caught by British vigilante squads were blown away from mouths of cannon to which they were strapped. Lord Canning was Christian aristocrat enough to forgive his wretched defeated adversaries, but the noble amnesty he announced only won the opprobrium of his own countrymen in India, who sneeringly dubbed him "Clemency" Canning for the remaining years of his Viceregal tenure. Few Englishmen could forget that White women's bodies had been butchered and stuffed into wells in Cawnpore, or that the Nana Sahib had treacherously ordered the remnant of the British garrison there massacred after it surrendered, having been promised safe passage downriver. Just as few Indians who lived through the indiscriminate burning of innocent Gangetic villages by Colonel Neill and his avenging band of British butchers would ever forget British racial intolerance or brutality. The wounds went too deep to be erased from the collective consciousness of either camp, even after scar tissue appeared to patch things over. Long after the bleeding actually stopped, seering memories remained vivid and continued to be passed down in whispers from generation to generation.

The ninety years of Crown Raj would not really suffice to exorcise those wretched memories. Never again would the British trust any Brahman or Kshatriya of Bengal or Oudh with weapons of any sort. Only "martial races" would be recruited into the Indian Army reorganized by the Crown, Sikhs and Muslims of the Punjab and North-West Frontier, Gurkhas of Nepal, and princely Rajputs who had remained loyal during the war. Loyalty was the only test of "martial birth," in fact, although British social Darwinians tried elaborately to invest their policy of fear and hatred with some facade of pseudoscientific rationality. The new Crown regiments were mixed promiscuously by race and caste as well as region, so that none would ever again respond to a single mutinous outcry, whether Hindu, Muslim, or Sikh. Even were it possible for them to rise again as one man, however, all scientific weaponry, machine guns and cannons, later tanks and planes, were kept strictly in White British hands, to cow the Native army whenever necessary. Never again would the British Raj be lulled into a false sense of security. Bravely its best lads sailed East to take up their "White Man's Burdens" as Magistrates, Collectors, Judges, builders of Empire, bearers of Civilization's bright mantle of Western Christian virtues to a land shrouded by heathen darkness, sunk deep in the mire of degenerate superstition and treacherous sloth.

Young India responded to the new Raj and its stricter, harsher, more suspicious ethos by cautiously retreating at first, withdrawing to allow the worst of its wounds to heal. The path of violent revolt had proved hopeless. Never again would it be tried on a scale approaching the magnitude of the Indian War of 1857. Some diehards remained irreconcilable, including the adopted last Peshwa, Nana Sahib, who apparently escaped to the jungles of Nepal, and India's Joan of Arc, Rani of Jhansi, who died fighting in her saddle. There would be others as well, one proclaimed himself Minister to Shivaji II and led his band of Maratha horsemen, followed by British troops who finally caught and killed them all. Most Indians, however, faced the reality of overwhelming British fire power and their own impotent disarmament, accepting the imperative of finding alternate paths to the future, if there was to be any future for their Motherland. In the anguished night of the aftermath of that dreadful defeat, young Indians began to awaken to the realization that before they could free India from the shackles of British rule they would have to unite themselves. And before they could accomplish that unification they would have to transform themselves.

So at least it seemed to the brightest of young India's intellectuals, the English-educated modernists of Calcutta, Bombay, and Madras, most of them Hindus of the new Zamindar and moneylending middle classes, who hoped to be teachers, barristers, newspaper editors, or entrepreneurs. They were all heirs to Macaulay's policy of creating a new breed of Anglo-Indian, "Indian in blood and colour," but "English in taste, in opinions, in morals, and in intellect." Many, indeed, became model "Englishmen," total collaborators in Empire, content to remain in the lower ranks of British official services or in the servants' quarters of private homes and clubs, living out their quiet lives in relative comfort and ease, the clerks and bearers, the station flag-wavers and tea-brewers of the new Raj, a few of them helping direct its Managing Agency Houses as well, its banks and its accounting firms, its mints, and its morgues. Some were not content with such tepid gruel, however, asking more of life, seeking tougher challenges to test their mettle.

The best among these, Mahadev G. Ranade (1842–1901), graduated at the top of his class from one of the three new British universities, and went on to become a High Court Judge in Bombay, but was also instrumental in founding the Indian National Congress. A Poona Brahman by birth, Ranade, for all his Anglophile learning and career, never forgot that his was the land of Shivaji long before Macaulay arrived. He devoted his free time to helping modernize and reform the Hindu faith, improving the status of Hindu women, and teaching generations of young disciples to commit their lives and labor to revitalize and reform their country so that India could stand on its own culture's two feet, free of foreign rule because its modern leaders would have made themselves as impartial and good, or better, than British officials who treated them so contemptuously. Gopal K. Gokhale (1866–1915), Ranade's foremost disciple, was also a Poona Brahman of such erudition and moderate restraint that he would preside over the Indian National Congress a full decade before his death, and become the leading unofficial Indian adviser to Britain's Liberal Secretary of State for India, John Morley (1906–1910), and one of the most courageous critics of Calcutta's Government of India from within its own legislative Council. He was also Mahatma Gandhi's "political Guru."

The moderate, Anglophile approach of Ranade and Gokhale was to remind all British Collectors, Magistrates, Governors, and Viceroys of promises made by their Queen in her royal Proclamation of 1858, on the direct assumption of the governance of India:

> We declare it to be our royal will and pleasure that none be in anywise favoured, none molested or disquieted, by reason of their religious faith or observances, but that all shall alike enjoy the equal and impartial protection of the law; and we do strictly charge and enjoin all those who may be in authority under us that they abstain from all interference with the religious belief or worship of any of our subjects. . . . And it is our further will that, so far as may be, our subjects, of whatever race or creed, be freely and impartially admitted to offices in our service, the duties of which they may be qualified, by their education, ability, and integrity, duly to discharge.

Other young Indian leaders, like Poona Brahman Bal G. Tilak (1856–1920), took a more militantly anti-British, basically Hindu orthodox but revolutionary approach, insisting that "*Sva-raj* ["Self-rule" or "Freedom"] is my birthright, and I must have it."[1] *Lokamanya* ("Revered by the people") Tilak and his many disciples learned enough English to be able to use it against British officialdom whenever they were brought to trial or taken into police custody, but the major thrust of their message to British foreigners was "Get out of my house, and give me the key before you go!" They put freedom before reform, whereas Ranade and Gokhale argued that before India was truly ready for the responsibilities connected with self-rule it was essential for all Indians to treat one another more humanely, with equality for all religions, sexes, castes, and outcastes. India's pluralism and historic legacies of conflict would also be exploited, although less ingenuously, by British officialdom whenever questions of greater freedom were raised.

Not that all Englishmen, even among those in the Civil Service, were hostile toward growing Indian aspirations for freedom. Indeed, the true "father" of India's National Congress, Alan Octavian Hume, who had devoted much of his life to the Indian Civil Service (ICS), seminally challenged the graduating class of Calcutta University to think "Nationally" in 1883, when he wrote to remind them: "You are the salt of the land. . . . And if amongst even you, the elite, fifty men cannot be found with sufficient power of self-sacrifice, sufficient love for and pride in their country, sufficient genuine and unselfish heartfelt patriotism to take the initiative . . . then there is no hope for India. . . . for 'they would be free, *themselves* must strike the blow.' "[2] And India's Viceroy that year, Liberal Lord Ripon, as well as his courageous Law Member, Sir Courtney Ilbert, were almost lynched by angry mobs of Calcutta English, who viewed them as "traitors" to their "own kind" for trying to enforce British equality before the Law for Indians as well as Englishmen in the backwaters of Bengal. Equally outspoken British Liberals, like Sir Henry Cotton and Sir William Wedderburn, early Presidents of the Indian National Congress, dedicated their energies and fortunes to helping young India assert her claims to enjoy all the rights, privileges, and freedoms of British subjects the world over. They were, however, exceptions to the rule of general indifference or malicious contempt that most Englishmen serving in India came to feel toward most of the educated Indians they met in the closing decades of the nineteenth century. By and large, Muslims, Princes, and peasants were better liked by British rulers. Was it because they were less "spoiled" by English education and the great expectations it seemed to impart to the young Hindu Bengali "Babus" who acquired it? Or were they consciously reaching out to Indian allies among the Muslim minority quarter of the population, the powerful Princes and silent majority of peasants, whose best interests British bureaucrats could always insist they had uppermost in mind, whenever pushy Congresswallas (Congressmen) accused them of indifference to Indian demands, needs, or political aspirations? Had they learned the game of divide et impera ("divide and conquer") from their Latin studies of ancient Rome? Was it just a modern extension of the old Nabob Game they knew so well? Or were they so truly altruistic that they simply wanted to remain in India to keep "the balance straight," and prevent Hindus and Muslims from slitting one another's throats? Perhaps their motives were a complex mixture of all these elements.

Before the end of the nineteenth century, at any rate, Muslim modernist voices were heard from, most powerful of which was that of Sir Sayyid Ahmad Khan (1817–1898), founder of the Anglo-Oriental Mohammedan College at Aligarh, who insisted that Congress did not speak for the Muslim "quarter" of India's population. Sir Sayyid argued at Meerut, in 1888:

> Now, suppose that all the English and the whole English army were to leave India, taking with them all their cannon and their splendid weapons and everything, then who would be rulers of India? Is it possible under these circumstances two nations—the Mahomedans

> and the Hindus—could sit on the same throne and remain equal in power? Most certainly not. It is necessary that one of them should conquer the other. . . . Now, suppose that the English are not in India and that one of the nations of India has conquered the other, whether the Hindus the Mahomedans, or the Mahomedans the Hindus. At once some other nation of Europe . . . will attack India. . . . Everybody knows something or other about these powerful kingdoms of Europe. . . . their governments are far worse, nay, beyond comparison worse, than the British Government. It is, therefore, necessary that for the peace of India and for the progress of everything in India the English Government should remain for many years—in fact forever!

This earliest public articulation of what would much later be called the "two-nation theory" must have been received most warmly by the British officers and their Muslim soldiers who heard it on the historic parade ground where the "Great Mutiny" had started. Small wonder that Sir Sayyid's Aligarh College, later Muslim University, was to become the intellectual cradle of the Muslim League, born in 1906, and four decades after that, of Pakistan itself.

Some young Muslims, especially Shi'ites of Bombay Presidency, attended early Congress meetings, and at least one of them, Justice Badrudin Tyabji, presided over Congress in 1887, insisting: "I, for one, am utterly at a loss to understand why Mussulmans should not work shoulder to shoulder with their fellow-countrymen, of other races and creeds, for the common benefit of all." But his was almost as lonely a dissenting voice among Indian Muslims as Hume's was among the tight and narrow ranks of British Civil Servants who disagreed with him. In 1905 British bureaucrats, who generally preferred Muslims to Hindus and highly valued their loyal service in the British Indian Army, were cheered as much as Aligarh and Dacca's Muslims by the Lord Curzon Government decision to partition Bengal. The line drawn just east of Calcutta created a new Province of British India, called East Bengal and Assam with a Muslim majority, to be administered from Dacca (now Dakha, capital of Bangladesh). The remaining half of the former province was called West Bengal, but included what are now the State of Bihar to its north and Orissa to its south, thus leaving its Bengali-speaking Hindu majority an overall linguistic minority in the new Western Province. Bengali-speaking Hindus were outraged. Indeed, most Indians, certainly most Congressmen, viewed that first partition of Bengal as proof positive of Britain's perfidious rule. A popular boycott movement against British manufactures was launched by Congress in response, and National bonfires burned Manchester cloth all over West Bengal—symbolic altars of political protest sacrificing goods of the hated British Raj to ancient Hindu Gods. As the positive side of boycott, a new *Sva-deshi* ("Of our own Country") movement gathered momentum from this time onward, supporting indigenous industries in cotton and everything else, from matches to iron and steel. India's young entrepreneurs, Parsi Tatas of Bombay, Hindu Birlas, and Sarabhais of Ahmedabad in their vanguard, became staunch supporters of Congress and its moderate leadership, among whose brightest new lights were two remarkable barristers of West India: a Muslim named Mohammad A. Jinnah (1876–1948) and a Hindu named Mohandas K. Gandhi (1869–1948).

The Impact of Mahatma Gandhi

Gandhi returned from South Africa in 1906 to attend the Indian National Congress in Calcutta at the end of that year, where Gokhale delivered the speech that Jinnah helped write for Congress' ailing Parsi President Dadabhai Naoroji (1825–1917). Gandhi's appeal on behalf of South Africa's beleaguered Indian community was warmly received by Congress, thanks to Gokhale's strong support and the publicity of Gandhi's first *Satyagraha* ("Hold Fast to the Truth") movement about to be launched in the Transvaal. As a Barrister of the Inner Temple, Gandhi had gone to South Africa in 1893 to represent a leading firm of Indian Muslims there, but soon experienced the traumatic shock of violent racial discrimination when he was thrown out of a first-class train carriage for which he had purchased a ticket, merely because of his skin color. The cold bitter night he spent reflecting on that experience changed Gandhi's life and subsequently altered the course of India's National Congress. Gandhi was inspired by early Christian concepts of love and self-effacing poverty, and the more recent struggles of such geniuses as Leo Tolstoy, in developing his revolutionary tactics to fight against South African discrimination and hatred. He organized the Indian Natal Congress and stirred the community of Indians settled there to heroic nonviolent resistance against the Transvaal Government's "Black Acts," returning to India at the start of World War I. He no longer wore Saville Row suits, adopting the dress (*dhoti*) as well as the simple diet of a poor Indian peasant. He reached back to the ancient Vedic belief in "the Real" as "the True," choosing *Satya* as the key word for the revolutionary movement he led, linking it inextricably to Jain and Buddhist, later Hindu, "Nonviolence," *Ahimsa*, which he also defined as "Love." By joining Truth to Love, Gandhi argued, one could "move the world." And he did.

The futility of the first World War helped *Mahatma* ("Great Soul") Gandhi to convince many of his followers that Western Civilization was "Satanic." The whole mighty structure of urban, industrialized society, Gandhi insisted, was a violent, repressive, monstrous machine that crushed human souls and destroyed all the good and beautiful things of nature. Like Thoreau and Tolstoy, he argued in favor of the simplest life, which put him in tune with most of India's village-based population. His appeal was, in fact, so traditionally Hindu in most respects that he came to be viewed as a Yogi or Sadhu and was worshiped by millions of Hindus as a Mahatma.

Most Englishmen and Muslims found Gandhi less comprehensible, certainly less appealing. Britain's Liberal Secretary of State for India during World War I, Edwin Montagu, considered him a "Trotskyite" and a "dreamer," failing totally to appreciate the mass appeal of his unsophisticated manner. Mohammad Ali Jinnah, in contrast, who had emerged as leader of the Muslim League as well as the brightest young leader in Congress by mid-World War I, was viewed as more brilliant than Viceroy Lord Chelmsford. "It is, of course, an outrage," Montagu confessed to his diary after meeting Jinnah, "that such a man should have no chance of running the affairs of his own country." Yet at Lucknow in 1916, Jinnah seemed close to achieving leadership over a united Congress–League National movement, whose joint "Pact" demand for postwar constitutional reforms he had been instrumental in drafting. Montagu, moreover, officially announced in the Commons in mid-1917 that 'the policy of His Majesty's Government, with which the Government of India are in complete accord, is that of the increasing association of Indians in every branch of the administration and the gradual development of self-governing institutions with a view to the progressive realisation of responsible government in India," all of which sounded as though Dominion Status for India were waiting only for the Great War to end.

Yet for India, Armistice was followed by more dreadful repression, triggered by more martial "law." The Rowlatt Acts, which Gandhi labeled "Black Acts," extended wartime suspension of civil liberties and Common Law safeguards, as the very first postwar legislation introduced by the Government of India. "The fundamental principles of justice have been uprooted and the constitutional rights of the people have been violated at a time when there is no real danger to the State," Jinnah wrote Chelmsford in resigning from his Legislative Council, "by an overfretful and incompetent bureaucracy which is neither responsible to the people nor in touch with real public opinion."[3] Gandhi called upon Indians to pray and vow never to obey such heinous laws. Satyagraha protest marches and strikes spread from Bombay to Delhi, from Bengal to Punjab.

The battle was joined in Amritsar in April 1919, where a walled "garden" (*bagh*) less than half a mile from the Sikh Golden Temple became the anguished birthplace of India's revolutionary Nationalism. Reginald Dyer, the deranged British brigadier who ordered his Gurkha and Baluchi troops to open fire without warning at thousands of unarmed people trapped at close range while celebrating a Hindu festival, later testified that he had acted to "produce the necessary moral and widespread effect." He murdered some 400 innocents, wounded at least 1,200, then hurried his troops out of Jallianwala Bagh without offering any medical assistance to the poor groaning, dying human beings shattered inside. Lord Chelmsford labeled such actions merely "an error of judgment, transitory in its consequences." Montagu at least insisted on Dyer's immediate recall, and early "retirement." But the British House of Lords amassed a small fortune to express their appreciation for Dyer's "valiant services" to the Crown, presenting the purse to him with a bejeweled sword on which was inscribed "Saviour of the Punjab." The Jallianwala Bagh massacre did have a widespread moral effect throughout India, convincing many moderate leaders of Congress that gradual constitutional devolution of power was no longer enough. Throughout the war, after all, Indians had been told that Britain and her allies were fighting against Prussian "barbarism" and "frightfulness." Now the British had behaved as badly; worse, from India's point of view.

Gandhi launched his first nationwide Satyagraha in August 1920. He called upon Indians everywhere to boycott British goods, British Courts, British schools, British honors, British jobs—in short, to withdraw Indian support from the vast, monstrous Machine of Empire until it ground to a halt. He tried to win the mass of India's Muslims as well as Hindus to his side, by adopting pan-Islamic demands on behalf of the defeated Turkish *Khilafat* ("Caliphate") as the first plank in his own movement. He called upon his disciples prayerfully to welcome suffering, to court prison, to face death, if need be, without flinching or violent response. "No country has ever risen without being purified through the fire of suffering," India's yogic leader reminded the millions who joined his revolution."Mother suffers so that her child may live. The condition of wheat-growing is that the seed grain should perish. Life comes out of death. Will India rise out of her slavery without fulfilling this eternal law of purification?" Tens of thousands filled the prisons of British India within the year. All of India seemed to have become a giant prison by the end of 1921, responding to the Mahatma's call. Then just a few months later, in Spring 1922, an angry mob of "Satyagrahis" immolated two dozen Indian police inside their own station at Chauri Chaura, which became a huge cremation pyre. When Gandhi heard that horrible news he publicly confessed to having made a "Himalayan blunder" by assuming that his illiterate followers were, in fact, sufficiently purified and disciplined to carry out a mass peaceful protest. The Mahatma-general called a halt to his campaign, leaving many of his most ardent young followers behind bars, wondering why they had courted arrest for such a leader. Gandhi himself withdrew to his ashram-village community to spin and weave, devoting his time and talents for most of the rest of the decade to his "constructive program" of socioeconomic reforms that included labor on behalf of "uplifting" Untouchables, whom Gandhi called *Harijans*, ("Children of God"). He would not lead another Satyagraha campaign until his 1930 Salt March.

Jinnah's frustrations at what he considered Gandhi's unrealistic, irrational, and unpredictable leadership of Congress after 1920 led first to his own withdrawal from politics, but later to his return as the president of a more militantly separatist Muslim League. Other conservative Anglophile Hindu and Parsi leaders abandoned Congress to found the small new Liberal party, or similar tiny political groups that had some influence in government circles, but no real following. Pandit Motilal Nehru (1861–1931), father, grandfather, and great-grandfather of three of independent India's Premiers, started his Swarajist party as a group within Congress, thereby permitting political pragmatists like himself and C. R. Das to win seats in the new Central Assembly "Parliament" of British India. From there they could frankly inform the Viceroy and other British officials of what they considered wrong with government, and of what needed doing to fix it. Motilal, a Kashmiri Brahman, had served as President of Congress and was one of its wealthiest backers, donating his palatial home at Allahabad to the Congress for its headquarters, and helping prepare his only son, Jawaharlal (1889–1964) to inherit his leadership of the Party as well as the Nation. A cosmopolitan, aristocratic lawyer as elegant in dress and manner as Mr. Jinnah, Motilal initially found Gandhi almost as hard to understand as Montagu did, but he was drawn to the Mahatma thanks in good measure to his son's admiration for Gandhi's revolutionary idealism.

Motilal Nehru chaired a prestigious committee that drafted a "Constitution" for an Indian Dominion in 1928 that would have been a secular democratic reflection of Britain's parliamentary system. Jinnah and his League insisted on more "safeguards" for Muslims as their price for endorsing the Nehru Committee's proposal. Jawaharlal and other young radical leaders of Congress like Subhas Chandra Bose of Bengal viewed Motilal's recommendations as too timidly conservative, on the other hand, making "Complete Independence" (*Purna Swaraj*) their goal. The Mahatma remained aloof from such matters, preferring to spin his cotton, waiting to be called upon to lead the next Satyagraha. Motilal's inability to rally the broad spectrum of Indian political parties to his constitution's support doomed it to an early demise.

In 1930 Gandhi led a loyal band of disciples from his Sabarmati ashram in Gujarat to the seashore near Dandi, where they gathered "illicit" salt from the beach, defying the British Government's monopoly on the use and sale of salt, all of which had to be purchased in Government shops and was heavily taxed throughout British India. Soon millions followed the example of their Mahatma, and once again British jails filled to capacity within months. At Jinnah's suggestion, Labour Prime Minister Ramsay MacDonald convened the first of a series of Round Table Conferences in London that December to tackle and seek to resolve India's constitutional problems. Princes, Muslims, Liberals, and British officials met in glittering array, but with Gandhi and other leaders still in jail Congress was not represented at the first London Conference, which was thus characterized as an attempt to stage "Hamlet" without the Prince of Denmark. Predictably, the prolix and costly effort failed.

The following year, Viceroy Lord Irwin released Gandhi and met with him till they agreed upon a truce-"Pact" that permitted the Mahatma, in good conscience, to sail off to London to attend the second Conference there, as sole representative of the Congress. It proved an equally futile gesture, for the Muslims and many princes each had proliferating demands of their own, as did the Anglo-Indians, Sikhs, Untouchables, the Liberals, and Civil Service officials. Everyone insisted upon "safeguarding" his precious constitutional turf. Yet how could so many divided, irreconcilable, often antipathetical interests reach agreement on anything in a matter of days, weeks, months, or decades? It was, of course, impossible. So Gandhi returned to India to his prison "ashram" cell, and much later, after medical release, to his "constructive program," hoping to rebuild the world in the image of his village community, a Hindu variant of primitive Christian communism. "The real 'White Man's Burden,'" Gandhi argued, "is to desist from the hypocrisy which is eating into them. It is time White men learnt to treat every human being as their equal. . . . 'Do unto others as you would that they should do unto you.' Or, do they take in vain the name of Him who said this? Have they banished from their hearts the great coloured Asiatic who gave to the world the above message?"

The failure of the Round Table Conferences presaged the Partition of India, for the gulf between revolutionary Nationalists leading the Congress and the far more conservative Muslims, and still more conservative princes, proved impossible to bridge. Liberal and Labour leaders of the British Empire were wise enough and farsighted enough to know that the years, if not days, of British rule over India were numbered. Tories like Birkenhead and Baldwin refused to admit that inevitability, as Winston Churchill would to his dying day. But the only real question by the mid-1930s, a decade before the end of Crown Raj, was how to wind things down. To whom should the batons be handed? How was it all to be accomplished without tearing up those thousands of miles of track, destroying all the dams and concrete canals, or burning the bridges that had cost so many hundreds of millions of pounds sterling to build? And who would lead the army? Who would control the police? How was that to be managed without causing riots that might annihilate half the population, because the other half felt outraged at the raw deal it received? How long would Muslim troops march when commanded by Hindu Brahmans or Banias? And what was to become of the Sikhs? Or Christians? The deeper one probed, the more impossible any single, or simple solution became. There were too many "Indias," it seemed, to be reconciled within any one constitutional formula. How on earth had the

British Raj survived as long as it had, many of those responsible for maintaining its existence now wondered, awed at their own achievement.

Then they did devise a Constitution, of sorts, an incredibly complex federal structure designed to bring Indian princes into harness with British Central and Imperial authority. Only it never worked, was never even dragged out to a test runway. Impossible to fly anything that cumbersome! So their superstructure was scuttled and in 1937 elections were held in British India's eleven provinces, and Congress, the Muslim League, and dozens of smaller parties ran candidates for what would become India's great pre–World War II experiment in "provincial autonomy." Nehru and Vallabhbhai Patel, India's first Deputy Prime Minister, managed the seven Congress provincial ministries. Jinnah was left to fume and revitalize his Muslim League by turning it into a single platform party for Muslims, demanding their own Muslim state, their own nation—soon to be called "Pakistan." Gandhi continued to spin at his new ashram in central India, where he lived in humble poverty, which cost the Congress High Command a small fortune for periodic pilgrimages to consult their Mahatma about most of India's problems, none of which disappeared.

World War II accelerated the process that brought an end to the British Raj with its transfer of power in the War's aftermath to two nations—India and Pakistan. The Viceroy's autocratic declaration that India was at war in September 1939 led Nehru and his Congress High Command colleagues to withdraw political support from the British Raj by ordering all Congress ministries to resign from provincial office. The seventy-year-old Mahatma went back on active duty as Congress' leader, organizing a series of wartime Satyagrahas that would return him, Nehru, Patel, and most other Congress activists to British prisons throughout most of the war. Jinnah announced a "Day of Deliverance" as soon as he heard of Congress' decision to resign its provincial power, urging Muslims throughout India to "Thank God" for having been "delivered" from the "tyranny" of a "Hindu Raj." While Congress and its Hindu leadership thus came to be viewed by most Englishmen, in India as well as in London, as "cowardly traitors" to the Crown, just when Britain needed help most, the Muslim League and its leader were perceived as staunch friends. Small wonder that British Viceroys and elder statesmen in Whitehall, Westminster, and Downing Street did everything possible to help meet what they considered the "just demands" of India's Muslim minority throughout the War at least. Muslim troops remained a disproportionately high number in all ranks of the Indian Army. From early 1940, *Quaid-i-Azam* ("Great Leader") Jinnah's Muslim League proclaimed "Pakistan" the only goal of their party, representing "all the Muslims" of South Asia.

In 1942, with Japanese troops fast approaching India's eastern gates, the British War Cabinet sent Labour's Sir Stafford Cripps to India to propose "Dominion Status" in the immediate aftermath of the war for India as a whole, but with the proviso that any province that voted not to join such a dominion could "opt out," thereby implicitly presaging the birth of a Muslim Pakistan. Gandhi and Nehru were most distressed by that offer, reading in it the thin edge of the wedge of partition. "If that is all you had to offer, why have you come so far?" Gandhi asked Cripps. Soon the Mahatma called upon every Englishman to "Quit India!" His mantra to his own people was equally simple, "Do or die!" Next morning, on August 9, 1942, he was arrested. In the tragic months of violence that ensued, the British Indian Army was ordered to bomb and strafe rioting Indians in several Northern provinces, especially Bihar and Bengal. Thousands of Indians were killed, tens of thousands wounded, a hundred thousand or more arrested in the undeclared war that was waged by the British Raj against what was no longer the "brightest jewel" in His Majesty's Crown.

Most of the Indian Army remained loyal, however, although some 60,000 British Indian troops taken prisoner by the Japanese in Singapore were released to serve under Subhas Chandra Bose in his *Azad Hind* ("Free India") Indian National Army, marching through Burma, hoping to "liberate" Bengal. Bose's force was stopped by monsoon rains just outside of Imphal in Manipur State in 1944, then driven back by Allied reinforcements flown in after the rains. When brought to trial in Delhi's Red Fort after war's end for "treason," Hindu, Sikh, and Muslim officers of the Indian National Army (INA) were defended by Nehru himself, and emerged national heroes. Britain's Field Marshal Viceroy, Lord Wavell, and his Commander-in-Chief understood at that moment in 1945 that the Raj was doomed, for all ranks of their Army that held it were fast "turning soft." Britain's final two postwar years were a holding action designed to maintain some "illusion of permanence," while the newly elected Labour Government desperately searched for a formula to make the imminent transfer of power to Indian hands as peaceful as possible.

The 1946 Cabinet Mission's three-tiered federal scheme was India's last hope for independent reincarnation as a single state. Jinnah actually agreed to accept it, even though his "Pakistan" remained only inchoate within its Muslim-majority "group" of provinces on the northwest and northeast. Gandhi had blessed the plan as a "faithful fulfillment" of British promises to India, but Nehru and Patel publicly refused to concede that it would in any way diminish the "total sovereignty" of the Constituent Assembly that was still to be convened in New Delhi, and would then be free to devise whatever Constitution its majority wished. After that fateful press conference, in August 1946, Jinnah abandoned hope of peaceful reconciliation with Congress, calling upon his Muslim League cadres to launch "direct action." It was the black dawn of a year of civil war, prelude to South Asia's Partition in mid-August 1947. Jinnah flew from New Delhi to preside over the birth of his own Dominion-Nation of Pakistan in its new capital, Karachi. Nehru raised the flag of the independent Dominion of India over the Red Fort that Shah Jahan had built for himself in Old Delhi, cautioning his countrymen to remember that "the service of India means the service of the millions who suffer. It means the ending of poverty and ignorance and disease and inequality of opportunity."

Mahatma Gandhi did not attend any of the festive ceremonies during that month of slaughter and pain, when 10 million refugees crossed lines that were hastily drawn on maps through the Punjab and Bengal, which overnight became international "borders," leaving all Hindus and Sikhs on one side vulnerable to Muslim attack, and all Muslims on the other just as vulnerable to Sikh and Hindu attack. As many as a million lives were estimated lost in the months of chaos and terror that followed Partition. Gandhi walked from village to village through the heart of that violent madness along the eastern border, trying to restore peace, preaching Ahimsa. Wherever he appeared, people bowed down to touch his feet and worship his visage, but when he moved on the madness returned, the mayhem and blood lust continued. In Delhi itself there were similar acts of brutality against Muslim families that had lived there peacefully for generations, as refugees poured in like locusts from the Punjab, telling of Pakistani Muslim murders and rapine that fired fresh cries for more blood. Once again the Mahatma tried to calm turbulent waters. Each night he preached Peace and Love and prayed, reading verses from the *Qur'an* (Koran) as well as the Bible and the *Bhagavad Gita*. Hate-crazed Hindu fanatics called him "Mohammad Gandhi," accused him of being a "Muslim-lover," a "traitor" to his own nation and people. He became disillusioned and lost interest in living much longer as he watched the violent madness spread around him. His dream of Ram Rajya appeared more remote than ever now that India was finally free, for her freedom had brought not peace but the sword of partition, hatred, and war. On Friday, January 30, 1948, shortly before the sun set over New Delhi, Mahatma Gandhi was shot to death by a crazed Hindu Brahman, who viewed the saintly Father of his Nation as India's "worst enemy."

Religion and Philosophy

On action alone be thy interest,
Never on its fruits
Abiding in discipline perform actions,
Abandoning attachment
Being indifferent to success or failure.

—The *Bhagavad Gita*
(trans. Franklin Edgerton) I: 25.

The last words Mahatma Gandhi uttered were "Heh, Ram!" They have been carved in Devanagari script on the polished black marble stone at the site of his cremation pyre along the Yamuna River in Delhi, which has become a place of pilgrimage. Hindus believe that one's last words help determine the next birth of one's soul; thus Mahatma Gandhi's "Great Soul" rose directly to merge with Rama's in Vishnu's solar heaven. The soul's immortality and reincarnation through many different forms of transient being and the interaction of a whole pantheon of gods with humans are central to India's greatest religion, which we call Hinduism. Hindus themselves speak of their faith as *Dharma*, a complex value-laden term, translated by us as-religion, law, duty, faith, and other virtues. We generally say that Hinduism emerged as a syncretism of Aryan and pre-Aryan ideas and doctrines, at around the dawn of the Christian era. Hindus believe that their Dharma is "Eternal" (*Sanatana*). Most of the world's Hindus inhabit India, representing about 85 percent of her population. There are, however, many millions of Hindus now permanently settled outside of India, a growing number of whom have converted to Hinduism in recent decades, especially among younger people in the United States during the turbulent decade of the 1960s.

About 10 percent of India's population continue to follow the religion of Islam; thus even since Partition India has remained one of the world's largest "Muslim" states. Jain, Buddhist, and Sikh religions, all born in India, are each practiced by additional millions of modern Indians, although Buddhism's many schools are far more popular and powerful outside India than within its borders. Bombay's "Zoroastrian" Parsis came in many waves to India's western coast, fleeing persecution in Persia. There are millions of Christians and several thousand Jews in India as well, yet these latter faiths remained peripheral to Indian life, having initially been so foreign to Indian soil.

Whatever their nominal "faith" may be, most (non-Muslim) Indians share a number of religiophilosophic values and beliefs that are by now almost "national" in character, having flourished so long in the special atmosphere of South Asia. This worldview is more an ideal model of behavior than the actual one followed in India's many bazaars of daily life or its often murkier corridors of power, but its components remain, nonetheless, widespread ethical goals among the majority of India's population. What we might call the "Indian spirit" presupposes a universal hierarchical model of life. That model is animated by a religious Spirit, reflected in countless invisible but undying "Souls," each of which inhabits some body for the interlude most of us call a lifetime, then moves along to another, higher or lower being on a continuum stretching from insect to divinity. Each soul's next reincarnation will depend upon the total "balance" in the action-account of its last body-shell whose deeds in sum may have merited spiritual advancement, or the reverse. One really has, therefore, no one to blame or thank but "oneself" for being born an "untouchable" sweeper or a wealthy merchant or a mighty prince. It never hurts, and indeed can often help, to appeal to one or more of the gods on high for aid, comfort, or compassion, offering gifts of flowers or food or copper or gold coins in the process, paying off their "intermediaries" as well, whether they be called Brahmans, sadhus, monks (*sanyasis*), or just "beggars." Who knows, after all, what a coin in some obscure cup might do to help clear one's deficit-karma-account? The most important asset to ensure "higher" birth, however, or better still, no rebirth at all, is to do one's "duty" without complaint or impatience, as best one can. Every good Hindu knows what that duty is from "birth," for each family, each clan, or what we call "caste" has its special place and tasks in the universal hierarchy. The ideal goal is "release" (*Mokṣha*), which Westerners might characterize as "escape," but Indians prefer to think of as "liberation" for the "soul," not simply a poor tired body's extrication from the otherwise painful imperative of rebirth.

Most Indians are gentle, nonviolent people, in part perhaps because they view all life as interrelated, and believe in the potential cosmic significance of individual deeds or actions and their implications, extending over a hundred or more lifetimes. One must thus be careful where one treads, for the very earthworm beneath one's foot shares cosmic connections. We never know where the ripple-current we set in motion could lead. Hindus have reported nightmares after eating beef, hearing a dead grandmother's voice crying out in agony at the pain caused by so violent a fall from vegetarian grace. Which is not to say that Indians never kill or wound others, only that, as a rule, they should regret doing so more than people less deeply committed to nonviolence unless they kill in the service of Goddess Kali or Durga! We also generally think of Indians as more "tolerant" of differences than most other peoples. Is that because they are truly "enlightened" beings? Or do they just care much less than most folk the world over about the plight, as well as the thoughts, of strangers? Have millennia of forced proximity to peoples of many races and disparate religions taught them that "withdrawal" or "indifference" is perhaps the better part of wisdom? We might say that "what they don't know can't hurt them!" Or is it their widespread belief in this world and its traumas, its follies and fortunes, as nothing more than "illusion"?

Indians generally take what is nowadays called a "holistic" view of life. They see connections not only between humans and animals and vegetation and demons and gods but also between actions and feelings, long-forgotten deeds or thoughts and future behavior, the past and present, all part of a process that goes on. Accounts are kept somehow, somewhere on the discs of distant galaxies perhaps, or the brainwaves of Brahman, where all is known, All is One, and the One is each of us, part of us, the same, in fact, even as the Real or True is God. God is whatever Name we recite, a mantra we may become if we chant it often enough, repeating a thousand million times a syllable that signifies this Universe. The rest is only illusion, a *Maya*-world to which we give name and form for fear of the Void that is All, or from sheer loneliness, perhaps, for even the greatest of gods gets lonely.

To Indians, in general, religion and philosophy are mother's milk, daily nourishment, not esoterica to be remembered only on Saturdays or Sundays, locked in books never read. Most Indians believe that the gods and stars affect everyone's fate, today, tomorrow, all part of the cosmic balance that includes Sun and Moon, Mars and Venus. To think otherwise would be "foolish" or dangerous, for how can we dare ignore such mighty gravitational forces? Which is why the exact moment of a Hindu's birth must be recorded as well as the day, month, and year, so that an "accurate" horoscope may be drawn up as soon as he is old enough to merit one. Otherwise how would one know when to marry, or the days on which one must avoid launching an important enterprise, or embarking upon a distant journey? Everything is connected, invisible "forces" everywhere act upon us, react to our every impulse and brainwave. That is why faith and philosophy are so important, for they are viewed as *real* powers, not mere abstractions. The crudest icon of a god *is* God, if one truly believes, devoutly, humbly, sincerely, with all one's heart, with the imperishable Soul that is a spark of the Transcendental Cosmic All. Then miracles do occur. Prayers are answered. There is "magic," and once the dark veils of ignorance and cynicism are drawn aside, the floodlight of wisdom will reveal Truth. So most Indians believe. For India is a Civilization predicated upon faith, built on belief. It has flourished on philosophy, and its most adept devotees can climb from the deepest troughs of despair to the highest peaks of pleasure with dispassion and equanimity achieved by their command of its oldest religious philosophy, Yoga.

Yoga and Shaivism

Yoga is a "discipline," which literally means "to rein in" or "harness." Its birth is shrouded in the deepest strata of preliterate remains, an ithyphallic figure seated in lotus position, carved on a seal 4,000 years ago, and phallic stones obviously used for ritual purposes at least as old. Do these represent Lord Shiva, modern Hinduism's "Great God," who is, after all, worshiped to this day in phallic form? Shiva is also depicted in painting and sculpture as a mighty Yogi, whether seated on his tiger skin atop Mt. Kailasa or standing within the ring of fire as "King of Dance" (*Nata-raja*), about to create, or destroy, the universe. His manifestations are numerous, his devotees countless. He is Lord of Beasts and God of Fertility. His name means "Auspicious," but beware the fire of his wrath, for his third eye alone could consume any human, and the very hair of his head is so powerful it breaks the force of River Ganga as she falls mightily from the sky, making her weight bearable to earth.

Yoga may have been ancient India's key to survival, amid such perils as those posed by heat, tigers, and cobras to unarmed and isolated humans. Disciplined concentration, deep breathing, balanced posture, meditation conducive to mental equipoise all helped yogis overcome pain, reining in receptors of feeling that sensitize human bodies to the usual hazards and discomforts of external environment. It is unclear whether yogis used desensitizing drugs or "weeds" to help numb their feelings, but over time they have observably taught themselves to bear without flinching walking barefoot over burning coals, lying atop beds of sharp nails or glass spears, or retaining rigid postures long enough to leave arms held overhead to atrophy, or allow their fingernails to grow out through the backs of their clenched fists. Yogis also claim to be able to slow down their metabolism and breathing enough to allow themselves to remain alive inside coffins buried deep underground for some time, although attempts scientifically to test such control over heartbeat have never established actual mental harnessing of the smooth internal organs. Other yogis claim to be able to transform themselves into soaring birds, leaping beasts, or mind-spirits capable of instant transmission to remote astral bodies throughout the universe. None of the latter claims can be impartially substantiated, although at least one prime minister of India believed in them strongly enough to wonder aloud why the United States and the Soviet Union "wasted so much money on space programs," since India's yogis could "reach the moon whenever they wish, and at no cost!"

Shiva is one of two leading male divinities of Hinduism, the other being Vishnu, whose images and powers have been almost equally worshiped in India for about two thousand years. As ancient lord of fertility, Shiva's sexual prowess was deemed inexhaustible. Myth has him running naked, seducing the wives of Brahman sages, until his eternally erect lingam was amputated. It is still worshiped in carved iconic form. Hindu myth credits Shiva with having ingeniously devised no less than 84 million sexual positions, although only 84,000 are still supposedly "known" to his greatest devotees! Shiva is also worshiped, however, as god of yogic asceticism, whose capacity for sexual abstinence at least matched his lascivious lust. As supreme Yogi, Shiva thus embodies the limits of "pleasure" and "pain," mastering opposites, rising above passions and restraint alike to a realm of control and disinterest so remarkably rarefied as to be considered divine. Precisely how long it took the pre-Aryan yogi to attain such powers of perfect control over his body's behavior and feelings is unknown. We assume, however, that by the middle of the third millennium B.C. yoga-powers were mastered, since so many Yoga artifacts datable to that era have been found.

The earliest meaning of Sanskrit "Soul" (*Atman*) was "breath." Ancient Indians must have noted that the most immediate difference between a living body and a dead one was the latter's loss of breath, hence their later exaltation of *Atman*, first to "Self," then to "Soul." Yoga has always stressed breath-control, intuiting long before the role of oxygen in purifying blood was understood that breath helped vitalize the body. Ancient Indians never correctly appreciated the function of lungs or the bloodstream, however, imagining that each breath circulated throughout one's body. Yogis long believed it possible to trace the progress of every breath through all their limbs and bodily organs. Many still do. They also focus on the spine as an organ of special powers that supports the body, and contains six invisible "wheels" within its column, the lowest among which is a "serpent" at the spine's base. Through proper concentration, yogis believe they can rouse the sleeping serpent, setting it whirling so swiftly that it rises high enough to twirl all six wheels at once, generating a state of bliss, that leads to the creation of honeyed nectar in the brain, much the same as semen. Several schools of Yoga focus almost exclusively on controlling "serpent power," using sex as a form of worship, practicing techniques for prolonging orgasm until the "pain" of that process matches the "pleasure" induced by its culmination or "release" (*mukti*). "Yoga of force" (*Hatha-yoga*) and "Yoga of dissolution" (*Laya-yoga*) stress such techniques, and hence have become quite popular in the West. Indian philosophers of every school have, however, used yoga as a generally valued method for helping to cleanse one's mind and prepare individuals of every predisposition for the enlightened clarity and calm prerequisite to Moksha.

Meditation, the technique of yoga most popular in the West, helps many individuals relieve pressures or tensions exacerbated by the speed and stress of urban industrial society. Not surprising that regular interludes of total quiescence for silent meditation should prove salubrious in an otherwise bustling day of rushing from one urgent task to another. Although some Western meditators insist upon calling it "hard work," Indian yogis usually manage to live longer than most people. Relaxing one's mind may not be as simple as it sounds, or insomnia would not be as common as it seems, yet by combining breath and posture controls with various other exercises, including mantra repetition, something close to a state of self-induced hypnosis can be reached remarkably quickly. And without strain. Millions of Indian practitioners have, indeed, achieved such unflappable, impenetrable calm through regular yogic exercise as to drive many Western visitors to distraction. British imperialists used to blame it on what they called "native laziness," trying to take up their "White man's burdens" bravely, using whips and other weapons only when provoked. English fiction as well as official reports from India through World War II are replete with accounts of "shiftlessness," "benighted natives," as "sulky" as they are "slow" to respond to orders. Modern American visitors feel similar frustrations, waiting for "quick" service in the posh restaurants of India's five-star hotels. As does any foreigner who has ever tried to buy an Indian railway or plane ticket, cash a personal check at an Indian bank, or mail a letter at an Indian post office. One soon learns the virtue of patience or must face a precipitously dangerous rise in blood pressure. Hindus generally believe that anything left undone in this lifetime can be accomplished during any number of future existences. Yoga is thus a great aid in a climate that makes patience a necessity to survival.

Shiva's premier position in the Hindu pantheon is based on his pre-Aryan yogic powers and his mythological identification with Vedic Indra as well as Agni, and a lesser Rig Vedic storm god of thunder and destruction named *Rudra*. *Tapas* ("Heat") is important to all of these divinities, whose potent powers give birth to countless offspring. Indra, like Shiva, was a "bull-god," castrated for his lechery, and with Fire-god Agni was forever overheating the sensuous wives of Brahmans and sages in the same wild forests where Shiva ran loose, using his lingam as a "weapon"—much like "demon-piercing" Indra's *vajra* ("thunderbolt weapon"). Shiva's first wife, Sati, immolated herself when her father spoke rudely to her divine Lord, thus proving her "True" devotion. *Sati* means "True One" in Sanskrit, and was later used to describe a Hindu widow's immolation on the cremation pyre of her departed husband, without whom her life supposedly lost all value and meaning. Sati was in theory called "voluntary," but British missionaries and civil servants were shocked to find Hindu women chained to cremation pyres screaming in agony to be released before being burned alive. The Company Raj outlawed Sati in the early nineteenth century, but Indian wives are at times still burned if their dowries remain unpaid. Soon after Shiva lost his first wife, however, he married her more famous reincarnation, Parvati, Himalaya's daughter, who was so beautiful that Shiva was tempted to love her divine body without respite for over a thousand years. Their children incuded the war-god Skanda (or Kartikeya) and elephant-headed Ganesh, most popular of Indian's terasomorphic deities.

Shiva is more popular in South India than in the North, which may reflect the deeper pre-Aryan roots of Dravidian peoples in that region, where Mother Goddess worship is also most intense. As Lord of Dance, *Nata-raja*, Shiva was said to have set the universe in motion from Chidambaram in Tamil Nadu, where his great temple serves as a magnet for Shaivites the world over, its laminated pure gold roof almost as blinding as the sun. Many of the more than 100 dances Shiva created were, however, dances of death and destruction; hence his dark side, when he haunts cremation grounds in ashes and rags or covered with the bloody hide of an elephant, bearing his trident staff in one hand as he taps the tandava drum with two fingers of another. Shiva's sadhu devotees wander every Indian byway, their untamed hair, ash-covered faces, inflamed eyes, and naked emaciatd bodies at once feared and revered by all who see them, even as the "Great God" (*Maheshvara*) they emulate. The duality of Shiva's role reflects universal realities, the inextricable merging of life and death, creation and destruction, good and evil. Shiva is Time incarnate, ever reminding humans of their fleeting moments. And he is Death, hence his preference for cremation grounds. But as India's greatest "sower of seeds" he generates Life, fires every womb with his penetrating powers, ignites passions that start the wondrous Dance all over again. Atop his tower of ice on Kailasa he sits in perfect calm, contemplating all, meditating upon the eternal, unchanged, unchanging. He is India's oldest God, ever young.

Mother Goddess Worship

The Mother Goddess is Earth incarnate. She is the field in whom every seed must be sown to live and grow. She embodies the creative, unmatched "Energy," *Shakti*, of the Life-force itself. Without his consort Mother Goddess, no Hindu god is of much use or value to anyone. He may strut about, but his powers are limited. To be complete he requires a *Devi*, "Goddess," who takes many different names and forms, but always embodies *Shakti*. Mother Goddess worship in India is also pre-Aryan, and possibly as old as Shaivism, for it is difficult to imagine Shiva remaining long without his Sati or Parvati. Hindu myth created the Mother Goddess from fires of wrathful indignation that flamed from the mouths of all the gods, when they contemplated the evil behavior of a giant demon buffalo. Those flames of divine wrath congealed to form the beautiful, invincible body of the eighteen-armed Mother of Power—Shakti. Armed with the fire of every god, Shakti cut off all the heads of the black buffalo-demon and crushed its instant incarnations until that titan-beast bled to death. Her strength was invincible, her vital heat had no limit to its fire. She embodies every female passion and power. Only Lord Shiva himself could satisfy her. Her progeny are countless, yet she nourishes them at her watermelon breasts, carries them lightly on her broad hips.

Hindu devotion to the Mother is both ancient and modern, for no relationship is stronger in a Hindu family to this day than that which binds sons to mothers. Mother-worship is often hailed in poetry and song as well as temple and household. India's first National "Anthem," *Bande Mataram* ("Mother, I bow to Thee!"), was originally a Bengali poem in a popular nineteenth-century novel by Bankim Chandra Chatterji (1839–1894), which inspired millions of young Bengali Hindus to court prison and risk death in the first wave of anti-Partition boycott and violent agitation:

> Rich with thy hurrying streams, Bright with thy orchard gleams . . . Mother of might, Mother free . . . Mother, I kiss thy feet . . . Mother, I bow to thee. Who hath said thou art weak in thy lands, When the swords flash out in ten million hands, And ten times ten million voices roar Thy dreadful name from shore to shore? . . . Thou art wisdom, thou art law, Thou our heart, our soul, our breath . . . the love divine . . . that conquers death . . . Mother sweet, I bow to thee, Mother great and free!

The paradox of mother-worship coexisting with general female subordination so prevalent throughout India may reflect differing pre-Aryan and Aryan values. Male-dominated Aryan tribes conquered matrilineal South Indians, and until quite recently matriarchal succession and inheritance survived along the Malabar coast in what is now the State of Kerala. Traditional Hindu customs like Sati, female infanticide, and dowry reflect the subordinate status of women throughout most of Indian History, as did the custom of Hindu temple female slavery. *Deva-dasi*s, "Slaves of the God," were unwanted daughters of the poor left on temple steps in their infancy, reared by Brahmans in the temple compound as their own courtesans or prostitutes. *Dasi*s, meaning "slaves," is the female form of the term used by Aryans for the "dark" pre-Aryans they had conquered. Those girls were taught Hindu dance among other arts from childhood, and by the nineteenth century South India's greatest classical dancers were *Deva dasi*s, whose most inspired performer of this century was Balasaraswati of Madras. Mother Goddesses themselves, however, had as many malevolent as benevolent forms, and the polarity of their qualities also reflects complex Indian ambivalence toward females in general.

Benevolent, loving, true goddesses like Sati and Parvati, include priceless Lakshmi (also called Shri), goddess of wealth, Lord Vishnu's consort, and Saraswati, goddess of the arts, Brahma's beautiful bride. Ushas, Rig Vedic goddess of Dawn, is a shining joy to behold, pink and golden her complexion, fair and fiery the portals of her body. Her rape by Lord Indra may reflect the conquest of non-Aryan peoples by the Aryan tribes and their divine warrior-hero. In her more violent forms, the Mother is *Kali*, "Black" goddess of Death, and *Durga*, the "Inaccessible," who rides her lion into battle and wears the skulls of her enemies around her neck. A malevolent Goddess's devotees must strangle and kill for her, since blood is her favorite drink, and the flesh of innocents her preferred food. Sacrificial goats continue to be offered up at Durga's altar during the prolonged bloody annual festivals that celebrate her birth at her temple in Calcutta (*Kali-ghat*). No fewer than 108 Mother Goddesses are named in "ancient" (*Purana*) texts of Hinduism, which also identify their sacred places throughout the subcontinent. The incomparable Meenakshi temple of Madurai is one of the best examples of Mother Goddess worship to be seen in daily practice in the heart of Tamil Nadu, where Mother remains supreme. Whatever Her name, She is Mother India. Every Hindu is Her child.

Nonviolent Buddhism and Jainism

Ahimsa, "Non-violence," or what Mahatma Gandhi preferr
Law of Love," emerged to historic light about six centuries before the dawn of the Christian Era with the birth of Buddhism and Jainism in mid-Gangetic India. Ahimsa was subsequently described in several Hindu texts as the "highest" law or religion (*dharma*), yet that was only after the Buddha became part of the Hindu pantheon. Nonviolence is so remote from the rough and ready mores of Aryan nomads and their Epic battles that we assume it has, like Yoga and Mother Goddess worship, pre-Aryan roots. Buddhism and Jainism were born as heterodox rejections of Brahmanic orthodoxy with its Vedic ritual fire sacrifices of lambs and goats as well as Soma and ghi. Ahimsa is so comprehensive an admonition against killing as to include animals and insects, even vegetative life in its prohibition, reflecting ancient India's concept of universal interdependency or what we call the balance of nature, what Indians see as the interrelatedness of all life. It is an important Indian premise, underlying many attitudes toward daily life and relationships. Thanks to Ahimsa most Indians have become vegetarians, and although the abjuring of beef may have been related to the specially high status of cows in Aryan society, all life was believed to be endowed with some form of soul that made it sacred. Was that uncommonly civilized virtue something yogis learned as a key to survival in the jungle?

The *Buddha* ("Enlightened One") set in motion his wheel of the Law by preaching Four Noble Truths about universal "Sorrow" and its causes, and the Noble Eightfold Path to its alleviation and ultimate elimination with the "blowing out" of *Nirvana*. Axiomatic to the Buddha's teaching was the concept of Suffering as an inescapable first Truth of life in the "transient," "soulless" world he perceived around him. From traumatic birth to death, through stages of sickness and old age, sorrow was everywhere. We suffer in our desperate longing for loved ones far away, and our dislike of others much too near. The universality of suffering is expressed in the mustard-seed parable of the hopelessly wretched young mother who brings her dead baby to the Buddha's retreat, seeking solace. "First go to yon village," he told her, "and fetch me a mustard seed from a home that has known no sorrow such as yours." So she goes from house to house on what turns out to be a futile mission, which nonetheless restores her sanity and enables her to bear ιe sorrow she has experienced, having learned that every village home has its own tale of loss often as terrible as her own.

The Buddha's genius, however, was not merely his appreciation of the universality of pain and sorrow, but his devising a "middle path" of disciplined action designed to help eliminate it. He taught that the combination of ignorance and desire invariably led to pain or disappointment. To escape those snares one had but to practice right views and aspirations, right speech and conduct, right livelihood and effort, right mindfulness and meditation. Ideally, one should give up the world of transience, struggle, and material possessions by becoming a monk of the Buddha's order, whose daily life was a regimen of disciplined abstention and self-denial, which included taking vows of truth, poverty, and Ahimsa.

Mahavira, the "Great Hero" founder of Jainism, stressed the virtue of Ahimsa as primary, since he believed that all things, including stones, dirt, and petrified trees, were "alive" with *Jiva*—"Souls." Mahavira also founded an order of monks, but his doctrines were much more extreme than the Buddha's middle path. He went naked and strove for many years to starve himself to death, since everything one ate, not simply meat or fish, was, according to his teachings, "murdered" through ingestion. Paradoxically enough, a devout Jain was encouraged to kill himself—but only by starvation. Invisible Jiva being everywhere, Jains often carry feather whisks to brush them aside before sitting down, and must be careful to wear gauze masks, and never to walk across fields after it rains, since so many earthworms and other forms of Jiva might be abroad. Jains really cannot use ploughs without committing mass murder, hence most of those who remained in the lay community turned to nonagricultural pursuits such as moneylending or banking, consequently becoming one of the wealthiest communities in India.

Ahimsa is the most sacred of Jain laws, and whether Mahavira learned of it from the Buddha's teachings or merely imbibed the same atmosphere of mid-Gangetic ideology, its importance among non-Brahman religions helped it to win acceptance within Hinduism, once that synthesis emerged. The Jain fast-unto-death became a modern political weapon in India during the last decades of the Nationalist movement, and has remained a potent provincial weapon against independent India's central authority, used most effectively in winning separate statehood for Andhra, and helping wrest some early concessions for Punjabi Sikhs. Mahatma Gandhi was always careful about invoking the "fiery weapon" of the fast-unto-death, however, insisting that unless one's motives were perfectly pure in doing so, it could become a weapon of "demonic destruction" (*duragraha*) rather than one drawn from the golden arsenal of Truth (*Satyagraha*).

Laws of Action and Reincarnation

The "Laws" of *Karma* ("Action") and *Samsara* ("Reincarnation"), first articulated about 2,500 years ago in Upanishadic dialogues, have remained axiomatic to Indic religiophilosophic thought and are widely accepted by modern Indian intellectuals, as well as most traditional Hindus. The idea of rebirth and redeath seems to have started as a form of extreme punishment for souls, whose deeds were deemed so vile that they could not properly be punished in a single lifetime. Once Samsara was accepted, however, it could obviously also be a reward for those of lowly initial status, who might be reborn into higher human, possibly even most exalted Brahman stations. The link between Karma and Samsara, once agreed upon, remained self-perpetuating. Every individual deed or action was viewed as a karmic input that would inevitably lead to an output in kind, good deeds ripening as good fruit, evil deeds as evil. The moral arithmetic was impersonal, and atheistic, for no god was required, nor could divinity really help change the balance once a deed had been done. Not even nepotism, India's most common weakness, could, in theory at least, alter an individual's karmic equation. There was no one to blame, no one to thank. The balance was always written in our own hand, sealed with our own lips, each payment falling due in our own blood. As ye sow so shall ye reap, not in high heaven or dismal hell, but here on earth, next birth round. Impersonally, then, every punishment would suit each "crime"—each action, that is, each deed—for Karma of every variety, good, bad, and indifferent, soon came to be viewed as undesirable. Karma, after all, required expiation, which meant rebirth, somehow to be avoided. The goal of Jains and Buddhists, and later of Hindus, was much the same "extinction" (*Nirvana*) of being, or "release" (*Mokṣha*) from rebirth.

How ingenious it was, how simple, yet how shrewd and seemingly logical a justification for the status quo. How could any Untouchable possibly complain, after all, about his lowly position in life? Surely he must have done many dastardly deeds in previous lives. Brahma alone knew what crimes he had committed! Now his own Karma was punishing him. To each the fruit of his own Karma was the universal Indian Law of cosmic justice. The poor and starving deserved their wretched plight. The rich and powerful were also deserving. So too the sick or healthy, the lame, the halting, the leper and the king, every one received exactly what he and she deserved by virtue of everything said, thought, and done from the beginning of time. Perhaps the ultimate key to Indian "tolerance" is Karma, for if one truly believes in its ethical imperative, why complain of your own plight, or envy another's? We are what we should be, because of what we have been in past lives. But does that mean we will always remain what we were born this time around? Obviously not. We can rise or fall in the hierarchy, by accruing merits and demerits, by the sum total of all of our virtues and vices, good or evil deeds and thoughts.

But part of the system's ingenuity was its amazingly long time-frame, the linking of past and future to present actions. An Untouchable could rise to Brahmanic heights of goodness and glory, but *only* by being a perfect Untouchable first! One must do one's duty without complaint, without hesitation, or doubt, or grudging, with no silent or vocal contempt. Sweep cheerfully, sweep carefully, and don't sweep any dust or dirt toward Brahman eyes or mouths, and perhaps next life you may be born a bit higher. Since 1950, of course, Untouchability has been outlawed by India's Constitution. Still its residue remains, despite judicial "teeth" of specified punishments for crimes spelled out in constitutional amendments, just as an acrid residue of racial hatred and intolerance lingers in the hearts and minds of many Americans, although our Fourteenth Amendment was enacted more than a century ago. Nowadays, moreover, in Gujarat and Maharashtra and Tamil Nadu and Andhra it is the Brahmans who feel "discriminated against," since affirmative action laws assure India's ex-Untouchables reserved seats in government chambers, medical colleges, and the higher ranks of all services. Laws can never eradicate feelings, however, and a century of modernity will hardly suffice to erase basic beliefs reinforced over 2,000 years. Even though Untouchability has been banished by law, India's caste system has never been officially dismantled, although its once impervious walls have been eroded by forces of change, some of its musty rooms are no longer entered, and many of its strictures no longer feared.

Modern Indians, who believe in Karma and still fear its consequences, such as possible rebirth in canine or mosquito form, are no longer limited to the ancient yogic assumption that the only way to eliminate Karma is to cease all action. Since it took Mahavira himself no less than thirteen years to starve to death, that path to "liberation" was obviously not easy. Even the Buddha was supposed to have tried it before attaining his Enlightenment, but at the sight of a beautiful young maiden and the smell of the steaming bowl of rice she held out for him, he was sufficiently distracted to opt for his "middle way" between hedonism and self-sacrifice. Upanishadic Vedanta opened a mystic path of philosophic insight as well, but that too is most difficult, requiring true understanding of the basic equation between one's immortal "Self" or Atman and the transcendental Brahman over-"Soul" pervading the entire Universe. Such mystic self-realization might take many lifetimes to attain, and various Yoga exercises could help prepare one's body for such enlightenment, or it might come in a flash of blinding instant illumination, that "All is One," that "Thou art That One" (*Tat tvam asi*). By thinking "This is I" and "That is mine, one binds himself with himself, as does a bird with a snare!" warned the *Maitri Upanishad* over 2,000 years ago. "Hence a person who has the marks of determination, conception, and self-conceit is bound. Hence, in being the opposite of that, he is liberated. Therefore one should stand free from determination, free from conception, free from self-conceit. This is the mark of Liberation (*Mokṣha*). This is the pathway to Brahma. . . . By it one will go to the farther shore of this darkness, for therein all desires are contained." In another Upanishad, achieving cosmic awareness of such truth is said to be as hard as walking barefoot "over a razor's edge."

But what then were mere mortals to do? Was there no hope of Liberation for the mass of India's populace who could not be monks or mystics? At about the start of the Christian era, the *Bhagavad Gita* introduced two new options that have remained the most important techniques used by Hindus for achieving Moksha, in this or some future lifetime. The first of these methods is called *Karma Yoga*, "Action Discipline," and the second is *Bhakti*, "Devotion." With the great popularity of Bhakti in the early centuries of the Christian era, Hinduism gathered strength throughout India, and since then "devotional" Vaishnavism especially has continued its appeal for hundreds of millions of ordinary people. Karma Yoga never attracted such a mass following, yet in some respects its impact has been as important as Bhakti, for it has given India's elite, especially its modern professional managerial and bureaucratic leadership, a brilliant method of integrating their traditional faith with modernity's secular demands. It has also armed India's youthful revolutionaries with an ideological weapon that proved most powerful during India's Nationalist movement, directed against the British, but has remained an explosive, thorny problem since Independence.

The *Gita* is a dialogue, supposed to have taken place on the field of battle just before the armies of warring Aryan cousins launched their bloody eighteen days of mortal conflict, the Epic *Mahabharata*'s finale. Arjuna, warrior hero of the Pandavas, recognized his old uncle and cousins in the serried ranks arrayed before him, and lost heart, laying down his weapons, until his charioteer, Krishna, restores his strength by the divine powers of his "Song." Krishna's "Blessed One's" (*Bhagavad*) message is that Arjuna as a warrior was born to fight, hence must always do his "duty," and, moreover, that those he sees "killed" in battle are only disposable bodies of little value, while their immortal "Souls" (*Atman*) can never be destroyed. "Yield not to unmanliness," Krishna argues. "For action is better than inaction. . . . Better one's own duty, imperfectly performed, Than another's duty, well done." The key is to act in so disciplined a manner that no Karma adheres to your Soul, "To whom pain and pleasure are alike. . . . He is fit for immortality." The method is to focus on the deed alone, never its fruits, to act dispassionately, without attachment of any sort, "Being indifferent to success or failure. . . . All whose undertakings are free from desire and purpose," Krishna informs Arjuna, "His actions are burned up in the fire of knowledge, Him the wise call the man of learning. . . . To whom clods, stones, and gold are all one. . . . To whom blame and praise of himself are equal. . . . Free from desires. . . . Action with the body alone Performing, he attains no guilt. . . . Doing acts for worship alone, his Karma all melts away."

Now everything can be done without fear of Karmic-punishment. The secret is to apply one's Yoga-discipline to action, rather than restraint of action, to disengage one's motives while remaining totally engaged in life's daily routine, to do any and all deeds with the same dispassionate selfless motivation. Kill, if need be, if duty requires it, but do so without hatred, malice, or passion, and even a flood of blood will leave no stain on your Soul. The *Gita* was invoked by Lokamanya Tilak in urging young Indian revolutionaries to "fight" the British. "Rise above the mentality of the Penal Code," Tilak told his ardent followers, "and get into the higher moral atmosphere of the *Bhagavad Gita*, and *then* decide upon your Duty!" It was a heady challenge, and two of his young disciples became the first Poona

Brahman assassins of recent Indian history. Half a century later another Poona Brahman, who also invoked the *Gita* in self-defense, murdered Mahatma Gandhi, and is still viewed by many young Indians as a "Hindu patriot." In Bombay, a fanatical group of revolutionaries recently organized what they call "Shiva's Army" (*Shiva Sena*), committed to "cleansing" India's sacred soil of all "polluting foreign" influences, especially Muslim and Christian. Karma Yoga has thus been used to justify the worst sort of antisocial behavior, and to invest modern Indian violence with an aura of religious rationale.

The method of disciplined action is, however, also used to positive advantage by many of India's brightest new professionals, physicians, physicists, business managers, officers, judges, and civil administrators, whose efficient "cool" is modeled on Arjuna's dispassionate devotion to duty. The admirable dedication of such new–old Indian leaders owes a great deal to ancient Hindu philosophy, whose message mirrors the British "public school" master's imprecation that it doesn't really matter whether you "win or lose" but rather "how you play the game" that counts. Playing their game with dispassion and disinterest concerning its fruits, with primary attention to doing the job well, is an important message for modern India's economy, polity, and security, one that new India's leaders can feel proud to have found in their own Civilization's brilliant ancient legacy.

Devotional Vaishnavism

"If your mind is on Me," Krishna also taught Arjuna, "you will cross over all difficulties by My grace. . . Be Me-minded, devoted to Me; Worshiping Me, revere Me; And to Me alone you shall go . . . I promise it—because you are dear to Me. . . . From all evils I shall rescue you." This Hindu devotional—*Bhakti*—path to Liberation was taught by no mere charioteer, of course, but an earthly emanation (*avatarà*) of great solar God Vishnu. The popular appeal of devotional Vaishnavism proved powerful enough to recapture the allegiance of most Indians lured from the costly, cold rituals of Vedic Brahmanism to Buddhism and Jainism. Indeed, the Buddha himself was brought into the Hindu fold as yet another of Vishnu's avataras, like Rama. Owing to Lord Vishnu's adaptable powers, virtually every popular cult hero found in India could be accommodated, made part of the greater glory that flowed into Hinduism's river of light.

Before the dawn of creation, Hindu myth has Vishnu asleep on the snake of a thousand heads at the bottom of the cosmic ocean, and from his navel grew a lovely lotus that bore demiurge Brahma aloft to build the world we inhabit, after which Vishnu flew to heaven to keep everything warm. Constrained as the Sun-god to remain on high, Vishnu arms himself with the capacity to delegate part of his powers to various avataras, each of whom "saves" the world, when demonic danger seems to be winning. Emerging as it did around the beginning of the Christian era, this Hindu version of divine "Saviors" coming down to earth might perhaps have evolved in emulation of Christian doctrine. Or was it Christianity that borrowed from more ancient Indian ideas? Possibly both concepts developed in remote independence.

In his first avatara, as a great Fish, Vishnu saved the world from flood. Then, as a mighty Turtle he dove to the bottom of the cosmic sea, which was churned by all the other gods, using Mt. Meru as their "pole" and a sacred snake as their "rope," until such wondrous things as the nectar of immortality emerged from the ocean's floor with Mother Goddess Lakshmi herself. Vishnu later appeared on earth in Boar and Man-lion incarnations, and as the magic Dwarf, who fooled demon Bali into granting him as much "land" as he could "cover in three strides," then transformed himself into a giant, spanning the universe, restoring heaven and earth alike to proper religious order. As King Rama he saved the world from Ravana, and as the Buddha he won back many of those who had defected to Buddhism, but Krishna was his most complete avatara, and still remains one of Hinduism's most popular gods. Krishna means "Black" and he is usually painted blue, often fluting, surrounded by cows and their adoring milkmaids, whose saris he playfully hides. He was most probably a pastoral hero-lover-turned-deity from the Mathura region south of Delhi. He is worshiped by Indians of every age, region, and station as the naughty child Bal-Krishna, the "butter thief," as the lover of beautiful Radha, Rukmani, and thousands of other maidens, and as the wise all-knowing guru of Arjuna. His worship has recently spread the world over, with the growing popularity of Swami Bhaktivedanta's Krishna-Consciousness movement.

As the Bhakti movement gained popularity, various schools emerged around saintly gurus and poets, who taught and sang or danced the joyous meaning of Shri Krishna's wondrous life, recorded for posterity in the most popular of all Hindu "Ancient" (*Purana*) texts, the *Bhagavata Purana*. Merely uttering Krishna's name was believed by some schools to suffice by way of worship and devotion, hence the repetitious "Hari-Krishna" mantra so commonly heard in the West. Bhakti cults devoted to Lord Shiva and Mother Goddess Shakti worship have emerged also, especially in Kashmir, Bengal, and Tamil Nadu, but the most popular Hindu deities worshiped with simple, devout, and passionate devotion are Rama and Krishna. The Bhakti movement opened the road to Liberation to low-caste and outcaste Hindus for the first time, and even to women and slaves. Anyone could appeal directly to God for aid, and if the appeal were pure enough, sincere enough, it would result in salvation, or at least divine attention to the particular problem addressed. Gods now acquired iconic forms, small images as well as giant figures, made of clay or wood as well as silver and gold, and Hindus brought *puja*-offerings, bananas and bits of coconut, flowers and milk, garlands and sweets; whatever looked, smelled, or tasted good became food for the gods. And with each offering went a prayer, hands clasped, body bowed low, in hallowed temple or at humble kitchen hearth, at a wayside stone daubed white or blue, or under a sacred banyan tree, worshipers go with bare feet, open souls, loving hearts, lowered heads. "O Lord of the Universe, help me to love you, teach me how to be more devoted to your wondrous nature and loving spirit!" Poet-Saints like the great Tukaram of Maharashtra, who lived in the seventeenth century, composed their love intoxicated lays of devotion to Krishna as they wandered from village to village performing ecstatic nocturnal kirtans, singing Lord Krishna's glory to the clang of cymbals and the beat of tiny drums. "Listen, O pious ones," sang Tuka, "Cast aside association with philosophers, Seek not the opinions of men, but worship the Lord!" To this day, villagers of Maharashtra worship giant goldfish, believed to be Tukaram's "descendants" in a shallow stream near his birthplace, so shallow, indeed, that the giant well-fed beautiful fish can barely move, only wriggle lethargically and eat the puja thrown to them.

A sixteenth-century Rajput princess named Mirabai fell so deeply in love with Lord Krishna that she left her husband to devote the remaining years of her life to writing poems and songs to her Lord-on-high. "I have forsaken family and friends," she sang, "to sit amid saintly souls. . . . I have watered the creeper of God's love with my tears. . . . My Raja husband has sent me a cup of poison to drink. . . . Everyone knows now that Mirabai has fallen in love with God!" Four centuries later, when Madelaine Slade, daughter of an English Admiral, moved to India to join Mahatma Gandhi's ashram, Gandhi renamed her *Mira-Behn*, "Sister Mira," reincarnating the memory of "Saint Mira" and her total devotion.

Chaitanya, a Bengali Bhakti-saint of the sixteenth century, was so intoxicated by the myths of Radha's unending adoration and passionate love for her Lord Krishna that he was supposed to have enjoyed a state of constant bliss by embodying inside himself that "most adored" and "most adorable" couple. Radha-Krishna cults flourished in Madras as well as Bengal, and countless *bhajanas* ("prayers" or "songs"), poems, plays, dances, and other forms of devotional art were created to celebrate the divine love affair of India's most popular god and his favorite consort. India's second President, a renowed Vedantic philosopher and flawless speaker, Dr. S. Radhakrishnan, was, like many other South Indians, named to personify their divine love.

Krishna worship, like so much of Hindu ritual, remains alive in India to this day, and is celebrated at joyous, noisy, ribald festivals that highlight the Hindu lunar calendar. *Diwali*, the "feast of lights," is the Hindu New Year, a three-day-and-night celebration of one of Krishna's youthful miracles, reported historically from at least the eleventh century, which generally falls either in our solar October or November. Mighty young Krishna hefted the huge Govardhana mountain on his small finger to serve as protective cover for all his cows and milkmaids during a thunderous downpour that might otherwise have drowned them. Diwali is a feast of joyous celebration and brilliant decor, when Indian homes everywhere are outlined with flickering oil wicks and the horns and heads of cattle are painted and adorned with bells and tinsel, commemorating brave Krishna, Savior of cows and fair ladies-in-distress.

Krishna's birth on the eighth day of the dark half of the Hindu month called *Shravana* (either our August or September) is also a Hindu national holiday, generally celebrated with fireworks and the public parading of beautiful images of Lord Krishna that are finally immersed next morning in the nearest body of water. E. M. Forster's literary re-creation of that "Gokul Ashtami" or "Krishna Jayanti" festival in his brilliant novel, *A Passage to India*, has given that festival its greatest fame in the West. "Where was the God Himself, in whose honour the congregation had gathered?" asks Forster in the concluding "Temple" section of his greatest work. "Indistinguishable in the jumble of His own altar, huddled out of sight. . . . His face could not be seen. Hundreds of His silver dishes were piled around Him with the minimum of effect. The inscriptions which the poets of the State (Dewas Senior) had composed were hung where they could not be read. . . . In a land where all else was unpunctual, the hour of the Birth was chronometrically observed. Three minutes before it was due, a Brahman brought forth a model of the village of Gokul (the Bethlehem in that nebulous story) and placed it in front of the altar. . . . Some of the villagers thought the Birth had occurred, saying with truth that the Lord must have been born, or they could not see Him. But the clock struck midnight, and simultaneously the rending note of the conch broke forth, followed by the trumpeting of elephants; all who had packets of powder threw them at the altar, and in the rosy dust and incense, and clanging and shouts, Infinite Love took upon itself the form of SHRI KRISHNA, and saved the world. . . . Some jumped in the air, others flung themselves prone and embraced the bare feet of the universal lover; the women behind the purdah slapped and shrieked."[1] So it continues, year in, year out, Hinduism's Christmas. And with rites of spring in late February or March comes the "Feast of Love,"[2] *Holi*, the Hindu equivalent of Mardi Gras, celebrating the passionate joys of Krishna's love for beautiful Radha by the flinging of colored powder and dung mixed with cow's urine at all who pass by, and wild dancing in the streets until dawn.

Rama is second only to Krishna in deistic popularity among Hindu devotees. With his own kingdom and an entire Epic tale about his exciting life that continues to be read with fascination and delight by and to Indian children of all ages, Rama remains an endless fountain of inspiration to artists of every genre, in every era. Rama is the Hindu prototype of valiant virtue, and practically everything he ever did is viewed as a lesson in right royal behavior for high-born Kshatriyas. Similarly, his beautiful wife, Sita, is idealized as the model Hindu wife. Wind-god Maruti and monkey-god Hanuman are Rama's divine servants, further proof of his almost super-divine status. Although his devotional cults and temples did not emerge to historic light until much later than Krishna's, Rama enjoys earlier nominal avatarship, being the seventh emanation of Vishnu, immediately prior to Krishna. The *Ramayana* has been translated into every Indian language, and Ram is one of modern India's most favored names, even as "Ram-Ram" and "Hari-Ram" are favored mantras. There is, indeed, a very popular cult of

Rama-Krishna worshipers, many of whom took the name "Ramakrishna," as did one of modern India's greatest Saintly Vedantists, whose "Ramakrishna Mission" disciples are now in many lands.

Rama's birth on the "Ninth" (*Navami*) day of *Chaitra* (March–April) is also a Hindu national holiday, and for eight days before those firework celebrations begin, the *Ramayana* is read aloud, and plays based upon its epic tale are performed in towns and villages. Ayodhya is then crowded with pilgrims from every corner of the land. More famous and most popular of the Rama festivals, however, are the "Nine Nights" (*Navaratra*) of Rama's dark struggle against demon Ravana, and the "Tenth Day," *Dasara*, festival in the Hindu month of *Ashvin* (September–October) that commemorates Rama's triumphant return to Ayodhya with his bride Sita. Soon after reaching home, Rama was consecrated Raja, and the ideal golden age of Ram Rajya began, coinciding with Krishna's youthful miracle, thus giving Hindu devotees double reason for lighting up homes and repainting their walls and cattle to celebrate Diwali New Year. It is a time of joy, spiritual rebirth, gift-giving, vow-taking, much the way New Years are celebrated the world over—only more so. For to most Indians Krishna and Rama live on, as do the dread demons Bali and Ravana, whose treachery always awaits us around the next dark corner. The struggle is endless, the balance precarious, and the gods need cheering on to help them do their best.

Devotional Hinduism, then, whether Vaishnavite, Shaivite, or Shakti in its theistic objects of worship, is a vital, personal form of passionate adulation and India's most popular stream of traditional religion. Hindu temples are built to house the God and His Goddess and their children and servants and attendants and animal or supernatural "vehicles" (*vahanas*) and the many Brahmans who live inside the temple walls or grounds with their families. Some of the temples are carved from a single rock; others are virtual cities, enclosed by walls that extend for a mile or more round the many structures and open spaces and bathing tanks inside. India is replete with more temples than have ever been tallied, and more than those that survive have probably crumbled over time or been destroyed by plundering invaders. Everywhere the gods can be seen, carved sublimely out of marble or softer stone, or painted garishly and overdressed, overdecorated with garlands of daily plucked, fresh-strung flowers, marigolds and jasmine, orchids, hibiscus, orange blossoms, and roses. Everywhere bells are being rung to call some god's attention to the latest barefoot suppliant just arrived at the temple entrance, desperately needy and in hope of a moment of divine time to plead a problem that may take fifty lifetimes to resolve.

A Hindu temple is a true microcosm, not only of the home of the gods to which it is raised at such lavish expenditure, but in some ways of India herself, replete with the sacred and profane, the extremes of golden wealth and abject poverty, of power and humble supplication, undying beauty and joy, unrelenting pain, sickness, sorrow. It is all there, vibrant with color and sound, wafting through one's nostrils on waves of incense mixed with dung. "Sita-Ram, Hari!" From broken-boned beggars to shining gods of many limbs that will never age, sacred-threaded, shaven-headed Brahmans chanting Sanskrit songs as they circle and wave flickering lamps before the wide-eyed divinities whose silence is matched by the awestruck faces of the true believers. They watch, with beautiful beseeching eyes more eloquent in their impoverished devotion than all the mantras chanted too rapidly by Brahmans bored with the repetition of their daily duties. Sacred cows are also there, and bleating goats, fluttering sparrows, crows, lizards, and mice, all part of the temple universe. "Sita-Ram—Hari!"

Higher Hindu Philosophy

Six classical "Visions" (*Darshana*s) of philosophic wisdom emerged with the first flowering of Hinduism during the era of Guptan Imperial unification. Higher Hindu learning generally began with memorizing one or more of the Vedas and seeking to achieve control over at least one of those six philosophic systems, as an aid toward attaining Moksha. Yoga, now given systematic form, would as a rule be studied by all "twice-born" Hindus, at least in its basic techniques. *Saṅkhya* ("the Count") was often studied together with Yoga, both systems considered very ancient, probably pre-Aryan. Sankhyan philosophers viewed the world as basically dualistic, consisting of "Matter" (*Praḳriti*), from which, in all, twenty-three "objects" of thought, substance, and sensory perceptions evolved, and "Spirit" or "Soul" (*Purusha*), which stands alone, much the way later Atman would from the body it animates. Purusha is masculine, literally meaning "Man," and Prakriti is feminine; hence the dualism is also sexual in nature. The system, very much like Jainism, is atheistic in its self-initiating, self-regulating, and self-perpetuating character, with as many "Souls" as there are bodies requiring animation. Three "strands" (*guna*s) of human nature were first posited by Sankhya, later to be reiterated in the *Bhagavad Gita* and other Hindu texts of more recent vintage: *sattva* ("true"), *rajas* ("passionate"), and *tamas* ("dark") qualities. Good people obviously have a preponderance of the *sattva guna*, passionate people of the *rajas*, and dull or useless folk, of the *tamas* strand. Such was the earliest Indian venture at psychological analysis, similar to the ancient Greek "humors" approach, or what we might nowadays call a chemical glandular analysis of human behavior.

Hindu logicians developed their own highly sophisticated "vision" of philosophy, called *Nyaya* ("Analysis"). Students of Nyaya hoped to attain Liberation logically, which is perhaps why that school attracted a much smaller following than several of the others, less rigorous in their epistemological analyses. The five-legged Nyaya syllogism is more complex than its Greek counterpart, providing evidence with another specific example to prove a general proposition, such as "The mountain is on fire." The reason of "smoke" coming from the mountain is not quite enough for cautious Indian thinkers; hence an example, such as "In the kitchen, where there is smoke, there is fire," follows. Then it is possible to apply that familiar example to the case of the mountain, concluding, "Therefore, there is fire on the mountain." Ingenious ancient Indian philosophers also reasoned that it was possible to feel *both* cold and hot upon entering the same room, since how one felt in a new environment really depended on the atmosphere in the place just left. Hence coming from a hotter room one would feel cold, and from a colder room, hot, in exactly the same temperature.

A fourth Indian classical philosophic system, usually compared to our "atomic" analysis of the physical world, is called the *Vaisheshika* ("Individual Qualities") school. All nature was viewed as composed of different "atoms," each of which is eternal, but combines with other atoms to form many differing substances that we generally call "matter." Like Sankhya, Vaisheshika posits a dualism of "soul" and everything else, but there is also a specified divinity, Brahma, who starts the atoms moving at the dawn of each cycle, and finally winds things down by fragmenting complex molecular structures, breaking them into primal atomic units at the end of his "day" of many millions of years. Logicians generally mastered this "Atomic" school as well, traditionally becoming science "majors," so to speak, helping to keep alive India's remarkable ancient precocity in mathematics and several other sciences that would in modern times reemerge with Indian Nobel Laureate leadership in several scientific realms of pure research.

Disciples of a Vedic *Purva-Mimansaka* ("Early Inquiry") school focused their attention narrowly on the study of Rig Vedic hymns and the re-creation of Soma altars at which ancient sacrifices to Indra, Agni, Varuna, and other Vedic gods would be performed. This residual Brahmanism has been of some use historically, linguistically, and ethnographically, but could hardly be expected to yield new philosophic insights. The last of the six "visions," *Vedanta* ("End of the Vedas"), did, however, prove fruitful in that regard, and its many schools have proliferated worldwide. Vedantists have been the most brilliant and famous of all Indian philosophers, starting with the great Shankara, a South Indian Brahman, who taught mostly during the first two decades of the ninth century, developing his "nondualistic" (***Advaita***) school of Vedanta, which was later elaborated upon by recent luminaries such as Swami Vivekananda, Ramakrishna's "Saint Paul," and Dr. S. Radhakrishnan.

Upanishadic mysticism was the basis of Shankara's teaching. His only "reality" was Brahman, the transcendental universal Soul, identical to Atman, the invisible human Soul. Everything we thought we saw in the world around us, the world of "name and form," was *Maya*, "Illusion." This grand illusion deceived us, played "games" and "tricks" on us, because of our cosmic ignorance. Shankara elaborated upon earlier Upanishadic arguments used to "prove" that invisible spirit alone pervades the universe as the Real, such as sage Uddalaka had developed in enlightening his son Shvetaketu:

> As the bees, my dear, prepare honey by collecting the essences of different trees and reducing the essence to a unity, and are not able to discriminate "I am the essence of this tree," "I am the essence of that tree"—even so, my dear, all creatures here, though they reach Being, know not "We have reached Being."
>
> Whatever they are in this world, whether tiger, or lion, or wolf, or boar, or worm, or fly . . . that they become. That which is the finest essence—this whole world has that as its soul. That is Reality (***Brahman***). That is *Atman* (Soul), That art thou (*Tat tvam asi*).[3]

Or consider another example: "Of this great tree, my dear, if some one should strike at the root, it would bleed, but still live. If some one should strike at its middle, it would bleed, but still live. If some one should strike at its top. . . . Being pervaded by Atman, it continues to stand." Then asking his son to "bring hither a fig," Uddalaka instructs him to divide it, and to divide one of the seeds he finds inside, asking, "What do you see there?" The son replies, "Nothing at all, sir." Uddalaka continues, "Verily, my dear, that finest essence which you do not perceive . . . from that finest essence this great Sacred Fig tree arises. . . . That is Reality. That is Atman. That art thou, Shvetaketu."

Next the sage tells his son to place some salt in a pot of water, and to bring it back to him in the morning. He has the son sip first from one side, then from the other, and then from the middle of the water, asking each time, "How is it?" Invariably, the answer is "Salt." "Verily, my dear, you do not perceive Salt here, but it is here. That which is the finest essence, this whole world has that as its Soul. That is Reality. That is Atman. That art thou."

Shankara sought to remove all veils of "superimposition" from the eyes of his students, to help them appreciate the unity of "subject" and "object," of "inner" and "outer" self, the total Oneness of Being as Soul. Many stories are told of his great teaching, including one about a rather "slow" student who could not comprehend the meaning of *Tat tvam asi* and its Brahman-Atman equation for the longest time, until one morning, in a flash of recognition, he saw it. Jumping up in excitement the student ran outside, shouting, "Yes, I am one with the trees and the air and the sky, I am one with the road and the birds." A huge elephant was fast approaching, and the driver shouted down, "Get out of the way, fool!" "I am one with the elephant," shouted the wisdom-intoxicated boy, and the elephant wrapped his trunk round his waist, raised him high, and hurled him down painfully on the side of the dusty road. Poor fellow could barely drag his bruised body back to his guru's hut. "My God, what happened?" Sadly, he told the story, concluding, "I'm afraid I don't understand *Tat tvam asi*!" "You almost do," Shankara explained. "It is true you are one with the trees and the road and the elephant, but you are also one with his driver, and when he told you to get out of the way, you should have done so!"

Similarly, later Vedantic mystics like the illiterate Ramakrishna, who lived in nineteenth-century Calcutta, reminded listeners: "You see many stars at night in the sky but find them not when the sun rises; can you say that there are no stars in the heaven of day? So . . . because you behold not

God in the days of your ignorance, say not that there is no God."[4] If we would "seek God," Ramakrishna taught, we must look for him in our fellow "man." He used the Upanishadic examples and analogies also, of course, some with variations, noting that although people who spoke different languages called "water" by different names, what they drank was the same substance, and while devotees of the various religions called "God" by many names, He was always the same sole God. Ramakrishna's messenger to the West was his greatest disciple, Swami Vivekananda (1863–1902), who came to Chicago in 1893 and electrified the World Parliament of Religions there with his golden voice and Vedantic wisdom. "If you cannot see God in the human face, how can you see Him in the clouds, or in images made of dull, dead matter," asked Vivekananda, arguing: "I shall call you religious from the day you begin to see God in men and women and then you will understand what is meant by turning the left cheek to the man who strikes you on the right. When you see man as God, everything, even the tiger, will be welcome. Whatever comes to you is but the Lord, the Eternal, the Blessed One, appearing to us in various forms . . . our own soul playing with us."[5]

Vivekananda's dream was nothing less than "the conquest of the whole world by India," at least philosophically. "Up, India, and conquer the world with your spirituality! Aye, as has been declared on this soil first, love must conquer hatred, hatred cannot conquer itself. Materialism and all its miseries can never be conquered by materialism. Armies when they attempt to conquer armies only multiply and make brutes of humanity. Spirituality must conquer the West . . . heroic workers are wanted to go abroad and help to disseminate the great truths of Vedanta. The world wants it; without it the world will be destroyed. The whole of the Western world is on a volcano which may burst tomorrow, go to pieces tomorrow."[6] His prophecy was uttered less than two decades before World War I. Mahatma Gandhi had only just gone to South Africa, and was still unknown, unheard from, but hardly a decade later Vivekananda himself was dead, worn out by the fever of his frenetic missionary efforts to save humanity from its own monstrous machines. The missions of Self-Realization he started, however, took root, and less than a century after he uttered his clarion call, mahatmas, maharishis, and gurus-galore would reiterate the higher Hindu messages of Vedantic wisdom and the powers of Love, the divinity of Soul, and the Real-Truth that is God.

Islam in India

The essence as well as the meaning of *Islam* is "Submission" to the Laws and will of *Allah*, "*the* God" in Arabic, Almighty, All-knowing, Merciful, Compassionate, Creator of the universe and all who inhabit it. He will preside over the Last Judgment, when every grave will open and every being on earth will appear before His throne to be assigned his eternal place, either in Paradise or in Hell, depending upon how well or badly he has "submitted," whether his life on earth was lived as a true *Muslim* or as a lost heathen soul, ensnared by Satan, hence left to burn in his wretched domain below. The true words of God Almighty were revealed to his final Prophet, Muhammad, in the seventh century of the Christian era, "recited" (*Qur'an*) to him by the Archangel Gabriel. Those sacred portions of God's message, which will only be completely revealed at the Last Judgment, have been preserved in Arabic in the Book of God, that all Muslims revere, the *Qur'an*.

To be a Muslim, one must merely affirm, with sincere conviction, and in Arabic, that "There is but one God, Allah, and Muhammad is the Prophet of God." As a true and devout Muslim, then, one should also pray five times daily, facing Makka, where Islam was founded by the Prophet in A.D. 622, when he "fled" (*hijrat*) to Medina. On Fridays, the noon prayer should be congregational, inside a mosque courtyard. Muslims also contribute a share of their wealth to the "democratic community" (*umma*) of the faithful and devout, and should give alms to the poor "for the love of Allah," and must fast during the ninth lunar month of Ramadan, from sunup till sundown. Finally, at least once in a true Muslim's lifetime he must make the pilgrimage to Makka, the Prophet's birthplace, where he was also buried. There are many other Islamic laws and traditions, for Islam is a faith built on laws and traditions, especially those of the Prophet; hence good Muslims must never eat pig products or drink wine, but are permitted to marry as many as four wives.

It is also important for Muslims to live in a land ruled by Muslims, one that is "Dar-ul-Islam"; otherwise they reside in what is called *Dar-ul-Harb*—a "Land at War," and then their duty is to wage *Jihad* ("Holy War"), if need be, against the infidels all around them. Nothing assures a Muslim a place in paradise as swiftly as to die fighting for Islam, for God Almighty. Since God is Almighty and so wondrous as to defy human imagination, He must never be depicted in human form, nor should any of His messengers or angels be so depicted, hence the only decorations on a Muslim mosque are geometric designs or calligraphic art, the *Qur'an*'s Arabic words often adorning high screen facades, carved in marble or stone, inlaid with precious gems, silver, or gold. On special days of the Islamic year, commemorating the Prophet's birth and the Archangel's revelation to him of God's Words, sacrificial festivals (*Id*s) offer thanks to God, and then goats or lambs or cows are beheaded at Muslim altars, the merest tokens of human gratitude to the Almighty.

Islam was born in Saudi Arabia and remains as remote from Hinduism as that desert land is from Mother Ganga's Varanasi ghats. No one can ever be sure of just how many gods Hinduism embraces, for every cow and Brahman at least is believed to partake of the divine. Some Hindus claim that no fewer than 330 million gods exist, although only thirty-three are named in the Rig Veda. Hindu temples with their towering gates and walls, often covered with naked gods and voluptuous goddesses, remain a source of constant provocation to Muslim eyes and minds, even as Muslim butchers provoke Hindu rage and fury, each time they lead a cow or her calf to slaughter. Hindus and Muslims have, however, coexisted now on South Asian soil for more than 1,000 years, and in countless Indian villages as well as small towns they still live side by side, temple and mosque within view of each other, Mullahs and Brahmans walking the same mud lanes or paved streets, shopping in the same bazaars.

Most of South Asia's Muslim quarter of the total population that emerged by the nineteenth century were offspring of mixed Hindu and Muslim parentage or descendants of Hindu converts to one or another of Islam's heterodox or mystic sects. The total number of Arabic, Persian, Afghan, Turkish, and Mongol Muslim invaders, who first conquered and then resided in India, was never more than 1 or 2 percent of the subcontinent's entire population.

Genetically speaking, then, most Indian Muslims are Indian, and many, who follow the mystic *Sufi* paths toward God as taught by saintly Islamic *Pir*s in Kashmir or Lucknow or Bengal, resemble Hindu devotees of Vaishnava saints much more than orthodox Mullahs. Why all the religious violence, then? How truly basic is the antipathy between Islam and Hinduism? Was Pakistan inevitable? And if so, has Pakistan's birth resolved anything?

Or has its existence since 1947 merely transformed and escalated what used to be an internal problem before that date into a more deadly and bitter international struggle for power ever since?

India has not been the only country in the world to be plagued by religious conflicts. More Protestants and Catholics have murdered one another in religious wars than have Hindus and Muslims. In Northern Ireland they continue to do so, even as in Lebanon, Jews, Christians, and Muslims seem committed to periodic, if not perpetual, warfare. Not that two or twenty-two wars justify any other, no more than one sort of prejudice can validate another kind. Hindu–Muslim antipathy is simply not unique, nor has Hindu–Muslim coexistence been impossible to achieve or sustain over long interludes in South Asia. Akbar came closest perhaps to providing the sort of strong, unbiased rule that made most of his subjects feel secure in the practice of their own particular faiths, during Mughal Imperial times. Several lesser Mughal Emperors were almost as tolerant as their "Great" forebear, and regionally some of the Muslim Nizams of Hyderabad proved adept at managing without much violent repression the mass of their own state's Hindu population.

The British Company Raj was also most successful at managing Indian pluralism as long as it kept official eyes and minds focused more on profits than the salvation of native souls, and maintained Dupleix's fiction of allowing most Indians to believe that they continued to be ruled by their own monarchs and tax-gathering aristocrats. Religious differences did not disappear during those intervals of relative internal tranquility, nor did Muslims who joined the British Indian Army become Hindus, or Sikhs. Such pluralism could be contained in India, much the way every other sort was within the Hindu caste system, by permitting different religious groups to manage their own faiths as they wished, without infringement or interference from any of the others. Lines were drawn, religious fences were staked out and maintained, defensive perimeters guarded by higher, or at least impartial, authority, and for the isolated fanatic who went wild and tried to take the law into his own hands, punishment awaited, swift, severe, unbiased. So the peace could be kept. As long as everyone wanted to keep it.

Communal virulence escalated as the political and economic stakes held out by Britain's Crown Raj to Indian aspirants for a greater share in power became increasingly attractive. Was it Liberal modernism then that turned South Asia into a field of religious warfare? Was it merely the prospect of democratic elections to some sort of Parliament? Obviously no single cause could have sufficed to generate as much hatred and bloody violence as finally broke loose on the eve of independence from British rule. But real political power has its appeals, again not only in South Asia. Yet in British India a seat on the Viceroy's Council or Legislative Assembly meant more than just one vote on legislation that might or might not affect the pocketbooks of millions, for its also meant influence, early access to financial news of every variety, easy access to the magistracy and all other branches of the law, and to the cumbersome complex machinery of bureaucratic rule and martial force. Unscrupulous use of such influence by members of one community could thus easily put members of the other community at comparative disadvantage, affecting one's chances of employment, or the education of one's children, or the tax levied on one's property, or access to water, or power, or new roads, or whether choice land in the heart of one's city would be used to build a new mosque or a new temple, or a new Anglo-Oriental Muslim College, or a Hindu university.

There were many ways to ignite the dry tinder of religious prejudice and difference that lay scattered in every Indian village, with the refuse searched by scavenger pigs in the darkest quarters of every town and city slum. There was always at least one malcontent Muslim ready to flare up at the first sound of raucous music approaching his mosque at noon on Friday as a Hindu wedding party or funeral went by, taking the worst possible route through town. And there was always a young Brahman ready to kill if need be to save the life of a sacred cow led toward the chopping block, or prepared at any rate to toss a squealing pig into the nearest mosque or Muslim home he could find. Such torches of doctrinal difference were always there, soaked in flammable kerosene, smoldering from the heat of despair and self-doubt. The impotent rage at watching one's wife smile at a male from another community, or seeing one's daughter swept away by a lover whose family, like Romeo's, came from the wrong side of town—whether real or imagined, invisible sparks were always in the air ready to turn cold torches into lethal weapons. Simply say the word, raise the cry—"That Muslim raped her!" "He's the Hindu who touched my wife's veil!" "See them taking my grandmother to the butcher's block!" "He spat on our temple!" "That one threw the pig in our mosque!"

Generally, the British tried to keep the balance straight. Peace was obviously in the best interest of those foreign officials who lived in India as well as for members of all indigenous religious communities in the land. Like Hindus and Muslims, however, the British had their own prejudices and preferences, individual as well as communal, personal as well as doctrinal. They were only human, although at times they tried to behave like gods, especially while in India. Or as devils. The first Partition of Bengal may have been an innocent error of administrative judgment. Or perhaps it was an unconscious or conscious case of pro-Muslim, or anti-Bengali-Hindu, prejudice on the part of the Viceroy, or his Secretary, or the new Lieutenant Governor, or one of the Secretary of State's Councillors, or all of the above! An academic question by now.

The real historic implications of the poisonous communal impact of that first Partition, however, proved more than academic. Just as the impact of the Jallianwala Bagh massacre of 1919 was crucial in galvanizing India's Nationalist "Revolution," derailing its prior moderate liberal course and leadership, so did the first Partition of Bengal whet the political appetites of Muslims for more power. Hence the birth of the Muslim League at Dakha (Dacca) the following year, and the creation of a bloc of Muslim politicians who would continue to press "Muslim demands" for more "Muslim seats" and more "Muslim votes" and more of a "Muslim voice" in India's political future. Similarly, the "separate Muslim electorate" formula introduced with the Indian Councils Act of 1909 reinforced growing Muslim awareness, at least among the elite, of the real political value of Muslim identity in British India. In the Government of India Act of 1919, and still again in the Act of 1935 and the Prime Minister's Communal Award (1932), the Government of Great Britain stressed and underscored its consciousness of Muslim separate interests, special interests, that made it mandatory for Muslim voters to vote as a distinct bloc divided from Hindu and all other Indians, for their very own *Muslim* candidates. How could Indians then hope to acquire a single sense of "National" identity when they were constantly being asked, every time they went to vote or were polled by government officialdom, whether they were "Hindu" or "Muslim" or "Christian"?

After 1937, moreover, Muslim leaders like Mohammad Ali Jinnah, argued that it would be more painful, humiliating, and dangerous for Muslims to live under a "Hindu Raj" than it had ever been to serve as subjects of the British Raj. Jinnah and his Muslim League lieutenants gathered reports from every province of British India run by autonomous Congress ministries, "proving" to Muslims that they had become "second-class" citizens at best, in the land they once ruled for centuries. Discrimination in employment, education, business, and the meting out of justice were all charged in several League reports. Congress leaders denied prejudice of any sort. Not only Nehru and Gandhi but Muslim Maulana A. K. Azad as well, an orthodox Alim who had served as Congress President throughout the war and would become Nehru's first Minister for Education, all promised to investigate every charge, to bring any culprits to justice, to change procedures that required altering, to do whatever needed to be done to restore Muslim confidence in the impartiality of Congress. But it was too late.

Jinnah, the League leaders who worked with him, and the Muslim voters who would overwhelmingly support them after the war, no longer trusted their Congress compatriots. "The present leadership of the Congress," Quaid-i-Azam Jinnah told his League at Lucknow in December 1937, "has been responsible for alienating the Musalmans in India more and more, by pursuing a policy which is exclusively Hindu. . . . Eighty millions of Musalmans in India have . . . their destiny in their hands, and as a well-knit, solid, organized, united force can face any danger, and withstand any opposition." Early the following year in Karachi, Jinnah spoke of the Muslim "national goal," but it was not until March 1940 in Lahore that he and the League finally committed to demanding a separate Muslim nation-state, to be called "Pakistan." "The Musalmans are not a minority," President Jinnah told his League at Lahore. "The Musalmans are a nation. . . . The problem in India is not of an inter-communal but manifestly of an international character, and it must be treated as such. . . . If the British Government are really in earnest and sincere to secure the peace and happiness of the people of this Subcontinent, the only course open to us all is to allow the major nations separate homelands, by dividing India into 'autonomous national States.'"

Mahatma Gandhi called that Lahore resolution to carve a Muslim "Land of the Pure" (*Pakistan*) out of India's body politic "vivisection of the Motherland." Other Congress leaders, like C. Rajagopalachari of Madras, India's first Indian Governor-General, considered Jinnah's proposal "a sign of a diseased mentality." Nehru viewed the idea as "fantastic." Most British officials also thought it "dangerous," "unrealistic," "ill-conceived," or simply "impossible to arrange." Jinnah insisted, however, that Pakistan was not only possible but also essential for the Muslims of South Asia, who could no longer contemplate living under "alien Hindu tyranny." In March 1945 Jinnah assured his fellow Muslims that though dark "powers" and "enemies" were always "working around us," "I have my finger on the pulse of Muslim India, and I feel confident that . . . Pakistan is within our grasp . . . *Insha-Allah* (God-willing), we shall win." The League's battle-cry, and by War's end a common Muslim League greeting, became "*Pakistan Zindabad!*"—"Victory to Pakistan!"

"Whereas Muslim India has exhausted, without success, all efforts to find a peaceful solution of the Indian problem by compromise and constitutional means; and whereas the Congress is bent upon setting up Caste-Hindu Raj in India with the connivance of the British," Jinnah and his League resolved in mid-Summer 1946, "the time has come for the Muslim nation to resort to Direct Action to achieve Pakistan . . . to get rid of the present British slavery and the contemplated future Caste-Hindu domination." A few weeks later the "Great Calcutta Killing" began, as "unbridled savagery with homicidal maniacs let loose to kill and kill and to maim and burn."[7] It was only the beginning of a year of slaughter, of Hindu–Muslim civil war that almost destroyed India even before the dawn of Independence. Religious differences and orthodox zeal provided ample fuel to keep the fires burning once the power, political ambitions, fears, and Machiavellian methods of the leaders of the Muslim League, Congress, and the British Raj sparked the initial blaze. Then all the pious words and goodwill of the Civilized World combined would barely suffice to hold back those unleashed forces of homicidal savagery.

The birth of Pakistan in 1947 did not "settle" Hindu–Muslim differences or end Hindu–Muslim conflicts. To the contrary. All the old problems remained, for the pig was still anathema to Muslims, the cow still sacred to Hindus, who continue to worship gods in many faces and beautifully depicted forms, while Muslims still bow only to one God Almighty. Some five million Hindus and Sikhs fled Pakistan in the weeks and months following Partition, and perhaps as many as a million of them never lived to resettle inside homes in India, dying en route to or in refugee camps hastily erected, inadequately maintained, insufficiently funded. Virtually the same number of Muslims fled in opposite directions, and possibly as many as a quarter of those, usually the oldest and youngest, also died within a year of their uprooting. Since then, of course, the major residual conflicts have assumed international, no longer mere national, dimensions. The 10 percent of contemporary India's Muslim population has, for the most part, remained loyally integrated into India's Republic, which is constitutionally "secular" as well as "democratic." Sporadic Hindu–Muslim riots continue, however, especially in the environs of pluralistic metropolises such as Bombay, Delhi, Ahmedabad, Lucknow, Calcutta, and Patna. The causes are familiar: interfaith sexual molestation, music near a mosque, cow-slaughter, pig-pollution, official prejudice or discrimination, poverty, insanity, drunkenness, enough to fuel a thousand and one fights. As a rule they run their course in a night or two, or a week or two, generally sorted out by local police, otherwise by the Indian Army that remains a National arm as yet untainted by communal passions, prejudices, or partisanship.

Sikhism

Sikhism, the religion of "disciples" or "students," was founded by *Guru* ("Divine Teacher") Nanak (1469–1539), who was born a Hindu in Punjab, where he learned Persian and Arabic as well as Sanskrit. Reared in a historic environment of devotional (*bhakta*) Hinduism and mystical Islamic *sufism*, Nanak absorbed many of the saintly teachings of late-fifteenth-century India prior to his own mystic illumination that preceded the birth of the Sikh faith.

"There is no Hindu, there is no Muslim," Guru Nanak taught. "There is only One Being Who is the Creator and the uncaused Cause of all . . . God is one." Repetition of the *Nam* ("Name") of God is one mode of Sikh worship, hard labor another, and sharing one's earnings from his hard labor with others of equal spiritual importance. The first Guru was a remarkable man of inspired wisdom, welcoming all disciples to his faith, women as well as men of every caste and creed, for Sikhism abolished the worst of Hinduism's sexual and hierarchical discriminatory practices. Eating meals in common, where all were welcome, strangers and family alike, was another Sikh habit that has remained one of its most egalitarian social practices.

Guru Nanak walked the length of North India to Bengal, preaching his inspired message as he went, winning disciples by the gentle goodness of his devotion to God. The first Guru was a great traveler, journeying to Sri Lanka in the south and as far west as Makka, where he slept in the mosque of the Qa'aba, then back through Baghdad and Afghanistan to Punjab. Nine Gurus succeeded Nanak, revered by all Sikhs as divine teachers.

Guru Angad (1539–1552) recorded the hymnal prayers of Guru Nanak and his life in the cursive Punjabi script that has come to be called *Gurmukhi* ("Script of the Gurus") and remains the script of all sacred Sikh writings. Just as Sanskrit is the sacred language of Hinduism, and Arabic of Islam, Punjabi is the language sacred to Sikhism. Since Guru Nanak believed that God is "formless," Sikhs worship no idols or divine images, but their most sacred "object" is the book containing divine scripture of the Gurus, which the fifth Guru Arjun (1581–1606) compiled and preserved as *Guru Granth Sahib*. Guru Ram Das (1574–1581), Arjun's predecessor, founded the sacred Sikh city of *Amritsar* ("Nectar of Immortality") in the center of which was a wellspring named *Amrit* ("Immortal Nectar") because of the curative powers of its fresh bubbling waters. Guru Arjun erected a beautiful Sikh temple of worship (*Gurdwara*, literally "Guru's Door") around the sacred pool. That most famous Sikh temple in Amritsar was named Harmandir Sahib by the Sikhs, but later came to be called the "Golden Temple" by the British, since its walls and Persian dome in the center of the sacred tank are covered with pure gold.

Soon after completion of Harmandir Sahib and the installation of the sacred *Guru Granth Sahib* inside its gold-covered marble temple, which is open on all four sides, symbolizing the universal openness of the Sikh faith, Guru Arjun was martyred by Delhi's Muslim Emperor Jahangir. "Of all religious Laws the highest Law is prayer to God and good behavior," wrote Guru Arjun, the first Sikh Guru to be martyred for his principled refusal to bow down to the Imperial Court of the Mughals or surrender his devout faith to adopt tenets of Islam. Guru Arjun's son, Hargovind, was just eleven years old when he became Guru, but, vowing vengeance for his father's murder, he girded himself with two swords, one symbolizing his temporal powers, the other his spiritual leadership over disciples who would follow him faithfully for thirty-eight years. Guru Hargovind erected a steel "Tower to Immortal God" (*Akal Takht*), facing Harmandir Sahib, and from within that new temporal headquarters of Sikhism, the seventh Guru presided over his increasingly martial court, armed and ready to confront any force sent by his Mughal adversary from Delhi to Amritsar. More recent martial confrontation and continuing conflict between Amritsar and New Delhi thus, like most of modern India's problems, has deep historic roots, extending back in this instance more than three-and-a-half centuries.

Guru Tegh Bahadur (1664–1675) was also tortured in Delhi but adamantly refused to renounce his faith, until he was finally beheaded by bigoted Emperor Aurangzeb's Mughal executioners. Martyred Tegh Bahadur's son, Guru Govind (1675–1708), was the tenth and final Guru, who wreaked havoc on Mughal Imperial forces throughout the more than thirty years when he led and transformed the Sikh community into an "Army of the Pure" (*Khalsa*), taking for himself the surname *Singh* ("Lion") and baptizing his foremost disciples with the same leonine designation that most Sikhs still retain. To help weld his Khalsa into a band of human lions, each of whom could easily recognize his brothers and all of whom could fight most effectively against Mughal tyranny, Guru Govind Singh adopted five signs that have come to signify his martial form of Sikhism: uncut hair, a comb to control it, a sword or dagger, a steel bracelet to be worn on one's right wrist, and shorts to allow Sikh-lions to jump onto horseback at any moment and gallop into battle.

Guru Govind Singh baptized his first five lion-hearted members of the Khalsa at Punjab's city of Anandpur in 1699. He chose the festival of Spring (*Baisakhi*), early in April, for that historic rebirth of the Sikh faith as a "Community" (*Panth*) of martial lions, and 274 years later Anandpur was again to be chosen as the venue for important Sikh communal resolutions, adopted during the same festive holiday. For recent Sikh political history, the Anandpur Sahib Resolution adopted in 1973 by the Sikh *Akali Dal* ("Immortal Party") would, in fact, prove almost as significant a turning point as Guru Govind's earlier baptizing had for his martial Panth. In 1699, however, the last Guru declared an end to the living line of Gurus, for all of his sons had been killed in battle or imprisonment, and to allow greatest martial flexibility to his Panth proclaimed that any five Sikhs in the presence of a copy of their *Granth Sahib* scripture would thereafter constitute a "Guru." Each Sikh panchayat was thus endowed with quasi-divine powers, every cell of the Khalsa becoming a virtual Guru-incarnate, hence considered practically invincible.

The last of Delhi's Great Mughals, Emperor Aurangzeb, had so huge an army that he was able to disperse the Sikhs, driving its fiercest fighters into Himalayan foothill heights seeking shelter. There, in the State now called Himachal Pradesh, whose capital is Simla, Sikh warriors defeated many hill Rajas and carved out their own little kingdoms. In Punjab's riverine plains, however, tough handfuls of Sikh guerrillas survived hidden in friendly Hindu Jat villages, converting many of the peasant families they met to the community of militant Sikhism that came to be called "Khalsa Panth," Govind's full-bearded and turbaned army of lions. Though Mughal Imperial forces hoped to drive Sikhism out of Punjab, their violent persecution and repression of that minority faith served only to help transform its tenacious disciples into a "Nation"-in-embryo. The last of the Gurus outlived his hated enemy, Aurangzeb, by a year, praying for "protection" to "God than whom there is no one better, no higher." Guru Govind was assassinated by two Muslims in October 1708, but almost a century later the first Sikh Kingdom was born in Punjab's fecund soil.

Maharaja Ranjit Singh (1780–1839), the one-eyed "Lion of Punjab,"[8] as his British East India contemporaries called him, proclaimed the independence of his Sikh Kingdom of the "Land of Five Rivers" in Spring 1801. Ranjit's courage and shrewd diplomacy secured his throne over a Punjab Kingdom, where only 10 percent of the population was Sikh, some 80 percent remaining Muslim, the rest being Hindu. The greatest Sikh Maharaja took counsel from Hindus and Muslims as well as members of his own Khalsa, creating a Punjabi State of remarkable communal harmony, although he ruled in the name of Khalsa Panth and had Guru Nanak's face stamped on every coin minted in his capital of Lahore. Ranjit's diplomacy kept not only the rapacious British Company at bay but warded off Afghans, Gurkhas, Marathas, and Rajputs as well, ruling Kashmir and Punjab from the Indus to the Sutlej with his grip of steel.

The British Company concluded its first formal treaty of "perpetual friendship" with Ranjit Singh in 1809, and their ill-fated "Tripartite" Treaty on the eve of the disastrous First Anglo-Afghan War in 1838. One-eyed Ranjit proved the most far-sighted of his regal Indian contemporaries, early recognizing that the British Company of merchants was destined to inherit Great Mughal Imperial power over India, prophesying as he pointed to a map on which the Company's still modest domain was painted red, "*Sab lal ho jayega!*" ("All will go red someday!") One decade after Ranjit's death his weak and squabbling successors proved the shrewd Maharaja's prediction all too accurate.

Sikh rivalries swiftly undermined Punjab's power, and British arms moved in to conquer the last bastion of independent India, absorbing Punjab in two hard-fought wars, the first in 1845/46, the second in 1849. British officers commanded East India Company armies that crushed the Khalsa Panth's forces, but the soldiers who fired their Brown Bess muskets across the Land of Five Rivers were Sepoys of the Bengal Army, high-caste *Purbaiya*—"Eastern"—Hindus for the most part from Oudh (present-day U.P.), Bihar, and Bengal. For almost a century, from before Robert Clive's landmark victory at Plassey in 1757, Gangetic plains Hindus were being recruited and trained in large numbers by enterprising Englishmen, who taught them modern European techniques of close-order drill and the proper use of new lethal weapons, rifles as well as cannon, that could blow away any adversary, no matter how brave or leonine he might be. With their Sepoy armies (the Company had three separate forces, one in Bombay, another in Madras, although the Bengal Army was by far the largest and most powerful) a handful of British merchants and soldiers-of-fortune thus "conquered" India.

So many thousands of Sikhs died fighting for their homeland that British officers came to admire and respect the courage as well as ferocity of those brave Punjabi soldiers, who were within a decade of their conquest to become staunch pillars of the British Indian Army. The brothers John and Henry Lawrence presided over the integration of Punjab into British India, and had the good sense to win Sikh support after their conquest, by trusting and recruiting them to serve the British Raj at what they did best, soldiering and farming. Sikh soldiers brought into the British service were permitted to wear their turbans and flowing beards and to carry swords or knives as members of the Khalsa were all expected to do. Those new Sikh sepoys were delighted to find that they would, after mid-1857, be asked to fight *Purbaiya*—"Mutineer"—sepoys of the Bengal Army, the same hated "Easterners" who had conquered Punjab less than a decade earlier.

For the British, reconciliation with the Sikhs came none too soon. After the "Sepoy Mutiny" ignited at Meerut in May 1857, no high-caste Hindu or Muslim Sepoy of the Bengal Army would ever again be trusted by a British officer. Sikhs, contrarily, were exalted as the finest example of a pure "martial race," for thanks to their loyal service under British leadership they quickly liberated Delhi and the rest of North India that had almost fallen permanent victim to treacherous Sepoy "rebels." Without martial Sikh assistance the British might not have recaptured their proudest Jewel to set in Victoria's Imperial Crown.

From 1858 through the end of World War I at least, Sikhs, and the martial regiments of the British Indian Army they manned and led into battle, remained the stout right arm of British Imperial power. Princely Sikh States, like Patiala and Nabha, added their own quasi-independent troops to the almost one-third of British India's regular recruits, whose turbans, beards, and ubiquitous swords proudly proclaimed their membership in the Sikh Panth. But if the Jat backbone of Punjab's Sikh population was primarily loyal to the British Raj and martially bolstered its ramparts the world over, there emerged with India's growing Nationalist movement a minority of Sikh revolutionaries, whose violent anti-British activities put them in the vanguard of assassins as well and those hanged by the British for sedition. One sect of Sikh extremists, called *Kukas*, because of the loud way they "shouted" God's name, advocated the boycott of all things British in the latter part of the nineteenth century, long before Mahatma Gandhi adopted the multiple boycott as his major post-World War I Satyagraha platform.

Sikh farmers who hoped to find more and better land to work in other parts of the British Empire were the first major group of Indians to migrate to the Western Hemisphere, settling in northern California as well as in Canada, but not without first confronting racial discrimination that initially prevented many of those valiant immigrants from even setting foot on Canadian soil. The *Komagata Maru*, a Japanese ship chartered to carry almost 400 Sikhs to Vancouver early in 1914, was never permitted to disembark its emigrants, and turned back to Bengal after almost a year at sea. Those painfully persecuted Sikhs returned to their Punjab villages confirmed anti-British revolutionaries, spreading word of Imperial intolerance and racism wherever they went, devoting their lives to the violent overthrow of the British Raj. In San Francisco a small band of ardent young Sikh revolutionaries started the *Ghadr* ("Mutiny") party, which tried to ship arms to India during World War I with German assistance. Har Dayal was the most famous Ghadr Sikh patriot, and Bhagat Singh (hanged in 1931) the most admired hero of all Sikh revolutionary leaders in the Nationalist movement.

Throughout most of World War I, the British Government of India had suspended Anglo-Saxon due process of law, previously introduced by the Raj, on grounds that martial emergency and wartime hazards required much tighter security. The Defence of India Acts, as those martial law ordinances were called, became, however, the first subjects of legislative business proposed by British officialdom for immediate extension after the War ended. Justice Rowlatt, who had drafted a Report on "Sedition" in Wartime India, proposed the preventive detention laws that bore his name, arguing that "seditious elements" in postwar India posed a continuing "threat" to

British rule, and it was "too risky" to abandon the simpler procedures of martial detention just because the Great War had been won.

Mahatma Gandhi labeled Justice Rowlatt's legislation "Black Acts," arguing: "To me, the Bills are the aggravated symptoms of the deep-seated disease. They are a striking demonstration of the determination of the Civil Service to retain its grip of our necks. . . . If we succumb we are done for . . . civil disobedience seems to be a duty imposed upon every lover of personal and public liberty."[9]

The most violent explosion in the wake of Gandhi's anti-Rowlatt Satyagraha agitation came in April 1919 in Amritsar. Gandhi himself was prevented by police order from entering Punjab, while his leading lieutenants in Amritsar were deported by British officials for "seditious incitement" under the very preventive detention measures they civilly opposed. Local martial repression in support of civil official refusal to meet with Punjab Congressmen seeking information about their deported leaders triggered violence that swept through Amritsar, bringing out the Army under Brigadier Reginald Dyer. April 13 was Baisakhi Spring Festival Day in Amritsar, and thousands of Sikh and Hindu peasants flocked to the sacred city from neighboring villages, gathering in Jallianwala *Bagh*, a large enclosed "Garden" within sight of the Golden Temple in the crowded center of the old town. Dyer had issued orders forbidding any public "meeting" that day, so when he learned of the gathering crowd he marched his Gurkha and Baluchi troops there double time and ordered them to open fire without further word of warning on the unarmed crowd inside the garden that had no exit (other than the one secured by his troops) and no shelter (except for a deep well into which many innocents plunged to their death). After ten minutes of point blank firing of some 1,650 rounds into terrified, helplessly exposed human targets, as his men's ammunition ran low, Dyer ordered his troops to return to barracks. Some 400 Indian corpses, and over 1,200 wailing wounded were left bleeding inside that garden as the darkest night of the British Raj descended over Amritsar.

Martial law with its "long horror and terrible indignity," as Jawaharlal Nehru put it, was then locked over Punjab's mortified body. "The Punjab was isolated, cut off from the rest of India," wrote India's first Prime Minister, "a thick veil seemed to cover it and hide it from outside eyes . . . individuals, who managed to escape from that inferno, were so terror-struck that they could give no clear account."[10] But before year's end martial law was lifted, and Congress held its annual meeting in Amritsar. Jawaharlal's distinguished father, Motilal Nehru, one of British India's wealthiest advocates, personally presided over that December 1919 Congress. Some 36,000 Indians, 6,000 of whom were elected delegates, attended the Amritsar Congress.

"We must do reverence to the sacred memory of the dead who were killed in Amritsar and elsewhere in the Punjab, and to the living who were put to indignities worse even than death," said President Motilal Nehru in his Congress address:

> The proximity of the Punjab to the frontier has enabled its administrators time and again to enforce their will. . . . The bogey of the frontier is exploited to the uttermost and the proposals made by the "man on the spot" seldom fail to secure acceptance at the hands of the higher authorities. . . . But repression and terrorism have never yet killed the life of a nation; they but increase the disaffection and drive it underground to pursue an unhealthy course of breaking out occasionally into crimes of violence. And this brings further repression and so the vicious circle goes on. No one can but deplore violence and political crime. But let us not forget that this is the direct outcome of continued repression.[11]

Three days after Motilal Nehru addressed the Amritsar Congress, the Central Sikh League met in the same city for the first time. That birth of a separate Sikh political organization presaged the modern dawn of Sikh political consciousness in Punjab. The following year, in 1920, more orthodox Sikh *Akali*s ("Immortals") joined forces to start their own party, supported by younger revolutionary Sikh students, inspired by Congress cries of *Svaraj* ("Self-Rule") to demand greater independence for Sikhs of the *Khalsa Panth* to live as Guru Govind had earlier taught them.

Punjab's rich alluvial soil, perennial river water, and a network of irrigation canals built by British engineers and enterprising Jat peasants had so enhanced the value of Punjabi land by the dawn of the twentieth century that peasant indebtedness rose alarmingly, just as Punjab started to emerge as Britain's Indian "breadbasket." British official preference for Jat peasants of every religion (especially Sikh), and intense personal dislike of "Banias" of every variety (especially Hindu) led to the passage of several Punjab

Alienation of Land Acts early in this century, designed to protect Sikh and Muslim Jats, who were also a fecund pool of recruits for the British Army, from losing their lands to urban Hindu moneylenders, who found it impossible to collect property for debt-default, despite holding the deeds as "collateral." Not all Sikhs were Jat peasants, however, some being urban Khatri and Aurora moneylenders and merchants, others belonging to the former "untouchable" Hindu menial and sweeper communities of Punjab, the Mazhabhis and Ramdasis. Although Sikhism, like Islam, had "abolished" caste, deeper currents of Indian social habits and preferences, especially in the selection of marital partners, were singularly slow to disappear.

In February 1921 the *Akali Dal* ("Army of Immortals' Party") launched its first peaceful "march" (*jatha*) against the Nankana Gurdwara, the Sikh temple where Guru Nanak was buried in what is now Pakistan, whose corrupt "Manager" (*Mahant*) was a Hindu who kept Sikh "untouchables" out of the temple and had brought many Hindu idols into it. The brutal hereditary Mahant hired thugs to butcher and burn the Akalis as they marched unarmed toward the Gurdwara, martyring 130 of them in Punjab's bloodiest confrontation since Jallianwala Bagh. Thousands of fresh Sikh recruits, however, now joined the Akali Dal and soon wave after irresistible wave of Akalis rolled across the Punjab, removing corrupt Udasi Mahants from every Gurdwara in the province, replacing them with devout Sikhs, selected by the Khalsa Panth's own chosen Management Committee of 175 Sikh leaders who came together within the newly founded *Shiromani Gurdwara Prabandhak* ("Central Gurdwara Management") Committee (SGPC), which first won legal status in 1925.

Master Tara Singh (1885–1967) emerged as the most important leader of the SGPC prior to Independence, and was jailed many times for his fearless opposition to Punjabi authorities as he marched at the head of Akali Dal jathas, leading them into Sikh Princely State domain, especially those belonging to Patiala and Nabha, as well as Gurdwaras inside British Punjab. In response to the Muslim League demand for a separate Pakistan, Master Tara Singh launched his own Sikh demand for separate nationhood, first raising the cry for *Azad* ("Free") Punjab in 1942. Asked what he meant by it, Tara Singh replied that his goal was "an independent sovereign Sikh state." Few leaders, even within his own community, took him seriously at the time, but in March 1946 the Shiromani Akali Dal resolved formally to demand a separate Sikh State of "Sikhistan" or "Khalistan"—if British India were partitioned. The British refused, however, to entertain such a demand and in the wake of Partition with its mass migration and slaughter of Sikhs, Master Tara Singh trenchantly remarked, "The Muslims got their Pakistan and the Hindus got their Hindustan, but what did the Sikhs get?" It was a question that was to ring louder in the minds of millions of Sikhs after more than a quarter century of Indian independence brought no peace but the sword of growing conflict to Punjab.

Modernist Religious Movements

Religions in India are always in flux, emerging, changing, integrating, dying, being reborn. India's soil and atmosphere seem especially conducive to divine inspiration; the birth of cults; the growth of exotic practices; devotion to Gurus, Mahatmas, Pirs, and Sheikhs; the blending of ancient with modern ideas and beliefs. Often it is difficult to say where one Indian religion ends and another begins, whether Jainism is merely a "sect" of Hinduism, or a separate faith. Aren't Sufis closer to Hindu Bhaktas than to Sunni Muslims? And where do "fire-worshiping" Parsis belong? They dress like Hindus, after all, and were an off-shoot of ancient Aryans' Persian Avestan cousins, who believed in the cosmic struggle between the "light and the dark," and still dispose of their dead atop Bombay's towers of silence, where special vultures pick every bone clean. And what precisely, religiously speaking, are ex-"Untouchable" Hindus now turned Buddhist? Or ex-Buddhist-Bengalis-turned-Muslim and then Christian? Are Vedantic philosophers really Hindus, or atheists? Perhaps all such lines blur under India's sun, in her timeless River.

New cults keep emerging, winning followers, sometimes moving off to test religious waters elsewhere in the world, in Sweden, Switzerland, Oregon, and California. Maharishi Mahesh Yogi lured millions to his side with the message of Transcendental Meditation, focusing silently at least for a few minutes each day on one's mantra, conducive to calm, probing the deep, silent unruffled waters beneath the often turbulent surface of life.

"Bhagwan" ("Blessed One") Rajneesh (1932–1990) created a new community and planted a city of pulsating life in what had been Oregon desert with his message of Love, physical as well as spiritual, open and uninhibited.

Radha and Krishna. Plate V of Lalit Kala Akademi's Series portfolio no. 21, New Delhi.

River Goddess Yamuna. From the Nasli and Alice Heeramaneck Collection. The Los Angeles County Museum of Art.

A burning ghat, Varanasi.

Ajanta Caves, Central India.

Two Indian children. Courtesy: Adam Wolpert.

Jama Masjid, Delhi.

The Taj Mahal, Agra.

Fatehpur Sikri

English Factory at Surat in 1638. Courtesy: India Office Library and Records, London.

English Sahib in Indian dress smoking hookah, Bengal ca. 1800. Courtesy: India Office Library and Records, London.

Qutb Minar, Delhi. Courtesy: India Office Library and Records, London.

Robert Clive of Plassey, 1725–1774. Courtesy: National Portrait Gallery, London.

Warren Hastings, 1732–1818. First Governor General of British India. Courtesy: National Portrait Gallery, London.

Lord Curzon, 1859–1925. Governor General of British India. Courtesy: National Portrait Gallery, London.

John Morley, 1838–1923. Secretary of State for India, 1906–1910. Courtesy: National Portrait Gallery, London.

By helping to release Puritanical Western sexual repressions through the passionate powers of holistic Indian consciousness, the "Divine King" of Love soon amassed his own fleet of Rolls-Royces and lapsed into long interludes of silent meditation on the "miracles" he had wrought in reteaching the meaning of "God is Love." Corruption and violence, however, soon brought official expulsion from the "Eden" of Rajneeshpur, and "The Bhagwan" moved back to India, followed mostly by his debts, and some of the faithful, to live his last years in his Pune ashram, changing his name to Osho. Yogi Bhajan, leader of a new youthful Sikh community of North America, has also opened doors to freer living and greater joy in passionate devotion to one another for some half million disciple converts, whose passion for vegetarian cooking and a chain of North American restaurants has proved almost as lucrative as the previously noted new cults. Krishna-Consciousness is another movement of Hindu modernist-devotionalism, whose chanting, dancing "Hari-Krishna" groups of barefoot, shaved-headed bhajana-bhaktas bring the story of Krishna with home-cooked sweets to travelers at airports and train and bus stations the world over.

At the other end of the spectrum, philosophic rationalism has grown out of traditional Vedantic thought blended with late-nineteenth-century Theosophy, and is articulated by such brilliant Indian thinkers as was Krishnamurti, "discovered" by Annie Besant in South India, and reared by her as the "Messiah," until he felt obliged publicly to renounce all claims to "divinity." Many disciples considered his humility proof-positive, however, of Krishnaji's "true Savior" status, but his probing rational mind did nothing but discourage such personal worship. Other yogic gurus, like Ma Anandamai and Sai Baba, have been worshiped by thousands of elite followers, who attest in detail to the countless "miracles" performed by these Saints of Hindu devotional modernity, most of whose "messages" have been transmitted in silence, or by a beatific glance, the faintest smile, one tentatively raised hand, or a mantra whispered so low it could barely be heard. Ah, India! Universe without end, seeking ultimately the release of Moksha, "Not this, not that," but "Truth, Pure Consciousness, Bliss," *Satcitananda*. OM!

Society

When the gods spread the sacrifice with the Man as the offering, spring was the clarified butter, summer the fuel, autumn the oblation.

They anointed the Man, the sacrifice born at the beginning, upon the sacred grass.

When they divided the Man. . . . His mouth became the Brahmin; his arms were made into the Warrior, his thighs the People, and from his feet the Servants were born.

—*Purusha-Sukta, The Rig Veda* X: 90
(trans. Wendy Doniger O'Flaherty)

Modernity, democracy, technology, urbanization have done much t transform the daily lives of India's huge and fast-growing population. Mos remote villagers today hear transistor-played rock music and watch satellite transmitted television broadcasts from New Delhi, tuning India's village int our world village. There are Indian astronauts as well as Nobel Laurea scientists, multinational tycoons, and international movie stars. Nonetheles India remains a family-centered, caste-oriented society. Marriage and pro eny, especially male, remain of basic, primary concern. Money and pow are important indicators of "class" in modern India as they are in Ameri and a new urban wealthy upper class of cosmopolitan fashionable consp uous Indian consumers is rapidly growing in Bombay, New Delhi, and other major metropolitan centers of sophisticated Indian society.

The most famous example of "caste" and family continuity merging into modernity's new cosmopolitan upper "class" is embodied in ex-Prime Minister Rajiv Gandhi (b. 1944), who "inherited" the position held for sixteen years by his mother, Indira Gandhi (1917–1984), and for seventeen years before that by his grandfather, Jawaharlal Nehru. Born Kashmiri Brahmans, the Nehrus long considered themselves the "highest caste" in India; the modern twist to Rajiv's family, however, is that his father, Feroze, was Parsi, while his wife, Sonia (nee Maino), is Italian. Less famous but almost equally powerful is the Birla family of industrial bankers, India's Rockefellers. Hindu moneylenders by caste, they easily shifted into modernity's fast lane, rising to new levels of affluent power by use of their traditional skills. Modern India's central cabinet has included several scions of old royal families: former Foreign Minister "Raja" Dinesh Singh, whose principality was near Varanasi; ex-Railway Minister "Maharaja" Madhav Rao Scindia of Gwalior; and present Prime Minister "Raja" Vishwanath Pratap (V. P.) Singh (b. 1931), adopted heir of Manda in U.P., whose popularly elected powers today are greater than all the inherited privileges once enjoyed by British India's 570-odd princes.

Caste and Class

Social hierarchy is most deep-rooted in Indic Civilization and remains vital to India's Hindu majority. The caste system has long been close to the heart of Hinduism, and even such enlightened Hindu reformers as Mahatma Gandhi never dared to attack it. Indeed, Gandhi insisted that caste was but a natural reflection of human differences. Some people were "born" to preach, others to fight, still others to handle money, or do strenuous manual labor, even as men and women were endowed with different natural functions. Modern Indians insist that freedom put an end to caste, even as a constitutional amendment abolished untouchability, but Brahmanic "purity" and ex-Untouchable "impurity" remain the polar stars of India's social hierarchy.

India's word for "caste" is *jati*, which means "birth." Jatis are kinship groups much larger than families, although not as self-sustaining as tribes or as unrelated as classes. There are thousands of jatis in modern India, and as intermarriage increases or conversion grows, new jatis are born. The Portuguese, who first used the word "caste," really meant India's ancient "class" (*varna*)-system, described in the Rig Veda's sacrificial myth of creation. According to that scripture, all Indians are descended from primeval cosmic "Man" (*Purusha*), who was sacrificed: from his "thousand heads" came the *Brahmans*; from his arms, *Kshatriyas*; from his thighs, *Vaishyas*; and from his feet, *Shudras*. Brahmans were bards and priests, Kshatriyas were warriors and kings, Vaishyas were merchants and landowners, and Shudras were peasant serfs or day laborers. The top three varna were "twice-born," their second "birth" a ceremonial initiation into the Hindu faith, when his "sacred thread" was tied around the naked torso of the young male initiate. Shudras, however, were too "unclean" to be born again, believed symbolically to have sprung from Purusha's feet, hence at once "dirty" and born to be stepped upon by the higher castes. Those original serfs of the three-class Aryan tribal conquerors of North India may well have been *dasas*, pre-Aryan "slaves." Subsequent expansion of Aryan Civilization brought more "primitive" peoples into the fold, who were so "barbaric" or "polluted" as to be added much beneath the four-varna hierarchy as "fifths" (*panchamas*), later known as "Untouchables."

If Aryan tribal divisions of labor and pre-Aryan conquests as well as fears of possibly polluted "foreigners" (*mlecchas*; *videshis*) were at the root of India's traditional class, varna-system, what were the origins of her true caste, jati-system? Fears of pollution or poisoning were doubtless one cause of ancient caste prohibitions and strictures. Walls of endogamy may have been erected after several daring members of important families ventured too far afield for brides, whose strange cooking may have poisoned their husbands, by either accident or design. Jati rules of commensality were thus made almost as strict as those limiting marriage options. Nowadays, with so many Brahmans working in city offices and factories, it is obviously impossible for them to continue to eat in ritually pure isolation, but they will usually take prepared food they have brought from home to an area reserved or cordoned off for managers or whatever category may equate to Brahman in the workplace dining facility. The higher one's caste, the fewer people one eats with or near. Some Brahmans are so strict about eating that they do not even eat with their own wives, who stand and wait outside the door until the husband has finished, then eat whatever he may have left on his *tali*-tray. Such practice is becoming less and less common in larger cities, but jati ranking is established and sustained by daily social behavior and inter-jati relations.

Caste hierarchy is thus established not only by the limits of one's potential marriage pool but also by rules of commensality daily observed and re-established in response to the question "Who takes food from whom?" Any Hindu will take food from a Brahman, which is why so many Brahmans work as cooks. The kitchen area in a Hindu home usually houses a shrine, where icons of the favorite family god or goddess are kept near the stove, propitiated each morning with some flower petals or fruit-offering as *puja*. The cooking area's floor is kept specially clean, and must never be entered by "unclean" visitors. When Brahmans embark on long pilgrimages, however, it may be necessary for them to taste food prepared by lower jati hands, but then they will take only "cooked" (*pukka*) grain, well parched and thus perhaps cleansed enough by Agni's fire to prove palatable. Never "raw" (*kucha*) food, however, nor water! Sensible advice for foreign visitors to India as well. The stricter one's Brahman-like behavior with food, the safer. Prime Minister Nehru always traveled throughout India with his own mobile kitchen and cook among his entourage. As a rational, secular modernist, Nehru was obviously most scrupulous about his health, and never risked eating "off the road," and hence rarely got sick. Nor was his premier-image ever hurt among the Hindu majority of India's electorate, who warmly approved of their Panditji's pukka-Brahman behavior.

Occupation is less strictly defined by one's jati than either the pool of potential marriage or commensal partners. But every jati has some special job or craft, at least historically identified with its members, even as every varna does. There are washerfolk, tillers of the soil, blacksmiths, moneylenders, warriors, goldsmiths, silversmiths, barbers, weavers, oil-pressers. The latter, called *teli*, are essential for providing not only cooking oil but also ritually required oil for temple lights and festive holidays like Diwali. The *Bene* Israel ("Sons of Israel") community is India's oldest Jewish community, and with several thousand households, still its largest. A Maharashtrian jati of oil-pressers, they were called *Shanwar teli*—"Saturday's oil-pressers"—by their neighbors, because they never worked on Saturdays, their *Shabbat*. The most favored Hindu explanation of India's caste system is, in fact, connected with divisions of labor it embodies, supposedly using "natural" human talents most "efficiently" in providing all goods and services required to sustain society.

Traditionally, India's village economy was sustained through inherited intercaste exchanges of grain for services, a ritual barter sytem that William and Charlotte Wiser first identified as the "jajmani system"[1] after observing it closely for several years in the North Indian village of Karimpur. A village jajman was usually a well-to-do landlord, possibly Brahman but at any rate born to the dominant jati of his region, who provided annual sustenance shares of his harvest to a network of artisans and village servants of every variety, each of whom repaid his jajman with labor-service in kind. Thus each landlord had his own barber, washerman, blacksmith, sweeper, accountant, and astrologer, and although all such specialists might serve several or many landlord households, each was expected to provide whatever services he performed on a regular required basis around the calendar and in perpetuity. Heirs to the landlord and barber or washerman would in turn continue the tradition-bound system. India's modern monetary economy has, for the most part, replaced the jajmani system with wages-for-work, but the residue of intercaste relationships going back for as many generations as memory serves is still found in most villages, where the same households are served by the sons and daughters of the same *dhobi*, *teli*, and *mali* families that have "always" worked for them. In most villages a mixture of jajmani and monetary economies coexist, field "hands" receiving partial payment in rupees, the other part in one or two meals during each day they work. The last time she returned to Karimpur in 1970, Charlotte Wiser noted that many traditional relationships, especially between oilsmiths and cotton carders and their *jajman*s, had broken down, becoming "casualties" of modernity.

Color prejudice appears also to have been connected with caste and class, at least in ancient India, for each of the four traditional classes was associated with a special skin "color," the original meaning of *varna*: Brahmans with white, Kshatriyas with red, Vaishyas with brown, and Shudras with black. The term for "slave," *dasa*, originally meant "dark" or "black," and was initially used by Aryan conquerors to denote their pre-Aryan enemies, who were subsequently enslaved. There thus seems to have been a racial aspect to caste hierarchy, still reflected in contemporary Indian aesthetic preferences for "fair-skinned" marital partners, a preference often noted in newspaper personal ads, usually run in weekend editions of India's major papers. Independent India's government has, however, always been vigorously antiracist, long in the vanguard of anti-Apartheid agitation at the United Nations.

Upper-class Hindus were ideally supposed to pass through four "stages" (*ashrama*s) in each lifetime. Their *dharma* ("religious duty") for each ashrama varied, even as every class's dharma was different, reflected in differing occupations. The first ashrama began only after the sacred-thread investiture ceremony was completed, usually between ages six and ten for Brahman boys, and slightly later for Kshatriyas and Vaishyas. That first "stage" of twice-born Hindu life is called *Brahmachari*, meaning "celibate Studenthood." The reason that celibacy was so important at this stage was that the young student went to live with his guru, in whose home he learned the sacred Vedas and other traditional studies, philosophy or grammar or the arts. The young student was usually closer in age to his guru's wife, since traditional Hindu marriage codes suggested that a wife be one-third her husband's age. Away from his own parents' home for the first time, moreover, the young student may well have been tempted to intimacy with his new "mistress." Gurus were much older, and supposedly deeply immersed in religious study or meditation. The emphasis on celibacy in so many legal textbooks (*dharma shastra*s) may indicate how often that prohibition was violated in practice. The first ashrama probably lasted between six and twelve years. After a student was tested by his teacher and passed to move on to the second stage of life, he took a ritual bath and returned to his parents' home to be married.

The proper form of marriage for a twice-born Hindu was one arranged by his parents in consultation with astrologers and matchmakers. Self-choice, or "love," marriages were known in epic lore, and seem to have been common among warriors in early Aryan times, but as classical Hindu culture evolved, the arranged marriage emerged as the most favored method for perpetuating the caste system and the Indian species. Suitable endogamous partners were always known to a matchmaker worthy of her title and commission. Parents of the bride had to be consulted most discreetly, of course, and details of the dowry agreed upon, after the horoscopes were checked so that the heavenly bodies were seen to be auspicious.

Our concept of romantic love and free dating, which has made considerable headway among India's "liberated" youths in most big cities, was viewed as chancy at best, potentially disastrous, and basically an abdication of parental responsibility, both for progeny and for their own prospects for salvation. Without grandsons to pray for him, a good Hindu's soul might wander hopelessly, eternally lost in perpetual reincarnation. Nothing was quite so important, then, as to arrange for the proper mating of one's progeny. Who was better equipped, moreover, to know which young men and women would be suitable as lifelong mates, their parents or the inexperienced youths themselves? Married love took time to blossom and grow, after all, as anyone with marital experience could appreciate. Nor was love the only, or even the most important ingredient in a good marriage, which required stability, loyalty, hard work, solvency, dutiful attention and proper action, respect and care for one's husband's parents, as well as loving kindness and devotion to one's children. The thousand and one chores and responsibilities of daily life took precedence in India over one's selfish sensual interest or carefree indulgence. To Indians, proof-positive of the misguided stupidity of most Western free-choice marriages is our high rate of divorce, which Indians find incomprehensible. To this day most twice-born Hindu marriages are arranged. The bride and groom, however, now generally see each other before committing themselves, and usually can veto a recommended mate, if they feel strongly negative. If parents and matchmakers take their work seriously, however, there should be no cause for rejection.

Following the marriage ceremony, which might last for several days and nights without abatement and has of late been known to cost millions of rupees in some notorious cases in Bombay and New Delhi, the young Hindu enters his second stage of life as a *Grihasta* ("Householder"). His dharma is now quite different from what it had previously been, for instead of remaining celibate, he must perform intercourse with his wife to ensure offspring. Birth is the first law of caste continuity. Without new generations to sustain it, traditions would die, and the gods themselves would soon be forgotten. Second only to his duty to future generations is a Grihasta's obligation to support Brahmans and their temples by generous and repeated donations. The ornate, elaborate temple institutions of Hinduism depend upon substantial funding, and this second stage in a good Hindu's life is really the only time when he can contribute financial support. Once again we see how practical and adaptable Hinduism is, both spiritual and material in its teachings. A time and place for everything. First study and celibacy, then marriage and procreation, with all the requisite feasts and ceremonies, all the chanting of mantras and propitiation of gods that require platoons and battalions of Brahman priests in attendance. Life in its many splendored moods and phases must be enjoyed to its fullest measure. Music and sweets, strong drink and dancing, all the passion and pain of what we might call the "high-life" or the "low-life" and which Vedantic philosophers call the illusionary life of *samsara*, need patronage. Grihastas pay the bills, allowing armies of Brahmans to perform the rituals that keep the gods satisfied and thus help maintain the cosmic balance. Nowadays, of course, many ceremonies are purely secular, with rock bands and movie stars taking the place of Brahmans, especially at weddings or birthday parties of rich and powerful ex-Untouchables, whose ostentatious public feasts are the envy of their "better" neighbors, but at times provide free sweets and drinks for as many as 50,000 to 100,00 delighted guests.

Traditionally, after a Hindu householder has seen his first grandson, he is free to embark upon his third stage of life, the *Vanaprasta* ("Forest-dweller") ashrama. Assured now of the continuity of his lineage and his own salvation, he begins the process of "letting go," or what we call "retirement." There are no longer many forests close at hand in India, but the ideal may be pursued through symbolic retreat or at least partial withdrawal from engagement in the hurly-burly of enterprise and festivities. The sons take over the business, their wives do more supervision of the countless household chores that have till now engaged the mother-in-law, who is permitted to retreat with her husband. In ancient times the elder couple went off together to a small shack in the forest-clearing, perhaps, not so far from their town or village home so that they could venture a visit, if they wished. The ideal was to move away from family connections, societal ties, seeking the strength to go beyond, toward the fourth and final stage, presaging release.

Was this Hinduism's way of accommodating Buddhism and Jainism? Are these last two ashramas the Hindu mode of integrating monasticism into everyday life? Or is this Indian society's ingenious preparation of elders for the inevitable conclusion of life, staged withdrawal, to help make the transition a bit easier, perhaps? Very few Indians actually retreat to a jungle hut anymore, but the ideal is important, for it alerts grandparents to a significant milestone in life's passages. Indians are, therefore, as a rule more ready to accept old age and impending death than most of us seem to be. There is a deeper tradition of letting go, of casting off one's material pleasures, if not actually wandering off into the woods, once your job is done, the third generation launched, the voice that will one day recite the requisite prayers to help save your soul heard at least in its undifferentiated cry or laugh. Yet that, too, is a transitional phase.

The fourth, final stage of a good Hindu's life is *Sanyasin*. As a wandering beggar the Hindu seeks Moksha by cutting all ties and karmic bonds, leaving his wife as well as children and friends, embarking entirely alone on the ultimate journey in search of a haven for his soul. "Salvation" means release, not paradise, and escape from commitment, present and future, and from rebirth, if possible—hence, the elimination of possessions of every sort, an end to earning and acquisitiveness, to wanting, ideally to caring, feeling, fearing. No tears, for they only bring new bonds, more karma to be worked off. No sorrow, no regrets. Hope not, remain passive and calm, and if you must continue to act, do so dispassionately. Much like the aging Eskimo who wanders off alone across the ice, the aging Hindu wanders alone to desert or mountain wasteland, or as a pilgrim to Mother Ganga, where he should, ideally, breathe his last out of human sight or sound, at peace with his past and the gods, wanting nothing, fearing nothing, regretting nothing. *Shanti, shanti, shanti.*

Traditional caste and class patterns have changed considerably over the past century and a half, under the impact first of Western modernity, then of independent Indian modernity. Most obvious and visible of the changes was the displacement of Indian princes, maharajas, and nawabs as well as Brahmans, by British Civil Servants, who emerged as the super-Brahman "Sahib" class of rulers by the late nineteenth century. By opening appointment to the coveted Indian Civil Service (ICS) through examination after 1854, having previously admitted Indians to the mysteries of the English language and Western learning, the British Raj gave a select number of brilliant young Indians access to super-Brahman status. Education thus appeared to displace birth as the key to power, although it was generally higher jati status that made access to such higher education possible in the first place. Hence the Banerjeas and Ranades, the Gokhales and Tilaks of India's first wave of nationalist leadership were all born Brahmans, whether of Bengal or Maharashtra, or Madras. Clever Parsis and Muslims, Christians and Sikhs could, however, also climb the class ladder to its slippery topmost rung if their brains were sharp enough and they could hold their seats in the saddle over some fairly high hurdles.

Well before Independence, then, and much more so since, a new elite class emerged and quickly acquired many of the characteristics commonly associated with India's caste system: endogamy, commensality, occupational or professional identity, and shared tastes in clothes, habitation, furnishings, amusements, vacations, and entertainments. They all went to the same Western or Indian "public" (i.e., private) schools, worked either as ICS (now Indian Administrative Service [IAS]) or army officers, lived in the same posh neighborhoods of the same big cities, belonged to the same clubs, holidayed in the same hill stations, and married among themselves. Thus a Bombay British Barrister like Mr. Jinnah, although born a Muslim, fell in love with and married a Parsi Baronet's daughter, Ruttie Petit, even as a Kashmiri Pandit's daughter like Indira Nehru would fall in love with and marry a Parsi lawyer like Feroze Gandhi, and then their sons would fall in love with and marry a young Sikh English major in New Delhi and an Italian student in Cambridge.

India's new upper class is thus no longer exclusively Brahman, Princely, or even necessarily Indian by birth, but it remains tightly exclusive, clannish, faddish, and has usually been "finished" at the same, or at least the "right" schools, which its families could afford. Much the same was true of physicians, lawyers, judges, and business managers, although since Independence, with affirmative-action quotas reserving places for ex-Untouchables in medical colleges as well as higher services, a more dramatic element of change has been injected into the highest class. Twice-born Hindus have not always taken this latter pace of change in nonviolent stride. Indeed more and more modern-day urban violence in Maharashtra, Gujarat, U.P., and Bihar has been triggered by rioting well-to-do Hindu youths attacking ex-Untouchables, many converted to Islam or Buddhism, and either burning their homes or otherwise violently intimidating them against trying to attend medical colleges.

For ex-Untouchables, however, affirmative-action opportunities have paradoxically only increased "untouchable"-consciousness, while designed to eliminate its historic injustices and its legacy of separateness. Other non-Brahman castes have experienced similar revivals of half-forgotten caste solidarity in the wake of India's emergence as a democratic nation-state. Politicians of all parties must seek election by appealing for votes after all, and what easier group to appeal to than one's own caste-brothers in their own regional languages? Predictably the response is usually enthusiastic, for reasons of both traditional loyalty and modern opportunity. Elected caste-brothers are naturally expected to "pay off" by hiring their jati-fellows for all patronage positions within reach, and by granting government contracts to their community cohorts, and helping them escape punishment for minor or even major offenses.

All the systemic weaknesses of modern politics that we associate with Jacksonian pork-barrelism, or the sort of ward-healing we connect with names such as Tammany Hall and Boss Tweed are alive and growing stronger in modern India. Which was why Mr. Nehru always cried out against modern India's "caste-ridden" society, for he had, after all, dedicated his life to the changes that were supposed to come with freedom: secularization, equality of opportunity, and an end to the corruption, exploitation, and social divisions detrimental to national progress and growth. Instead, with freedom from foreign rule came a return to ancient Hindu caste and clanship loyalties, a back-to-the-*biradari* movement. All for one's caste and evil-karma to every other became the unwritten law of local elections. Minority Brahmans, who for millennia had enjoyed unique semidivine powers, suddenly found themselves being discriminated against by dusky illiterates who managed to muster enough votes to get themselves elected to provincial legislative assemblies and even to Lok Sabha in New Delhi merely by force of populist appeal to the lowest common denominator of greed, fear, corruption, or sheer prejudice.

Democracy was "ruining" India, the deposed traditional elite complained. The underworld—in ancient as well as modern meaning—was taking charge! Thugs, a word coined from the name used by gangs of Hindu ritual stranglers in the service of Goddess Kali, were often elected to high office while still serving time behind bars. Even at the national level, tradition-bound caste-leaders surfaced, men like Chaudhary Charan Singh (1902–1987), born a Jat peasant, who never forgot his roots or failed to appeal to his community for votes. He rose to be home minister, deputy prime minister, and for almost a month, prime minister in the dismal last days of Janata party rule during the bleak winter of 1979. Half a million of Charan's Lok Dal peasant community loyalists from Haryana and U.P. drove their bullock carts into New Delhi to honor their caste-master in the art of power politics on his seventy-fifth birthday, all but stopping motorized traffic in the heart of modern India for a day as proof-positive of the powers of her tradition-bound past. A decade later another half million mourning Jats walked solemnly to the former prime minister's cremation site in Delhi near the sacred

Rajghat of Mahatma Gandhi. His son, Ajit Singh, who first entered politics in 1987, was appointed to the federal cabinet as Minister of Industry in 1990.

So the wheel has turned, bringing many who once stood high to positions of obscurity, if not actual persecution, elevating others from the subsoil of ancient Indian society to the five stars of modern India's posh hotels, where business luncheons and banquets are enjoyed in air-conditioned comfort to the tune of strings. Caste patterns vary from state to state, although basically they fall within what may broadly be called Brahman, non-Brahman, and ex-Untouchable jatis, whose relative status is always defined by social intercourse or its proscription, partial or total. About 7 percent of India's populace today was born to one or another of her hundreds of Brahman jatis, from Kashmiri Pandits in the North to Namboodripad Brahmans of Kerala, from the Chitpavins of Maharashtra to the Vadama Smarthas of Tamil Nadu. Another 18 percent were born as pariah ex-Untouchables, and they, too, have many endogamous jatis, each considering a few others just a bit lower in status. The vast majority of India's Hindu population, however, were born somewhere between exalted Brahmanic sacrosanctity and traditionally shunned "untouchability." Most of these middle castes are "twice-born" merchants and landowner farmers, many of whom have in recent generations moved into urban professions attained through modern and higher education. The remaining quarter or so of India's Hindu majority are landless laborers and urban menials, whose lowly Shudra birth or darker skin or lack of resources have long relegated them to the bottom rungs of hierarchical social ladders, once more rigid than they have recently become but still very much in evidence across the landscape of village life and urban poverty that fill India's complex continent with long-suffering, struggling humanity.

Untouchability

Fears of pollution, carried to their ultimate extreme, gave birth to the dreadful outcaste group called "Untouchable," who emerged as the lowliest members of Hindu society. Without Brahmans, of course, we might think there could be no Untouchables, since only those who considered themselves "gods on earth" might be arrogant enough to believe that the mere touch of another human being brought defilement. Yet the Burakumin in Japan, blacks in South Africa, and Jews in Nazi Germany have all been treated in the same sort of inhuman "outcaste" manner, making such barbarisms of "civilized society" seem almost universal.

Article 17 of India's Constitution has, fortunately, abolished untouchability since 1950, explicitly forbidding its practice "in any form." Deep-rooted, irrational prejudice, however, dies slowly. Dr. B. R. Ambedkar (1891–1956), India's greatest Untouchable, who chaired the committee that drafted India's Constitution, was a British Barrister, who received his Ph.D. from Columbia University and served as Nehru's Minister for Law. Ambedkar was so bitterly disappointed toward the end of his life, however, in how most upper-caste Hindus totally ignored Article 17 of their Constitution, that he converted to Buddhism. More than half a million of Dr. Ambedkar's fellow ex-Untouchables joined their leader in this renaissance of Buddhism in India in the mid-1950s. Millions of others who were born Untouchable Hindus had earlier converted to Islam or Christianity.

Mahatma Gandhi tried to remove the stigma of "outcaste" status from Untouchables by renaming them *Harijans*—"Children of God" (*Hari*)—and one of the journals he published weekly was called *Harijan*. Ambedkar never trusted Gandhi, however, especially after the Mahatma's "fast-unto-death" to keep Untouchables officially Hindu in the eyes of the British Raj. But Gandhi knew that if the Untouchables won separate electorate status, such as Muslims, Sikhs, and Christians enjoyed and as the British were ready to grant them after the 1932 Round Table Conference ended, they might well next demand separate "Nationhood," as the Muslims won, and some Sikhs have done. His fast, called off only after he and Ambedkar had agreed upon their own Pact granting Untouchable *Hindus* twice as many reserved seats in central and state parliaments as the British promised them, thus probably saved South India from a caste-based civil war. Gandhi's strategy, however, left independent India with a legacy of continuing commitment to affirmative action, which has of late elicited its own bitter backlash.

Traditionally, Untouchables have always performed services vital to "caste Hindus," including sweeping, caring for cremation grounds, disposal of carcasses, leatherwork, even blacksmith work. Their deep-rooted pariah status reflects twice-born Hindu fears based on occupational taboos, as well as "racial" differences that go back to the pre-Aryan origins of many Untouchables. Perhaps the ancient Brahmans who saw them handle dead bodies feared that they were contaminated by death themselves, especially if they caught some infectious disease from the corpses of which they disposed. Perhaps other Untouchables developed immunities to such Black Deaths, or were strengthened by eating beef, which most other Indians abjured. That too would have contributed to Brahman fears of polluting pariah powers. Untouchables usually ate sacred cow meat, and often lived on polluted cremation grounds. At any rate, custom and experience appeared to validate prejudice, which among high-caste Hindus became more deeply entrenched, more inhuman. Fear bred hatred, reinforcing fear. Strange rationalizations followed, as generations learned from whispered warnings of elder generations to "beware" of those dark, lurking shadows beyond the field, never to go near the sweeper-lady, or the tanner-man, or the village smithie. They were "Demons" as dangerous as Ravana, their touch as lethal as a tiger's. Soon, in fact, the most "polluted" of all South Indian Untouchables came to be feared at even distant sight by Namboodri Brahmans. Those dreaded poor people were obliged to wear warning bells, like cattle, so that at first sound of their remote approach, Brahmans might shield their eyes to avoid possible "piercing" by "poison arrows" of an "Unseeable's" glance, or simply run indoors and lower the blinds.

Originally, Untouchables may have been captured slaves of Aryan tribes, or failures from within the social system, "misfits," possibly drunkards, obliged to do the hardest manual labor that no respectable herdsman or cultivator would do for himself. Others, however, might have initially opted to withdraw themselves, not to meditate in forests as yogis to develop brilliant Upanishadic philosophies, but to sulk, to hide, out of fear or madness or hatred for the Raja or the Panchayat, or for any number of reasons that continue to drive people off what we think of as the "tracks" of conventional social development and generally accepted behavior. Many may have started as drop-outs and after going "wild" long enough, no one inside a village's dominant caste cluster invited them in. But as long as they slept far enough away not to be troublesome, odd jobs would be thrown to them, a carcass to be skinned, a corpse to be burned.

With more than 1,000 jatis of their own, Untouchables have found it impossible to unite in opposition to twice-born dominance, themselves reflecting all the fragmentation of Hindu society that has always been its greatest weakness. "The wall built around Caste is impregnable," Ambedkar often insisted, arguing that Hinduism at its core had nothing to do with either "reason" or "morality." Ironically, however, his own Mahar jati of Maharashtra looked down upon "Untouchable" *Chamars* (leatherworkers), and both groups looked down at "scavenger" *Bhangis*, almost as much as all three were despised by Brahmans.

Ambedkar's ultimate "remedy" for the Hindu caste system, which he viewed as a curse, was "intermarriage." "Nothing else will serve as the solvent of Caste,"[2] he wrote, practicing what he preached by marrying an American woman. Mahatma Gandhi also believed that intermarriage would help remove the "curse of untouchability," advocating it within his own family, to his sons and closest disciples. He adopted a Harijan girl, in fact, and seriously proposed that one such young Harijan might serve India as her "best first President." But none of the leaders of India's Congress party agreed. Since Independence intermarriages have occurred, of course, but indicative of how rare they remain, the Government of India once offered a gold watch as a gift to every twice-born and ex-Untouchable married couple yet long found it impossible to expend their scant supply of such presents.

Millions of Bhangis continue to remove night soil from India's urban drains and streets, daily carrying it away on their heads. Until all Indian homes are built with modern toilet facilities, and most Indians believe that urination and defecation should not be practiced in public, such scavengers will remain as vital to modern India as they were to ancient and medieval India. The problem is not merely to educate young Indians, moreover, since enlightened teachers who attempt to instruct them in modern public health and private sanitation become the targets of irate parents. Those outraged parents want to know by what "right" such "trouble-makers" teach their children that what *they* do every day is "dirty." Mahatma Gandhi insisted on daily latrine-cleaning as part of his personal "religious service" and thus helped remove such work from the exclusive realm of Untouchable-scavengers to an area of higher Hindu consciousness, if not general respectability. Laudable as such individual reform efforts might be, however, they did not adequately address the issue of public, open defecation and its causal connection to several of India's most persistent health hazards, especially water-borne diseases such as cholera and typhoid.

Untouchability is abolished by law in modern India. But wary ex-Untouchables know better than to try as yet to draw water from twice-born Hindu wells in many villages, some of which now have fine new "Scheduled Caste" (Constitutional schedules list the names of the ex-Untouchable jatis) wells to provide separate but equal water for those of "impure" birth. They also know better than to try to rent apartments or purchase homes in the more affluent urban neighborhoods, for the first question anyone managing such buildings will ask is usually "What is your jati?" They must still keep their distance from many village shrines and temples. Nowadays, however, in Madras and other regions of South India where ex-Untouchables have been elected to chief ministerial posts of power, some of the most beautiful areas, including the beach, traditional home of "outcaste" fisherfolk of the Coromondal coast, are dotted with ex-Untouchable low-cost high-rise housing. Children of ex-Untouchable jatis understand the rules of their modern status. Often they look much cleaner than high-caste Hindus, wearing beautifully pressed white shirts and trousers, but they would never dare to enter fine hotels or homes, for the gate guards instantly recognize them, know their pedigrees, and shackles of tradition weigh heavily on their minds, inhibiting even the young from venturing too quickly toward India's promised future of equal opportunity.

Still, change is in the air. Law is on the side of progress, the machinery of justice opposed to prejudice of this most inhuman sort. Millions of Scheduled Caste children now attend schools everywhere in India, well over 50,000 of them enjoying special admission status in technical and other institutions of higher learning, including medical colleges, where the total numbers admitted for each class are so small compared to those applying that "backward class" admissions have triggered many riots. India's affirmative action policy toward Scheduled Castes has generated much the same passionate controversy as American minority policies. Higher-caste Hindus argue that such special treatment serves only to drain the nation's precious resources, diminish its higher talent pool, and perpetuate "backwardness" rather than eliminating it, since all ex-Untouchables now have vested interests in proclaiming and proudly affirming their "backward" status. Some Constitutional lawyers argue, moreover, that special privileged treatment for Scheduled Castes is antithetical to Article 16 of India's Constitution, which promises "equal opportunity for all citizens in matters relating to employment or appointment to any office." That same Constitutional article, however, explicitly states that nothing in it "shall prevent the State from making any provision for the reservation of appointments or posts in favour of any backward class of citizens."

India's Constitution clearly reflects the ambivalence of the Nation itself, which remains sorely divided on this issue of untouchability, whether it be dealt with under the Sanskritic euphemism of Harijan or the English one of Scheduled Caste. The problem is still too hot for most Indians to handle rationally. Modernists, who argue that their only desire is to see India move forward toward a more secular, truly democratic society, insist that by focusing on "backward castes" and "tribes" for special treatment, India's Constitution inadvertently reversed the process of assimilation, reinforcing caste differences that traditionally kept one-fifth of India's society "backward," and now gives those very communities powerful incentives to remain that way.

More ex-Untouchables enter Parliament at each election, however, where close to 100 now hold seats in the highest legislative assembly of the land (Lok Sabha). Others move closer to central executive pinnacles of power (Jagjivan Ram was in four Cabinets and almost became prime minister in 1979). Still others work as physicians, lawyers, business executives, and IAS officers in every corner of the country. The former untouchability of such leaders has, therefore, come to be seen by an increasing number of Indians for what it was, is, and will always be: a "problem" of high-caste Hindu prejudice and narrow-minded fear that relegated human beings with all the potential, intelligence, and talents of humans the world over to a horribly wretched status lower than that of worshiped animals like the cow, or indeed cobras, and monkeys.

The Family

No institution in India is more important than the family. Family life is in many ways the heart of the caste system, since that is where caste values are taught and learned, and where the way of life called "Hinduism" is daily perpetuated. The traditional joint or extended Hindu family was something of a microcosm of ancient Indian society and remains to this day India's most vital social unit of continuity, the stuff that caste communities are made of, more important than the individual at one end of society's spectrum, or the Nation at the other.

For at least three thousand years, most North Indian families have been patriarchies, ruled by elder males whose word was law, and whose sons brought home brides to live jointly under their father's roof, within his domain. Work and its fruits, entertainment and its pleasures, were jointly shared by members of the extended Indian family, which usually embraced three generations, sometimes four. Nuclear urban families are now becoming more common, but old patterns persist even in India's largest modern cities almost as much as in her half-million ancient villages. The family head—the father or the grandfather—is generally treated almost as a god, approached by children who bow to touch his feet, given deference and respect virtually unknown any longer in the West, empowered to make decisions that must be obeyed at the risk of family ostracism. The best family heads, of course, use such powers sparingly, wisely, and will consult their wives or adult sons concerning money or property decisions of importance, although ultimate power is by tradition vested in them and may be used autocratically. Indians for the most part are an obedient, deferential people, accepting of "higher" authority, even when vocal in their objections to what they may view as "grossly unfair" or "intolerable" restriction, regulations, or orders. Such obedience is family-inculcated. Authority figures, moreover, are traditionally older males, although divine authority images are always youthful gods and beautiful goddesses.

In royal families inheritance was by primogeniture; otherwise all land and most other Indian property would be divided equally among sons. Daughters now are empowered by law to enjoy equal shares in inherited property, but must first have the courage to assert their legal rights and then the good fortune to win judgments in some high court and have such claims to property executed in practice. Filial–fraternal solidarity is an Aryan tradition reinforced throughout India every time the *Mahabharata* or the *Ramayana* are read and enacted. Brothers stick together and fight to support one another, at times even sharing the same wife. The Hindi word for "brother" (*bhai*) also means "cousin," and within the extended family, the sons of one's brothers are the same as one's own sons in virtually every respect.

The typical Indian family live together under a single roof and eat food prepared in the same kitchen. There is very little privacy in an Indian household, nor does it seem to be missed or much desired. Indians as a rule appear to have less-developed privacy needs than do Americans, and usually miss the bustling human contact if they opt to leave their joint-family home to establish an isolated nuclear family in some modern apartment. Most Indians find life in America much too "lonely," even as Americans usually find India much too "crowded," especially if they get close enough to an Indian family to live in their home. "Private" rooms are rarely equipped with doors that fully close, and if they can, indeed, be closed, they can hardly ever be locked. Joint families are used to sharing, not just food, but possessions of all sorts as well, including TV sets and VCR movies. Newlyweds rarely find any privacy at home. Nor do they seem to require much. Only eating is viewed as a specially private sort of act by Indians, and then only if one is a very strict Brahman. Living in and being raised among large families endows Indians with a great sense of security and group identity, but relatively little initiative or what we would call "rugged" individuality. There is, indeed, more "passivity" in Indian personalities than we generally find among Americans of comparable age and status, a product in great measure of lifelong accommodation to the many competing voices, needs, demands, and aspirations of the large extended family. If all clamored at once, none could be heard, nor would the more pressing demands ever be met. Indians learn early in life to wait their turn, to be patient.

A Hindu family shares its sacred moments and celebrates its most important events as a unit. Births, marriages, and deaths are all family events. Prayers for ancestral souls are recited by the eldest son, but the commemorative rites of *shraddha* are attended by all male descendants, each of whom offers his "balls of rice" (*pinda*) to Brahmans on behalf of the deceased ancestor. Thus the sons and grandsons are united and linked to the fathers, all "co-pindas," members of the family. The Hindu family, of course, is like ancient Roman and other Aryan patriarchal families: a blood bond of males who live to help and support one another and would die to defend one another. At least such is the ideal that animates this tightest of all Indian social groups. In practical reality there are naturally deviations and problems, the lazy ones or the lame, the jealous and the inept, those who work too hard and others who work not at all, knowing in any event that food will come, shelter is assured. Why sweat, then, or strain? The ideal hierarchy is only one of males in order of age, but there, too, deviation is not unusual. Many women are, in fact, much wiser than their husbands, and some younger sons are more aggressively ambitious than their elder siblings. We need once again only look at modern India's recent "first family" for some such familiar examples: Indira Gandhi and her husband Feroze, Sanjay Gandhi and his elder brother Rajiv.

In recent decades, young professional couples generally move away from parental homes as soon as they marry, starting their own smaller, nuclear, family units. Often at least one of these suddenly isolated people feels so lonely that they either actually move back "home" or spend as much time as possible in the larger parental house, enjoying dinners there with the rest of the family, and staying to watch TV, perhaps, or to listen to music with their siblings and others. Extended families remain most common in villages and among wealthier twice-born Hindus, whose status is visibly enhanced by large families with many sons and sumptuous marriage feasts. Through the family, jati connections are maintained and developed, daughters given to or taken from other families, usually in neighboring villages, sufficiently removed on both the paternal and maternal sides to ensure against incest taboos. As families grow in size and wealth they naturally gain greater power, and their elder may be invited to join a Panchayat or to become village Headman. But continuity is more common than change in Indian village life, just as doing one's duty (*dharma*) is far more important than "enjoying" individual freedom of will.

Conformity to authority, to the family, to the jati, becomes the first law of Indian life and a major limiting factor to creative growth, radical change, or independent initiative. India's multifaceted search for consensus, its overall impulse toward finding some means of preserving unity, maintaining traditions, integrating diverse points of view, reconciling differences, and harmonizing polarities are public extensions of joint-family life to the larger sphere of polity. The family is the nucleus, the matrix, the model from which all else that is Indian grows, often in direct emulation or imitation of what is learned, expected, found there; hence, the continuity that is India, the comforting stability, the security, and all the conformist limitations and modern Indian weaknesses as well.

Roles of Women

Ancient Indian law (especially the code known as the *Laws of Manu*, compiled c. 200 B.C.–A.D. 200) treated women as perpetual minors, requiring "protection," first by their fathers, next by their husbands, and finally by their sons. Women could never be "trusted" to care for themselves or live alone. Even prostitutes became "slaves of the god," kept by temple Brahmans. A Hindu husband, however, "though destitute of virtue," as Manu's law code put it, "or seeking pleasure elsewhere, or devoid of good qualities," must always be "worshiped as a god" by his wife. Women were generally viewed as "weak-natured" and "lascivious," and hence were confined to the "rear quarters" of homes, watched carefully when they went outside, and closely guarded.

Much has changed since then. Widows are no longer burned, infant or preadolescent girls are no longer forced to marry, one woman served as prime minister of India for more than a decade and a half, and more young Indian women now become doctors, scholars, and scientists than do American women—indeed, many of them come to the United States to pursue their professions. Nonetheless, most Indian women remain subservient to their closest male relatives, and although village women as a rule work harder than men, few of them ever receive either wages or respite. The rate of divorce is lower in India than almost anywhere else in the world, but suicide rates for married women are higher than anywhere else and an alarming number of young Indian brides are daily reported "burned to death" in kitchen "accidents." Such tragic "accidents" usually occur to young women whose parents have failed to remit adequate dowry payments.

The "duties of a woman," as traditionally expounded in Epic Indian lore, include being

> beautiful and gentle, considering her husband as her god and serving him as such . . . obedient even if commanded to unrighteous deeds or acts that may lead to her own destruction. She should rise early, serving the gods, always keeping her house clean, tending to the domestic sacred fire, eating only after the needs of gods and guests and servants have been satisfied, devoted to her father and mother and the father and mother of her husband. Devotion to her lord is woman's honor, it is her eternal heaven.

Manu added: "The production of children, the nurture of those born," and "the daily care of men," to a woman's duties. Procreation was viewed as so important a female function that if a wife "failed" in that vital role, her husband was permitted by Indian law to take a second wife, or a third, who could bear his children. Some orthodox Hindus, like Mahatma Gandhi, believe that having intercourse with one's wife for any reason other than procreation is sinful. That is hardly, however, the sole Indian male attitude toward sex. It is not the one expounded in such ancient classics as the *Kama Sutra*, "Textbook of Love," whose eighty-four most favored "positions" have been carved in stone on many a Hindu temple's facade and preserved there for almost a thousand years.

Matrilineal families appear to have been widespread throughout most of South India until quite recent times. Dravidian names often have the inherited matrilineal name as a first initial, followed by the given name, as in the case of India's second president, Dr. S. Radhakrishnan, a distinguished philosopher, whose son, Dr. S. Gopal, is a distinguished historian. In both cases the "S" stands for their matronymic "Sarvepelli." In the Southern State of Kerala, matrilinear inheritance was continued through the early decades of this century, with, for example, a Nayar daughter participating in ritual marriage to a "husband" front-mate, who was then immediately sent away. The young married woman was now free to pick a lover from among the eligible men in her neighborhood, bringing him into her household without any need for further ritual of a public character. Their offspring took the mother's name as their initial of identity. Male consorts did not inherit any part of their wife's property, and might be "dismissed" at any point in the relationship when the almighty matriarch lost interest. That Malabar system is illegal in modern India, but is probably still practiced in remote areas of the South by those who consider the Mother not only a Goddess in heaven above, but the only true leader on earth.

Women in patriarchal Indian families are much less powerful. Mothers retain personal power over their sons, and wives become quite influential and respected after they have borne sons. But "a bride is given to the family of her husband, not to the husband alone," according to Dharma Shastra law. The dowry was "arranged" with the marriage and is still often deemed its most vital contractual term. No self-respecting Indian woman would agree to a dowry nowadays, nor would any truly modern family ask for one. Mrs. Gandhi campaigned vigorously against the dowry by insisting that it was "humiliating" and "demeaning" for any man to allow himself to be "purchased" for a price. Most Indian males still appear more willing, however, to accept such humiliation than to forsake what is often a substantial amount of money or valuable goods upon marriage. Tragic bride immolations in several parts of North India have recently shocked the outside world, but underscore the callous materialistic motives of many arranged marriages. Some Indian women are treated more as chattel than human beings, toys of their husbands and slaves of their mothers-in-law, whose venality is exceeded only by their brutality. Rarely, moreover, are the culprits in such brutal murders brought to justice. Village or jati communities as a whole usually close ranks to defend what we view as barbaric behavior meriting the most severe punishment, but what is often judged through traditional Indian eyes as appropriate "self-help" and as exemplary or a "good lesson" to others.

Daughters are thus still viewed for the most part as a liability. Their birth is hardly heralded with the festivities attendant upon the birth of a son, and the work they can do is limited. By the time they are old enough to prove truly useful, they must be married "off" and with them goes whatever fortune in cash or clothes or jewels has been amassed by a poor man's family. Then new in-laws often keep badgering for more, until such tragic finales as the above-noted immolations. Until fairly recently there have been reports of female infanticide in the deserts of Rajasthan or Central India, where life remains most harsh, the soil least fruitful. Since Independence, however, many new laws, collectively known as "The Hindu Code," have been enacted, legally arming women with rights of divorce, inheritance, and overall equality of opportunity with Indian men. Hindu marriage since the Act of 1955 has been strictly monogamous, although Indians generally still believe that it is both kinder and more civilized for men who can afford to do so to take in, keep, and care for women who have provided them with offspring or periodic pleasure than merely to "love them and leave them." In barren mountainous regions of the high Himalayas, including Ladakh and Nepal, polyandry is still practiced as the simplest, safest way of controlling population growth. India's women have made important contributions to every profession and science, as well as public life, up to and including the office of prime minister. "But to a woman," Prime Minister Gandhi insisted, "motherhood is the highest fulfillment. To bring a new being into this world, to see its tiny perfection and to dream of its future greatness is the most moving of all experiences."[3] She was speaking then of her first-born son, Rajiv, who was as yet but an obscure airline pilot.

In the last quarter of the nineteenth century, Mahatma Gandhi was married at the age of thirteen to Kasturbai, who was also thirteen. "Marriage among Hindus is no simple matter," he wrote in his *Autobiography*, subtitled "The Story of My Experiments with Truth":

> The parents of the bride and the bridegroom often bring themselves to ruin over it. They waste their substance, they waste their time. Months are taken up . . . in making clothes and ornaments and in preparing budgets for dinners. Each tries to outdo the other in the number and variety of courses to be prepared. . . . It was only through these preparations that we got warning of the coming event. I do not think it meant to me anything more than the prospect of good clothes to wear . . . rich dinners and a strange girl to play with. The carnal desire came later.[4]

At about the same time, a sensitive Maharashtrian girl of ten, named Lakshmibai, was married to eighteen-year-old Narayan Tilak, and later wrote in her autobiography, *I Follow After*: "According to the Hindu standards of those days, I was now quite a big girl, for I was fully ten years old. In those days children were married to each other at the age of five and six or younger, and to have a girl to eleven years unmarried was an unheard-of thing."[5]

Orthodox Hindus believed that if their daughter was left unmarried after she started to menstruate, they were "guilty" of "abortion." Thus in 1891 when the British decided to raise the marriageable "Age of Consent," below which all intercourse, whether "married" or not, would be considered "rape," from ten to twelve, Hindu orthodoxy raised a hue and cry of opposition. Enlightened Indians like Justice Ranade, however, argued in favor of such humanitarian reforms, insisting that "these institutions, which had grown as excrescences upon the healthy system of ancient Hindu society, were checked and could be checked, only by the strong arm of law."

Widow remarriage was another prime cause for Hindu social reformers of the late nineteenth and early twentieth century. Widows might no longer be burned as Satis, yet were obliged to remain luckless shadows lurking in the rear quarters of Hindu homes, prohibited from wearing anything but a white shroud of mourning, no jewels, no perfume, no makeup, no laughter or parties, no contact whatever with members of the male sex. The British Raj passed a Widow Remarriages Act in 1856, but hardly any widows had sufficient courage, nor suitors brave enough, to take advantage of that enlightened law for decades. Anandibai Karve recalled in her memoirs in *The*

New Brahmans that she was first widowed at age eight, four months after being married, and she was still a teenager when her second husband died. Then Maharshi Dhondo Karve, one of Pune's leading reformers who would live more than a century himself, decided to marry her, but each day for years she feared "that somebody might do physical violence to him, because he had violated tradition."[6] For decades the Karves, Chitpavin Brahmans, were treated as "outcastes" in their own native city, by their own jati. The Karves founded and maintained a Hindu Widows' Home Association in 1896, and through it helped thousands of other widows to overcome the plight of their social status, to live useful, productive, relatively happy lives. The Karves' daughter-in-law, Irawati, became a famous professor of Indian anthropology and was the first woman to drive around Pune, on her own motor-scooter, dressed in a sari. "How fortunate I am that I am the daughter-in-law of such a man!" Dr. Irawati concluded in her memoir of him. "And how still more fortunate that I was not his wife!"

Weddings are always noisy and often grand in India. For the elite they remain outdoor events that rival religious festivals, and to this day the groom will arrive at his bride's home on horseback, or if wealthy enough, atop an elephant. In 1916, when twenty-seven-year-old Jawaharlal Nehru was married to sixteen-year-old Kamala Kaul, the Nehru "Wedding Camp" left Allahabad a full week before the scheduled wedding day and entrained for Delhi, where many spacious tents had to be pitched and added to the houses filled with invited guests. "Each day there was a party somewhere or other," Jawaharlal's younger sister, Krishna, recalled in her autobiography, *With No Regrets*, "and after ten days the wedding party returned to Allahabad, where there were some more festivities."[7] Nehru's closest sibling, Swarup, renamed Vijaya Lakshmi Pandit after her own marriage, the first woman President of the United Nations, recalled that "a brother . . . is the guardian and protector of his sister, whose attitude to him borders on adoration." In her *The Scope of Happiness: A Personal Memoir* Madame Pandit also recalled her brother's wedding, writing that "the real celebrations began with the coming home of the bride, when evening after evening there were feasting and gaiety in which it seemed as if no one in the whole province had been left out."[8] Little more than a year later, when "Kamala's baby was born . . . the expectant grandparents . . . presumed that it would be a boy." Indira's arrival then proved disappointing, even to so enlightened and Westernized a family as the Nehrus.

Village Life

Three-fourths of India's population still live in more than half a million rural villages, averaging from 500 to 5,000 inhabitants. The village is India's smallest territorial unit and its headmen or panchayats are drawn from traditional leaders, who reside within its community. Most villages include families from up to twenty or more jatis, thus providing a majority of the basic goods and services required to sustain life within village boundaries. But Indian villages have never been totally self-sufficient, nor autonomous. Myths of Indian village "republican independence" were started by early-nineteenth-century British administrators who never spent enough time in villages to note the extensive ties, marital as well as economic, that every village had with others in its environs. Almost a century of more recent anthropological field research has, however, provided us with the more accurate picture of an Indian village as one of many mutually supportive, interdependent rural cells in the vast body of Indic Civilization. Patterns of village settlement, architecture, and governance vary greatly from North to South, and each region of India has its unique customs, ceremonies, dress, food, and languages that distinguish its villages from all others. Yet in some respects every village shares in the all-Indian Sanskritic cultural ideals and divinities that constitute India's "Great Tradition."[9]

Like India itself, then, her villages reflect the fragmented diversity of many jatis and faiths coexisting within an overall unity imposed by geography and ancient traditions. There is usually only one dominant landowning jati, whether Brahman, Kshatriya, or Vaishya in origin, that presides over the political as well as economic fortunes of each village. But jati fortunes, like individual family fortunes, change, and competing groups are always in the wings of village power, seeking more land or greater access to water or mineral rights, or whatever may provide the key to village power. Nominal village identity is shared from birth by all its offspring, yet primary loyalties remain rooted in family and jati institutions. Girls born in most Indian villages, at least, know that after marriage they must move on to the villages of their husbands, which may be either less than a day's walk away or quite distant. They return to ancestral homes on some holidays and before the birth of each of their own children and for weeks or months afterward, but their new permanent homes are with their husband's parents. Many young men also leave villages nowadays to seek their fortune in neighboring towns or cities.

The accelerating pace of Indian urbanization depends in good measure on village labor. After some time spent in cities, with high wages and prospects for future advantage, most young village defectors opt to remain, even in crowded urban slums. But the lures of open land remain potent enough to hold the vast majority of India's sons close to her fecund or grudging soil. Nor is that surprising to foreign visitors who often find Indian villages the most beautiful, serene, and in some cases the "cleanest" parts of India. The rich deep green of rice fields before harvest or the gold of mustard surrounding the lime-washed white huts and well-swept lanes of a prosperous village appear so peacefully integrated into the natural environment of many regions of India's countryside that it is almost too easy to wax romantic about the pastoral beauty of village life. However, the Hindu ashram ideal, a Utopian village life of natural harmony, has successfully been put into actual practice by great religious teachers like Sri Aurobindo and Mahatma Gandhi in Pondicherry South of Madras, at Sabarmati in the outskirts of Ahmedabad, and at Sevagram in Central India.

Most Indian villages provide only grudging, marginal sustenance to their laboring sons and daughters, who work as required by the inflexible calendar of crops, following the backs of their bullocks from sunup until sundown. Much the same as other peasants the world over, Indian villagers generally distrust strangers. The speech, dress, and officious manner of foreigners, "townies," or Delhi-wallas usually add up to "trouble" in a peasant's mind. Like the proverbial Missouri farmer, they view change of any sort with skeptical eyes. When missionaries William and Charlotte Wiser first drove into Karimpur Village in 1930, its peasant population retreated, disappearing *Behind Mud Walls* (the title of their study of that Indian village from 1930 to 1960, with a sequel by Charlotte Wiser in 1970). The first villager to approach them was an ex-Untouchable Christian, whose baby was dying of dysentery but was saved by the medicine they supplied. Soon other villagers emerged from their defensive walls to seek aid from those ingenious intruders from afar. The Wisers' patient wisdom helped them win the friendship of Karimpur's populace and allowed them to map and immortalize the life of their Indian village in more accurate detail than had ever been done before.

The title of the Weisers' fine book symbolized not only the dark walls behind which most villagers would retreat at the first sign of strangers; their crumbling mud also represented traditional village fears of any display of wealth. For there was always some moneylender or tax collector waiting to be paid off, hovering until he noted or was informed of any outward sign of affluence among his peasant debtors. The decades brought many changes to Karimpur, however, including new seeds, new tools and wells, education, and security enough to allow many families to replace their crumbling mud walls with *pukka* ("solid") brick that stood firm after the rains. Winds of change continue to blow, but cautious peasants and their conservative leaders fear that like the harshest or hottest of nature's winds, too fierce or searing a pace of change might perhaps destroy their village entirely. India's villages thus remain tight little bastions of traditional Indian religious values and institutions.

Most villagers traditionally related to one another according to strict rules of jati hierarchy and *jajmani* economic traditions. Not every service was village-based. A single goldsmith, for example, might service as many as five or ten villages, as a Brahman astrologer might, and eventually work only for those who came to his "shop" in town, and for payment in cash. Some village servants might, at the other extreme, be supported entirely by one wealthy landlord; others, like blacksmiths, were patronized by many members of the dominant jati, receiving a fraction of their annual sustenance from each. The system was designed to be self-perpetuating over generations, although in the face of modernization it is breaking down more and more rapidly, a village barber's son opting to work in a nearby mill; hence the need to "import" a new barber or else go to town for one's haircut, shave, and pedicure.

A *jajman* was viewed as much more than one's economic "patron," traditionally seen as something of a god, worthy of being served night or day, generously rewarding his humble servants with food. Most jatis in modern Indian villages now interact monetarily, in a more formal modern economic sense rather than by ritualistic tradition. Friendships across jati lines are still rare, however, and the social distance between Brahman or dominant caste families and "unclean" or "outcaste" families remains for most villagers unbridgeable. Yet there are exceptions to every rule of tradition, and satellite-TV broadcasts daily conspire at present with India's secular Constitution and modernist leadership to accelerate the pace of change and bring fresher winds of democratic consciousness even to the most remote regions or hill tracts of rural India.

Most villages continue to have resident headmen and panchayats, but subdistrict and provincial officials, tax collectors, police officers, and development planners as well as central office-seeking politicians drive more and more often down dusty roads or over muddy trails to remind those local leaders of how minimal their once extensive powers have become.

Central Government commitment to economic planning has since 1954 helped revitalize ancient rural "Council of Five" (*Panchayat*) rule, but only for suggesting planning priorities, not to punish infractions of traditional jati "laws," their ultimate power in "olden times" having been the awesome force of ostracism. Nowadays caste elders retain considerable influence owing to their age, wealth, and Brahmanic or dominant landowner caste status, but they have none of the residual police or judicial powers that their ancestors enjoyed. Village headmen (there are often two, three, or more in large villages) still exercise various administrative powers, usually connected with tax collection or keeping local police informed of the whereabouts of "strangers" or the activities of "vagrants," in return for which they may enjoy tax-exempt status. Headmen are also greatly respected, of course, by virtue of their advanced age and jati-exalted birth, or landed wealth, and are usually consulted by provincial officials and candidates for Lok Sabha just prior to election time. As more Indian villages come within range of orbiting satellites that daily beam TV news from Delhi, and as more all-weather roads link the remotest corners of India to increasingly rapid modern transit, modern bureaucrats and degree-holding scientists as well as heavily guarded politicians whittle away at the traditional powers of local leaders. Still, India remains a society deeply respectful of tradition, remarkably worshipful of age and inherited religious status. Neighboring cities with their factories and relatively high wages reach out more and more to magnetize village youth, especially enterprising and restless young men, who have learned enough about the modern world to want to see more of it. More noteworthy, however, than the rate of change in India's rural society is its degree of continuity and the continuing hold so many village communities exercise over their patient, hard-working sons and daughters.

Market centers are generally within a few hours' walk or bullock-cart ride of any village. Weekly marketplaces offer villagers ample opportunity to buy whatever products they may require that are not available within their small communities and to sell any surplus handicrafts or crops. Markets are usually based at crossroads, often the original locus of Indian towns today, many of which have recently blossomed into small factory cities with large bazaars. In more remote regions markets remain mobile and merchants often shift their venue from week to week among half a dozen villages with enough merchandise piled and rolled up on their bikes to make them look like circus jugglers or stores-on-wheels. Indian villagers, especially women, often develop remarkable balance and dexterity from early youth, daily walking with several jugs of water or other precious goods stored in brass or clay vessels stacked on top of their heads. Before dawn, peasants are found walking or bicycling to the nearest market or city with fresh milk, still considered too great a luxury to lavish on village children, for sale in town.

Markets, like religious fairs and festivals honoring local deities, are important opportunities for social intercourse as well as economic gain or religious merit. Indian women often have no other legitimate reason for leaving their homes, and readily venture far afield to markets and fairs, meeting their sisters or other close relatives, with whom they spend much of the day gossiping, catching up on all that has happened. Men take spare goats or bullocks or cows to the cattle markets that usually are more remote and less regularly held than local produce markets. There, too, important social contacts are consolidated, arrangements for marrying off one or more children begun or consummated as part of the long journey's "business." Market days thus become major holiday outings for the entire family, usually a full day's trip in a crowded, creaking bullock cart.

The most important vehicle of change in village India today is education. The Constitution of India committed that republic to "free and compulsory education for all children" up to the age of fourteen as one of its "directive principles." Full realization of that ambitious goal has yet to be achieved, but at least 50 percent of India's children receive some schooling, and at least half of those will continue to study through the age of puberty. Every Indian village has its "school," which may be no more than a cleared patch of dust under a special tree, but is often a recently constructed room, either baked brick or concrete, where students learn their alphabet and start to read, write, add, and subtract. At planting or harvest times, of course, classroom attendance is minimal and most other days it is all too brief by our standards, but progress is being made, literacy expanding.

Once that first window has been opened, moreover, and a peasant child learns to read by himself, there is no telling how far his mind, ambition, and intellect may lead him. First to the nearest town's high school, and then to a provincial capital's college, possibly on a government quota provided for ex-Untouchable children. After those hurdles have been taken, New Delhi itself is within accessible range, or Bombay, possibly even London or New York. Education and talent remain the swiftest elevators to pinnacles of modern Indian power and opportunity, but competition is fierce, the odds greater than one in a hundred thousand for village lads, to achieve urban fame or fortune by this most common Western highroad to "success." The total number of young Indians currently enrolled in primary and secondary schools throughout India is well over 100 million, approximately 6 million of whom go on to colleges for university degrees. Although the ex-Untouchable literacy rate is still only about half that of upper-caste Hindus and the female literacy rate remains much lower than that for males, rapid progress has been made since 1961, when barely 10 percent of ex-Untouchables could read or write their own names. If the current rate of increased literacy continues, virtually every Indian should be able to read and write by the year 2050.

All of the problems endemic to our own affluent public educational systems are naturally compounded in the environment of India's rural world of poverty and pluralism. Teachers are underpaid, and in many cases themselves so inadequately educated that it is something of a miracle if their students ever learn anything. There is never enough funding for textbooks, slates, chalk, or pencils. Upper-class families who can afford tuition invariably send their children to private schools, many of which are run by missionaries or modeled on the British "public" school system. Obviously few such families live in villages, but even there, if a wealthy landlord can afford it, he will hire a private tutor to teach his sons at least to read at home.

Indian schools remain carefully segregated as to sex, boys sitting on one side, girls on the other side of a room, with a substantial distance between them, usually where the teacher stands or patrols, keeping the neutral zone clear of adventurers. Segregation by caste is no longer permitted by law, but is nonetheless often practiced, at least as much by the timid and self-conscious children of ex-Untouchables as by those of overbearing Brahman or Kshatriya jatis. Muslims in many villages are so small a minority that they too feel reticent about taking full advantage of the equality of opportunity before the law that all Indians should enjoy. Human Rights are one stage in social evolution; finding the courage to assert those precious rights is a more difficult achievement. India's peasant population remains deeply mired in traditions based on hierarchy and respect for authority. No remote legislature can inject self-confidence or self-assertiveness overnight into the hearts or minds of those reared to remain passively obedient. The process, however, has begun. The rules, at least, have been changed. Now it is for the players, individually as well as collectively, to learn to play differently, without losing faith in either themselves or the greater system of which they are just a small part.

Some regions of India have been more radical than most in altering things politically, calling for rural revolution to give land to the landless and jobs to the unemployed. West Bengal, Kerala, and Tripura have voted Marxist state governments into office, but none has been able to overcome the grim realities of India's rural penury or to reduce population densities that limit available land or bring happiness and the fulfillment of useful labor to those without education or skills. No more than the Ford Foundation or Margaret Sanger could convince India's average peasant family, at least its male-dominant side, that birth control and family planning were wiser and better for all concerned than having as many sons as possible. "A son is born with two hands for work and only one mouth to feed," Indian peasant shrewdness argued. And though daughters were economically far less desirable, most peasant elders knew from the experience of others that even bearing a dozen children did not necessarily insure adequate support for parents in their sunset years.

Village architecture and general physical arrangements vary considerably throughout India. In the wheat-growing, prosperous States of Punjab and Haryana, nuclear villages, often electrified with tubewells and tractors in abundant evidence, are dominated by Sikhs or Jat Hindus. In Rajasthan and Madhya Pradesh the villages are also nuclear, often walled, but much poorer; and houses, often in general decay or ill-repair, include the larger compounds of ruling Rajput families. With more rain in the Ganga Valley of central U.P. and east through Bihar and West Bengal, rice is the major crop and population densities so high that villages are dispersed to permit use of more land. Thakurs and Varendra Brahmans and Kayasths generally function as the dominant jatis. In Bengal and in the Malabar State of Kerala peasant homes are often raised above rice fields on bamboo stilts to allow maximum exploitation of rain-rich paddy land. At least two, usually three, crops are grown annually. Mixed village clusters are found in Karnataka and Maharashtra, with Okkaligas or Lingayats dominant in the former State, long called "Mysore"; and Marathas generally predominate in villages of the Deccan. Cardboard-like millets as well as cotton and sugarcane are the most common crops in that central region of peninsular India. Oriyas control most of the coastal villages of Orissa, while tribal Konds dominate in the rugged hills. Farther south in Andhra and Tamil Nadu, ex-Untouchable Adi-Dravidas are becoming increasingly dominant, leaving Smarthas and Sri Vaishnava Brahmans to complain of iniquitous discrimination. Modern caste associations and mass electorates are thus gradually but inevitably transforming India's rural society, even as stronger and deeper processes of change rumble through her new factory towns and fast-growing, overpopulated larger cities.

The Urban Revolution

Accelerating urbanization is the most powerful complex process currently contributing to the transformation of Indian society. About one-fourth of India's population is "urban," inhabiting towns or cities of over 5,000 residents, with population densities of 1,000 or more per square mile. At least 75 percent of the adult male populace of these urban areas are employed in nonagricultural occupations. Many Indian villages have populations larger than her smallest towns, and shades of difference between those two regions on the rural–urban continuum are obviously marginal, since larger villages usually have small factories, if only for manufacturing bricks, within their boundaries. More than 50 percent of all urban-dwellers, however, live in cities of over 100,000 population, with India's top ten multimillion or over one million megalopolis complexes at the upper end of that group, as remote from rural village life as the freeway system of New Delhi and the monster steel mills of Jamshedpur.

Cities have been firmly rooted in South Asia for at least 4,000 years, dating back to the high tide of Indus Valley culture. The plains around Delhi are strewn with rubble of at least seven cities, each of which once functioned as capital of some long-departed dynasty. John Company brought with its mercantile trade the impetus to build port cities around early British Presidency forts at Calcutta, Madras, and Bombay, which have evolved over the past few centuries into modern urban complexes of magnificent and terrifying dimensions. Following Manchester's industrialization, nineteenth-century India initially experienced deurbanization, millions of her town-dwelling artisans forced back to dependence upon tilling soil of ancestral villages by Britain's industrial competition. By century's end, however, new milltowns sprang to life in Gujarat, Bombay, Bengal, and Madras as indigenous cotton, jute, and other cloth-manufacturing centers emerged to challenge cheap British imports.

India's industrial revolution was long inhibited by British imperial rule, which denied tariff protection to indigenous entrepreneurs as long as possible. But during World War I Great Britain needed Indian produce more than it worried about thwarting Indian profits. Far-sighted pioneer Indian industrialists like Jamshed N. Tata (1839–1904) launched iron and steel mills without government support. By World War II Tata's giant complex at Jamshedpur in Bihar, India's Ruhr, had grown into the largest such mill in the British Empire. Since Independence many more iron and steel, electrochemical, electronics, and nuclear atomic urban centers have blossomed on Indian soil. India's larger cities are growing at twice the rate of smaller towns and villages. New Delhi has more than tripled its population in the last twenty years, with over six million now living on the sprawling plain around that modern capital magnet, whose shabbier sister-city, Old Delhi, reflects all the poverty, congestion, and pluralism of ancient India with as many people crammed inside its narrow precincts. More than 30 percent of Delhi's new residents, however, are impoverished squatters, *busti*-"slum"-dwellers, with none of the amenities found in the posh heart of India's modern capital. Indeed, even many well-to-do middle-class suburbs to the south, west, and east of New Delhi's palatial official and diplomatic centers have no fresh water available after 6 A.M., and must share limited electricity in the "rolling brown-outs" that have long been familiar to greater Calcutta's populace, where "modern" suburbs enjoy electricity only one or two nights a week.

Urban caldrons serve in India, as elsewhere, as pressure-cookers of social change. Peasants, who flock to cities and find work in office buildings or factories, transported on overcrowded buses, trolleys, and commuter trains, are forced into close proximity with millions of others, whose jatis, religious persuasions, villages of origin, and moral values remain unknown, impossible to ascertain. There is never time for the amenities, curiosities, or courtesies of rural habits and provincial manners in the hustle and bustle of big-city life. Merely crossing a street in Bombay or Calcutta could bring an otherwise pure Brahman into touch with so many outcaste or "polluted" bodies as to set back one's struggle toward Moksha several incarnations. City-wallahs learn to carry on by compartmentalization of their lives, however, washing up and changing clothes at night when they return home, saying a mantra or two, or dropping a puja garland over the proper icon. Many of India's cities have more than 1,000 residents per acre in their most densely packed neighborhoods, and those are often places with a single tap for water and no septic tanks or covered drains. The industrial slums of Ahmedabad, Madras, and Bombay, as well as Calcutta, are among the worst such areas.

In most respects New Delhi is atypical of Indian cities, more a world metropolis than a "third world" capital. The lavish expenditure that created Asia's largest illuminated stadium and more than doubled the number of five-star bedrooms in New Delhi in 1982 for the Asian Olympiad added freeway fly-overs and fountains to the central government's spacious modern heart and helped transform India's gracious capital into a modern symbol of power. Traffic patterns, however, remain almost as hierarchic and precariously chaotic as elsewhere in India. Some crossroads have street lights, but neither they nor the handsomely attired traffic police, dressed in white, standing in circular boxes with gloves and whistles, seem to have much impact on the chaos of cars, buses, motor scooters, and cyclists, as well as pedestrian and animal traffic swirling round them.

India's roads, even in the heart of New Delhi, are like her varna-jati system, hierarchically run. Curtained Mercedes or air-cooled Marutis, with ministerial flags flying from forward fenders or hoods, are the pukka-Sahibs of any road. They are the equivalents of our siren-sounding and light-flashing ambulances, squad cars, or fire engines, stopping traffic as they sail through, rolling ahead at high speed. Next come the Kshatriya-Vaishya private cars without flags, for they, too, belong to the very rich, symbols of the powerful ruling class, who can afford to pay for such luxury. Next come the chartered air-conditioned buses, filled with tourists from abroad, twice-born beauties of modern technology. Sacred cows, of course, like Sadhus and Brahmans on foot, go where they will, when they wish it. New motor-scooters take similar liberties. Old trucks and muncipal buses, three-wheeled lambrettas, bullock carts, and hand-drawn carts (bicycle rikshas) are the Shudras and outcastes of the road. When trucks are heavy and a road remote, however, they barrel down dead center, like ex-Untouchables just recently elected to high office, fearing nothing, moving aside for no one! Small wonder that India's fatality rate from road accidents is twenty times higher than America's.

The approximately 800 square miles of metropolitan area round Delhi's plain accommodates the vast migrant populace that has flocked to India's burgeoning capital from neighboring Punjab, Rajasthan, Haryana, and U.P. In the wake of Independence and Partition millions of Sikh and Hindu refugees from Pakistan settled in camps around Delhi, which have since evolved into suburban satellite towns built under the auspices of the Ministry of Rehabilitation. In the nightmarish orgy of violence that followed the assassination of Prime Minister Indira Gandhi in late 1984, several of the predominantly Sikh settlements on the outskirts of Delhi were turned into crematorium pyres by rampaging mobs of frenzied Hindu supporters of Congress, leaving thousands of innocent Sikhs dead within seventy-two hours of vengeance-fired violence.[10] Even the main business districts of New Delhi as well as the "Silver Area" (*Chandni Chawk*) artery of Old Delhi were subjected to torch and brick-bat destruction by rampaging hoodlums, unrestrained by passively watching police. The most modern of India's urban centers seemed to have become overnight the most barbaric place in the entire nation, a hazard of urbanization long familiar to Westerners who have witnessed race riots in Chicago, Philadelphia, Detroit, London, Belfast, or Beirut. Delhi's tragedy, nonetheless, was a grim reminder to everyone concerned of the inadequacy of urban planning in India. Within a month of that nightmare, an equally chilling example of the hazards of rapid industrial urbanization struck the sleeping inhabitants of Bhopal, Central India's petrochemical capital, whose population had grown with cancerous speed around a huge Union Carbide "fertilizer" plant erected close to its center in the 1970s. Deadly poisonous gas billowed silently from inadequately protected storage tanks at that plant, claiming the lives of at least 1,700 slumbering innocents, and polluting the eyes and lungs of an estimated 200,000 others, who barely managed to survive that worst of modern India's industrial accidents. Bhopal is the only major Indian city whose population has been reduced of late by migration back to the countryside and to smaller townships.

India's largest city remains Calcutta, whose Metropolitan District includes some 100 urban units with an overall population fast approaching 15 million. Calcutta City, at the heart of this sprawling complex of towns and cities on both banks of the Hughli River, was begun by a British merchant trader named Job (Charnock) in 1690, and prophetically dubbed "City of Dreadful Night" by Kipling two centuries later, when it was still relatively safe and uncrowded. Calcutta was the first of India's cities to be granted "Municipal" status by the British. Its population reached one million early in this century, and remains India's premier city in size as well as the proliferation of urban problems. More than three-quarters of Calcutta's families live in single-room squalor or unsheltered out-of-doors, without running water or adequate lavatory facilities. Yet it is the first of India's cities to have expended a fortune on a mile of modern subway in the best part of its posh Fort district. West Bengal's Marxist State government thus proved itself no better at solving India's enormous and urgent problems of poverty or urban inequities than did any of its Congress rivals. Calcutta's inadequately filtered water supply runs through badly eroding pipes installed by British engineers in 1870, with a maximum survival expectancy of 100 years. The central municipal sewerage system, initially designed to service 600,000 people, is now being used by more than five times that upper limit. Howrah, Calcutta's industrial twin on the west bank of the Hughli, is still linked to its sister by only two bridges, over which traffic barely moves for most of each day. Calcutta may die of gridlock, if none of its waste or water-borne epidemic diseases strike first.

In recent decades Bombay has emerged as India's premier financial metropolis as well as its major center of trade and commerce. The western capital of Maharashtra displaced the eastern capital of Bengal at the top of India's mercantile mountain of wealth in the late 1970s. But in the process of dethroning Calcutta, Bombay may fall victim to all the same diseases of urban blight and unplanned growth that have so sadly crippled Calcutta. Its air is now heavily polluted with oil fumes and industrial waste, its water supply dangerously limited and equally fetid, its streets and byways jammed with traffic, its fields and marshes crowded with squatter-bustis filled by the daily flood of penurious rural migrants. In barely a decade Bombay has begun to change from India's most prosperous and promising city into its most precariously endangered one. Not that the glitter of its Marine Drive necklace by nightfall has lost its beauty, or the Bombay stock and commodity exchanges their profitable buoyance. Bombay's harbor, moreover, remains one of its most attractive natural assets, with the unique ancient stone artifacts on the island of Elephanta a continuing tourist magnet. The neighboring island of Tarapur with its modern Atomic Research Center is India's major bastion of modern power. An uncontrollable blaze at the nearby offshore oil complex of Bombay High in 1983, triggered by the collapse of a drilling platform, not only wasted countless millions of gallons of precious oil and gas, but burned for weeks, shrouding Bombay harbor in blinding smoke, a grim reminder of the far more dreadful potential explosive hazard hovering just beyond the placid waters at the steps of the Imperial Gateway to India.

Bombay's international airport is second only to Delhi's in handling express traffic to and from India, sharing the total national revenue from airborne trade and claiming more than 40 percent of India's sea-borne revenues. No other Indian urbanists pay half as much income tax as do the affluent residential community of Bombay, whose leading Parsi, Marwari, Jain, and Shi'i Muslim trading houses are solidly based in this truly cosmopolitan center. Some 5,000 industries, ranging from huge cotton mills and chemical plants of machinery and transport vehicle factories, employ close to a million workers around Greater Bombay. The new restricted industrial area called "Trombay" contains the Homi Bhabha Atomic Research Center and several oil refineries, thermal power units, and fertilizer as well as petrochemical plants. Bombay's inner city now has more than 100,000 people living in each of its square miles, almost a third of them with no permanent shelter, no running water, sewerage, or sidewalk, squatting on marshland recently reclaimed from the sea, filled in with refuse and waste.

Madras remains the major center of urban buildup and increasing sprawl in South India, and is rapidly acquiring the characteristics of its two larger models, Calcutta and Bombay. The once sleepy town around Fort St. George, built by the East India Company along one of the loveliest stretches of sand and sea on the Coromandal coast in 1639, has turned into a mushrooming growth of squatter slums, bustling bazaars, snarled traffic, and polluted air and water. Pressures of population continue to mount as more and more of Sri Lanka's Tamil minority flee that troubled Island just off the shore of Tamil Nadu, to the comfort of Madras's "Land of the Tamils" State. Rural migrants flock toward Madras from north and west as well, hoping to find work in its fast-proliferating factories or by building more of its high-rise structures that require armies of unskilled labor to carry the bricks and often too-watery cement up scaffolds of bamboo that somehow survive the construction process, raising multistoried barracks, desperately needed to house Madras's growing populace. Petrochemical, truck, and rubber factories and other industries stretch their bands of steel and smoke to the north of Madras's commercial and residential heart. In the southwest quarter of the city are major film studios, where many South Indian political stars first skyrocketed to fame and fortune. "N. T. R." Rama Rao, the most popular star of the Dravidian screen, emerged in his 1980s role as Chief Minister of Andhra, national opponent of Congress, but was defeated at the polls in 1989, returning to the Silver Screen to star as Lord Vishnu. Another former matinee idol, M. G. Ramachandran (M. G. R.), ruled Tamil Nadu's political roost at the head of his Dravidian Progressive Federation (DMK), until his death in 1988.

Every major city of India faces the same proliferating problems: inadequate housing, transport, sewerage, water, schools, and hospitals. There is virtually no planning, except for such "model" cities as Chandigarh, designed to be Punjab State's capital by Le Corbusier, and personally nurtured by Prime Minister Jawaharlal Nehru as an urban symbol of New India. Yet even Chandigarh, centrally administered since 1966 as joint capital of Punjab and Haryana, has fallen victim to India's complex congeries of urban diseases, ringed by squatter slums, overcrowded, ill-housed, ill-serviced. It is becoming more difficult to deliver mail in any Indian city, since few people live in areas with sequential street addresses or numbered houses—outside of the heartland of New Delhi, Bombay, Madras, Calcutta, and other major centers like Bangalore, Mysore, Pune, Patna, Allahabad, and Chandigarh. Lack of power leaves most suburbs in darkness much of the time, even when electric wires, switches, and outlets are, in fact, built into homes.

Indians, of course, learn to adjust; hence much that happens in Indian cities seems "mysterious" to Westerners. People often appear at one's door at exotic hours, "sensing" that the person they are visiting wanted to see them, merely wanting to chat or have tea. Cities are more unpredictably violent than the countryside, their hazards more contagious. Every decade another Municipal Planning Board or Commission sets to work, devoting precious time and resources to studies that project impossible needs for an urban future that swiftly becomes part of India's past, without implementing even the highest-priority proposals.

Yet with plans or without, India's Urban Revolution continues to gather momentum, swift and loud, slow and silent, with steady streams of vehicular traffic and migrant squatters moving by day and night toward the nearly 100 magnets of light and power, money and hope that are India's largest cities, diminishing their luster as they settle down to choke off green space and add pollution. Unconsciously, insidiously, without pause or reason, the countless daily, hourly changes induced by city lights, city traffic, city sounds and smells make their impact on rural minds and hearts. Jati fears and prejudices fade before new terrors of much higher orders of magnitude as the steel factory or cloth mill replace fields of rice and millet as centers of work and life. Symbiotically, the presence of so many recent rural arrivals in even the largest of India's cities inhibit the pace of urbanization, or at least diminish the speed at which the "modernizing" process as we know it in the West occurs. Indian-modern is, however, a variant all its own, just as Indian-English is a language distinct from American or English, "isn't it?" Urban planning and development in India is at best fragmented, uncoordinated; at worst, basically nonexistent, anarchic. India's cities keep growing with alarming, dangerous, explosive lack of direction, control, or intelligently guided effort.

By the twenty-first century, India's population will be well over one billion. Approximately one-third of that vast population will reside in urban areas, which means adding the population of another Calcutta, Bombay, or Madras to India's already overburdened cities each year until 2001, and still more thereafter. Unless some rational urban planning, with central coordination, is undertaken, that Urban Revolution may prove more hazardously polluting to India's future potential than all of its other problems combined.

Arts and Sciences

Mother, I bow to thee!

Thou art wisdom, thou art law,
Thou our heart, our soul, our breath,
Thou the love divine, the awe
In our hearts that conquers death.
Thine the strength that nerves the arm,
Thine the beauty, thine the charm.
Every image made divine
In our temples is but thine.

—*Bande Mataram* ("Hymn To The Mother"); Bengali original by Bankim Chandra Chatterji (trans. Sri Aurobindo)

Art pervades every facet of Indian life, is found on every byway of Indian Civilization. A spice or cosmetic stall in any Indian bazaar is a palette of dazzling color, blood-red henna, turmeric, coriander, and saffron, piled in perfect pyramids by gnarled hands of merchant vendors unconscious of their artistry. Garland-weavers nimbly string fresh flowers into stunning fragrant works of marigold, jasmine, or rose colored art to be offered as puja at countless Hindu temples. Enter the meanest hovel of any weaver in Kanchipuram, and watch shimmering silk threads as fine as a spider's turn into diaphonous garments worthy of draping a Mother Goddess. Or climb the dismal stairway of a "factory" loft in Varanasi, where exquisitely embroidered works of art are woven with gold and silver into patterns complex and enchanting by the fingers of artists whose names will never be known to the fortunate women adorned with their miraculous creations.

Descendants of the very craft-artists who constructed the Taj Mahal sit patiently in its environs, chipping away at marble and semiprecious stone to repair eroded "flowers" on the facade of that most magnificent of mausoleums, kept in almost pristine condition by the reincarnated talents of its creators. So too are the Hindu temples at Khajuraho continuously repaired, loving figures of gods and goddesses lured from blushing stone by artists, whose genes are imprinted with techniques of sculpting learned more than a thousand years ago by their ancestors. Every Hindu festival is a living work of transient art, a drama of worship improvised by casts of thousands, who wend their merry way through village and town, dragging carts with images of gods draped in silk, adorned with jewels, crowned with silver, or made of basest clay covered with painted chips of glass and tinsel, yet bright as the dawn that brings most such festivals to an end with immersion of the icon in river water.

Indian art in its purest form is Yoga, a disciplined style of worship and self-restraint that may also be thought of as India's oldest indigenous "science." Shiva, the "Great God" of yogic practice, visually represented as "King of Dance" (*Nataraja*), is the most remarkable single symbol of divine powers ever created by Indian artistic genius. Lord Shiva stands perfectly poised inside a mandala-ring of cosmic fire, one leg lifted gracefully, the other crushing down on the back of the evil dwarf of darkness. Armed with four hands, the Great God holds a drum of creation in one, a flame upon another, and points with his two empty hands toward his raised foot as well as toward the sky above as he embarks upon the Dance of Life, ready to launch our universe upon yet another cycle of divine creativity. South Indian Chola artists from at least the tenth century produced their priceless Natarajas by the same lost wax process first mastered by Indus Valley sculptors some 3,000 years earlier. Indian metallurgists contributed their scientific talents to the creation of these bronzes now recognized the world over as on a par with Italian Renaissance art. The bronze dancing girl found at Mohenjo-daro attests not only to the antiquity of Indian sculpture and metallurgy but also to multimillennial roots of the art of dance in Indic Civilization.

"The man who knows nothing of music, literature, or art is no better than a beast," ancient Indian wisdom warned, "only without a beast's tail or teeth." The arts are Civilization's armor, her weapons and shield against all the pitfalls of life, lighting the darkest corners of the trail, helping us to cross its most dangerous passes. Indian wisdom has always extolled art as a key to the salvation of ultimate release sought by all good Hindus. Art has also obviously provided a pleasant, amusing escape from dark realities that press so compellingly around one on every Indian street and highway. There is a holistic quality about Indian art, moreover, a unity of many forms and artistic experiences that helps transcend the drab or sorrowful world, to experience deeply and comprehensively artistic pleasure with all one's senses. Indian art is like the all-encompassing clamor of simultaneously ringing bells and reverberating drums inside a crowded temple to the Mother Goddess, where a cacophony of sound, the smell of incense, and the glare of circling lamplights mix with chanted mantras, creating waves of sensation at once bewildering, transporting, and terrifying, yet beautiful. Much like everything else in India, her arts are abstractly wonderful and mundane, exhilarating, engaging, ethereal, sensual. Like the microcosmic universe of a Hindu temple, they help us to climb from terrestrial trials and samsaric fears up to a realm of gods and goddesses that seems as chaotic and cluttered as our own, but is adorned with immortals in flesh carved of stone that never ages, finding external pleasure in the adoration of one another's nubile naked bodies as they while away millennia waiting for Moksha.

India's greatest artist of the twentieth century, Rabindranath Tagore (1861–1941), called by Mahatma Gandhi *Guru-Dev* ("Divine Teacher"), epitomized the unity of Indian Arts. Tagore won the Nobel Prize for Literature in 1913 for the beautiful poetry, fiction, and dramas he wrote with equal facility in English and Bengali, but he was also a fine painter, creative educator, and musical composer. His life was a blend of every artistic impulse. The scion of Zamindari Bengali wealth, Tagore personified not only Indic Civilization in its most ethereally creative spirit but also the peak of Western sensitivity. He was India's greatest modern artist, transcending all bonds of birth and region or nation to dwell on the highest plain of art, where the most beautiful products of creative spirits from all climes and times inspire one another in the only truly universal "language." Tagore turned to painting quite late in life, noting that "words are too conscious; lines are not. Ideas have their form and color, which wait for their incarnation in pictorial art. . . . My morning began with songs and poems; now, in the evening of my life, my mind is filled with forms and colors." Gurudev Tagore explained how "love" carries so much "joy" that it can only be "expressed in a form of art. . . . Love gives evidence to something which is outside us but which intensely exists and thus stimulates the sense of our own existence. It radiantly reveals the reality of its objects." Great artist that he was, Tagore was also a supreme lover, even as Kalidasa long before him had been. His *Gitanjali*, published in 1913, immortalized the Nobel poet's passion:

> Light, my light, the world-filling light, the eye-kissing light, heart-sweetening light!
>
> Ah, the light dances, my darling, at the center of my life; the light strikes, my darling, the chords of my love; the sky opens, the wind runs wild, laughter passes over the earth.
>
> The butterflies spread their sails on the sea of light. Lilies and jasmines surge up on the crest of the waves of light.
>
> The light is shattered into gold on every cloud, my darling, and it scatters gems of profusion.
>
> Mirth spreads from leaf to leaf, my darling, and gladness without measure. The heaven's river had drowned its banks and the flood of joy is abroad.[1]

Dance, Drama, and Music

The *Natya Shastra* ("Textbook of Dance, Drama, and Music") is India's oldest exposition of the arts, attributed to sage Bharata. Classical Indian dance, whose purest practitioners are from the South, is called *Bharata Natyam*, named for that ancient text and its author. The *Natya Shastra* dates from about the second century of the Christian era, but is sometimes called a "fifth Veda," teaching that all arts were "created by the Gods," first for their own diversion, and also for the entertainment of mortals, including lowly Shudras. The latter, never permitted to hear or recite Vedic mantras, were thus allowed to dance, reaching toward God through gestures and gyrations, singing devotional charts of love as they moved. The *Bhakti* ("devotion" has as its secondary meaning "sexual love") movement of Vaishnavism opened gates of salvation to low-caste Hindus and women, much the way song and dance-drama provided employment and amusement to virtually every Indian. Shudras and even outcastes joined roving bands of singers, dancers, and entertainers, like the Gypsies of Rajasthan, who staged performances in open fields at night, or, if good enough, in royal palaces. Hindu temples became venues for Bharata Natyam dances by *Devadasis* ("Slaves of the God"), abandoned girls, left on temple steps by parents too poor to feed them, reared by Brahman priests for their own pleasures.

Bharata's 100 sons were supposedly the first Indian actors, accompanied by a chorus of divine nymphs, sprung full-blown from Lord Brahma's mind. Most Indian actors, however, like dancers, seem to have been of humble birth, even outcastes, forced for some reason to leave the security of their villages, whether because of marrying below their jatis or for other anticaste causes, to wander and seek their sustenance for a song. Folk and tribal dance-drama long anteceded "Great Tradition" compilations such as the *Natya Shastra*. Indian folk art remains vital and varied in every remote region of the subcontinent, and has only recently become part of recorded tradition, thanks to modern tapes, transistors, and video cameras. Wandering minstrels and dance-drama troupes served as blood-cells of the arts circulating throughout the body of Indic Civilization, refreshing its most remote limbs, carrying Epic and Puranic messages to the illiterate mass of its populace in forms more vitalizing and accessible than any Brahmanic mantra or turgid text.

Indian Civilization developed its own style of aesthetic appreciation as well as unique forms of dance, music, and sculpture. Indian art is believed to reflect varieties of "taste" (*rasa*) and "states of mind" (*bhava*). The *Natya Shastra* originally noted four basic rasas, the erotic, heroic, violent, and odious, from which evolved nine major taste-moods that span the spectrum of India's artistic palette: love, courage, joy, hatred, fury, pity, terror, surprise, and spiritual peace. Each of those rasas has many transient bhava-states of mind, the latter varying with time of day or night, state of health, weather, and other factors. There are at least thirty-three bhavas, perhaps as many as forty-nine. Love, not surprisingly, is generally associated with happy states of mind, although separation from one's beloved, however brief the interlude, induces a bhava closer to pain. Fatal illness, on the other hand, is so odious as to lead generally to "pathetic" states of mind, as does loss of fortune or captivity, although even such tragedies may elicit responses closer to courage or ennobling spiritual peace.

Classical Indian artists must, of course, internalize each rasa and bhava to convey it properly, but the audience is also enjoined to try its best to appreciate every performer's art by learning the varieties of taste and mood-state being enacted. This symbiotic sensitizing generates so powerful a field of aesthetic appreciation that its force can be felt by true Indian artists and artistic-appreciators alike. Thanks to a sensitized audience's good taste, an otherwise mundane Bharata Natyam performance or sitar and tabla recital may thus be transformed into what we might call a magical or divine experience. Indian afficionados of fine arts will, therefore, never hesitate to exclaim vocal appreciation during a performance or recital, often beating time, shaking their heads in visible satisfaction, smacking their lips, or otherwise participating in the event. What highly refined Western audiences might consider bad taste or offensive noises are viewed in just the opposite light by connoisseurs of Indic arts.

Natya is a Sanskrit word that means both "dance" and "drama." Classical Indian dance forms are, indeed, highly stylized dramatic presentations that tell Epic stories through a complex language of "hand gestures" (*mudras*) and body movement, including no less than thirty-six specific ways of lifting or opening the eye, eyelids, or eyebrows, and twenty-two poses of head and neck, listed in the *Natya Shastra* alone. Hundreds of additional mudras have been added over time, and every great Bharata Natyam artist must not only master all traditional forms, but tries to add a mudra or two of her own, as Balasaraswati did in depicting the flight of a Bhakti's winged heart toward the lips of Lord Krishna. No wonder that classical dance form takes so many years of daily practice to master, and continues to recruit very youthful Indian talent, much the way ballet does in the West.

The finest schools of Bharata Natyam remain centered in Madras, although New Delhi has also become a major modern center for both the teaching and performance of that art. Bharata Natyam dancers are usually beautiful women, garbed in tightly draped multicolored silk saris, adorned with knotted hair garlands of jasmine, elaborate head-jewels, golden bracelets, and noisy ankle-bells clasped over painted bare feet. Individual performances may take a few hours to complete, opening with a devotional *allarippu* ("floral decoration") to Lord Krishna. The next segment is a series of graceful body gyrations punctuated by the loud stomping of belled feet, followed by a number of devotional "songs" (*padas*), which may be rendered by a singer in Sanskrit, Telugu, or Tamil, or sung by one of the accompanying musicians, possibly an old man playing a bellow-pumped harmonium. Devoutly worshipful, the padas are addressed to either Lord Krishna or the

Mother Goddess, and often consist of no more than a line or two of poetry repeated in many rhythmic variations, affording the dancer ample time to catch her breath while she translates the words into mudras. Once the soulful singing ends, however, the last and most exhausting portion of Bharata Natyam dancing begins, a physically taxing climax of swift whirls and accelerated stomping, until the entire stage rocks and vibrates as though Lord Nataraja himself were setting the universe into motion. That climactic burst of explosive energy (*tillana*) often leaves an audience almost as breathless as the artist, whose sure-footed dexterity is truly remarkable.

Another classical South Indian dance form is called *Kuchipudi*, named after the Andhra village where it originated in the seventeenth century. A delightful blend of sacred and profane emotion, Kuchipudi has become very popular in modern India, and now flourishes in New Delhi as well as in the States of Andhra and Tamil Nadu. The favorite dance-drama of this classical art form is the tale of Krishna's jealous wife, Satyabhama, who hated sharing her Lord with 16,000 other women. Foolish Satyabhama hoped to keep Krishna for herself by donating him to sage Narada as the learned Brahman's ascetic "assistant." When Krishna's other consorts learned of Satyabhama's treachery, they implored the sage to release their divine husband, and Lord Krishna returned to the bedchambers of his favorites, Radha and Rukmini. Then Satyabhama entered the "anger-closet" in Krishna's palace, reflecting the actual practice, no doubt, of many a jealous harem-maid, obviously ringing a responsive chord, moreover, in modern Indian hearts and minds. Krishna himself was finally obliged to lure Satyabhama back to brighter quarters by going down himself to release her from the dungeon of her jealous despair with sweet words and far sweeter kisses.

Most elaborate of the dance-drama forms of classical India is the *Kathakali* ("Recited action") that emerged from the palm-fringed Malabar coast in what is now the State of Kerala. Kathakali productions may take as long as twelve hours, and employ an entire company of artists, all male. The dramas are as a rule drawn from Epic material, either *Ramayana* or *Mahabharata*. The costumes and makeup are so ornate and intricate as to require many hours to put on. Huge monstrous masks are worn by the dancers, who jump around and shriek wildly to the rhythms of drums and cymbal-clapping singers. Long, painted fingernails endow Kathakali mudras with exaggerated power, and virtually every character looks like a demon, although villains can be recognized by well-trained audiences, differentiated from heroes by their ugly bulbous facial warts. Superficially all the characters look alike, but those who know the Epics can tell Rama from Ravana, and Sita from Lakshman. Deafening drum beats and piercing howls usually herald the start of a Kathakali drama, generally staged outdoors. A simple curtain divides audience from actors, and there are rarely any props on "stage," only dancing actors and musicians.

North Indian classical dance forms were strongly influenced by Islamic court tastes, and are still performed by female dancers wearing diaphonous harem-silks and veils to the accompaniment of Persian musical rhythms. The popular *Kathak* ("Story") dances of U.P. and Rajasthan were the favorite *nautch* style of harem-dancing that British officials enjoyed so much in the heyday of the old Raj. Dancing "girls," sometimes played by young boys, pirouette lithely around, waving long arms and veils, revealing naked thighs and buttocks as they twirl faster before collapsing in a heap of spent passion, flowing silk, and uninhibited hair. Devotional padas are often chanted, sentimental love poems, in either Persian or Urdu, to punctuate the pathos of these dance-dramas that usually tell a tale of unrequited love.

Manipuri dance-dramas are the northeastern classical art of Manipur State, bordering Burma. The graceful gentle swaying of Manipuri dancers, whose regional costumes and straight striped skirts, more Burmese than Indian, make them look like toy dolls on rotating stands, delighted Rabindranath Tagore. Thanks to his personal interest and patronage, Manipuri dancers emerged from their provincial obscurity and have attracted world attention and renown. Of all India's classical dance styles, Manipuri is least demanding technically and is often mastered by amateur imitators, throughout the West as well as in other parts of India. Manipuris themselves must all dance, since they believe that unless every villager dances at least one month each year, gods become so angry that either floods or fire, common Manipur disasters, may destroy their region. Esoteric *Ras Lila* ("Love Plays"), re-creating Krishna's seduction of his adoring milkmaids of Mathura, are performed in Manipur on three full-moon nights every year. Those sensuous eighteen-hour-long operas are considered sacred mysteries by the artists and should never be performed in the "profane" world beyond Manipur's borders, although several such productions in much abbreviated form have recently been produced in New Delhi. A single male drummer usually accompanies Manipuri female dancers, his naked torso and the sharp percussion rhythms of his drum a dramatic contrast to the fully clothed, easy undulating motion of the chorus.

There are almost as many styles of Indian folk dancing as there are varying types of villages. Perhaps the most colorful of these many rural art forms is the wedding folk dance that emerged in Rajasthan. The groom, his torso draped with a brightly painted "horse" made of papier-mâché and hung over his shoulders, gallops with eager enthusiasm toward his cowering bride, sword drawn and raised above her veiled head. The symbolic conquest is, of course, completed only after seductive chasing and a few near misses with what is happily also a papier-mâché sword. Most villages have special dances designed to ward off dreaded diseases, such as smallpox, artists first modeling and dressing up the goddess of that sickness, and putting her into a colorful cart that is then accompanied by the dancers and musicians to the village boundary, and pushed, not very considerately, onto the land of a neighboring village. Folk stick dances are equally common, concentric circles of men and women holding two sticks each, which they strike against one another's sticks as they move round in opposite directions at ever-increasing speed. Great dexterity is required to avoid sorely bruised bones. Flaming-sword swallowing and burning-coal dancing are familiar acrobatic dance performances, often the specialties of roving Indian acrobats, who attract large crowds in town or city parks and open spaces where they perform on festival days.

Indian folk dance-dramas generally tell bawdy tales of rural seduction and the abandonment of maids-in-distress by lecherous lovers. Monstrous mothers-in-law and greedy landlords are the most common villains of such dramas, reflecting traditional stereotypical prejudices as much as the rural realities of modern-day India.

India's huge and enormously profitable film industry continues to pander to such familiar stereotypes, introducing pastoral bullock-cart rides with buxom singing peasant girls eyeing naked-torsoed lads as they labor in furrowed fields. Raj Kapoor (d. 1988) acted in, produced, and directed more Hindi films than any other movie Mughal of Bombay or Madras, premier sites of the more than seventy Indian studios that grind out about 850 films a year. Raj's younger brother Shashi Kapoor has become a Mughal on his own, a star of international acclaim in the Ivory-Merchant production of Ruth Jabhvala's story, *Heat and Dust*. Amitabh Bachchan, India's superstar of the 1970s and early 1980s, opted for Lok Sabha's stage in 1984 and was easily elected as a member of Prime Minister Rajiv Gandhi's Congress team, but felt obliged to resign in 1988, when the Bofors arms' "kickback" scandal and reports about his brother's supposed Swiss bank account became daily news in New Delhi.

India is not, of course, the only democracy whose movie stars have turned their box office appeal into political launching pads. Color TV and the more than half million videocassette recorders and players now in use in India have cut into film profits, but have hardly diminished the enormous crowds and lines outside big-city movie palaces, especially in Bombay, Calcutta, and Madras. Movies offer, after all, magic get-away gardens amid urban India's blight. More than a third of a million Indians are employed in the "Industry," but most films are of such poor quality, not to speak of taste, that they rarely recover costs of production. Blockbusters of Bombay and Madras are, however, as profitable to those studios as *Jaws* and *Rocky* have been to Hollywood. India's greatest director-producer, Satyajit Ray, has created over a dozen works of cinematic art, from *The Apu Trilogy* to *The Chess Players* and *The Home and the World*, based primarily on life in Bengal. His films, like the best of Indian art, are experiences of holistic pleasure, gratifying to all senses and sensibilities, but have to date been far more appreciated and popular in France and the United States than in India.

Music and song emerged integral to classical dance-drama and continue to be part of all such performances. Basically improvisational, Indian music is melodic and rhythmic, but lacks harmony or counterpoint. Melodic *raga*s ("colors" or "passions") are usually five or seven notes in ascending or descending scale. Each raga has its principal mood: erotic, heroic, pathetic, or tranquil, and each is also associated with time of day or year. No two ragas are precisely the same, since improvisation plays so important a role in Indian music. Myth endowed Krishna with no less than 16,000 ragas, but only a few hundred survive, and six of those were considered basic enough to name: Bhairava, Kaushika, Dipaka, Hindola, Shriraga, and Megha. Like the Hindu gods, masculine ragas were always coupled with female raginis, generally two in number, but for Bhairava no less than five. He was obviously a most powerful raga, but should only be played at dawn, for his dominant moods are awe and fear. Hindola is the raga of love, to be played at night; Megha is the music of peace and calm meditation. Ragas and their consorts are each adorned with special notes and melodic phrases that sometimes lead to prolonged improvisational interludes, enchanting afficionado audiences. Nowadays there are always new ragas being developed to reflect modern times, including "Swing," and "Intoxication," or "Nuclear Disaster."

Indian music is accompanied by a drone, usually played by an upright gourded instrument called a *tanpura* with four or five strings, to establish each raga's tonic note, as well as its fifth. The rhythmic element of Indian music is called *tala* ("time-measure" or "rhythmic cycle") and ranges from three to more than 100 beats. Bharata's ancient text listed twenty-two talas, but many more have been created since, and continue to be added to the repertories of great Indian tabla artists. Most famous and commonly used talas are *Dadra*, a cycle of six beats divided in two equal parts; *Rupak*, a cycle of seven divided 3-2-2; *Jhaptal*, a cycle of ten, divided 2-3-2-3; and *Teen-Tal*, sixteen beats divided into quarters.

A classical instrumental group may consist of only three performers, a sitarist and tabla-drummer alternating solo improvisations, inspiring each other with the passion of their performance, and a drone sitting unobtrusively behind them on stage. Or there may be as many as six artists, generally no more. The *sitar*, a double-gourded multistringed instrument, has evolved from the ancient single-gourd hundred-stringed lute called *vina*, supposedly created by sage Narada to comfort the gods with its heavenly sounds. Anyone who has heard Ravi Shankar "breathe life" into that lovely instrument can well understand its virtuosity and remarkable range of appeal. The *sarod* is an instrument that resembles a sitar, but is more resonant, and is often played in duet with the sitar. Ali Akbar Khan, the greatest sarod artist of this century, joined Ravi Shankar in their scintillating performance at the gala opening of the Festival of India in Washington, D.C. in mid-1985. Ala Rakha, the tabla virtuoso, whose hands are so swift as he accelerates his drumbeat to reach a climax that they appear invisible, also played at that historic Kennedy Center event. Several centuries ago, violins were imported to India from the West, but are usually bowed on the floor as secondary, rather than leading, instruments. Many classical groups use a hand-pumped harmonium, called *shruti*, instead of the tanpura lute drone. The Beatles and other Western musical stars have integrated Indian music and its instruments, especially sitar and tabla, into modern global musical forms that have recently emerged from a harmonious syncretism of Indo-Western arts.

Worship in Bronze and Stone

Indian artists have celebrated and immortalized the beauty of human bodies in bronze and stone for more than 4,000 years. Hindus have always worshiped youthful gods, but their male figures have an almost feminine softness about them, and are at times hard to differentiate from Mother Goddess images. The voluptuous full-bodied fecundity of the Mother is, however, usually quite apparent in the countless naked images dedicated to her worship everywhere on Indian soil and in museums the world over. No other society, not even classical Greece or Rome, has produced so many godlike figures of humans as did India.

Our earliest bronze and stone figures date from Indus Valley times, but are few in number, enough merely to establish the dawn of an artistic tradition that reaches flood tide only after the Christian era. Metallurgic skills, stone-working caft techniques had, however, been mastered and were brilliantly practiced long before the Aryan invasions. Greco-Bactrians wrought Gandharan variations in the northwest, thanks to which we still have Hellenistic temples in Pakistan and countless Buddhas and dark stone friezes depicting the Buddha's life, where he looks more Greek or Roman than Indian.

But the mainstreams of indigenous Indic tradition that started in Mohenjo-daro and Harappa flowed underground during early Aryan times and resurfaced in the Mathura and Oriya and later Guptan schools during Mauryan and Andhran and Guptan Imperial times. Other rivers of art flowed south and burst into brilliant historic light in post-Christian Pandyan and Pallava art and in the immortal bronzes of Chola dynastic genius. There are as many regional and local variants in artistic styles of sculpture as have been noted in dance-drama and folk music, as anyone who travels into India's hinterland swiftly recognizes. Market bazaars and village crafts reflect local visages, images, and talents, even as the Hindu temple changed most dramatically from North to South and within each major region from East to West.

Although the greatest works of visual Indian art are inspired by religious worship and were designed primarily for temple, sacred cave, or palace shrine decor, those figures are mostly sensual, often sexually embracing maithuna naked beings, remarkably realistic images of youthful humans. The Buddha image and his ethereal Jain Thirtankara reflections are obvious exceptions to this general rule as to the singularly secular nature of Indic "religious" art. Buddhism and Jainism, however, as monastic faiths, would hardly be expected to foster full-fleshed sensual figures of their divinities. Mother Goddess worshiping in Hinduism is, of course, a far different sort of inspiration for artists, who, like the adorners of Khajuraho temples, were confronted with the challenge of somehow seeking to celebrate the primal power of Shakti, whose passion-born offspring fill the earth. Or how was the Bhakti-devotee of Lord Krishna adequately to depict his stunning form that excited milkmaids to abandon their chores for orgiastic pleasures as soon as they turned their lotus eyes toward the alluring sounds of his sacred flute? And where was the artist to find stone enough for Lord Shiva and his mighty phallus? Clearly, Hinduism posed challenges to Indian artists that no other faith has ever raised. No Gothic Christian attenuation of blood or bone under India's sun. No Semitic retreat before the blinding face or form of God. No Islamic iconoclasm.

The earliest full-bodied Mother Goddess images in stone are from Diganj and other North Indian sites, "watermelon-breasted" women, with hips to match their bosoms, over 2,000 years old yet as bright as their living models, seen to this day working in many a field of rural India. Modern fashion may dictate a sari-paddar draped demurely over ample bosoms at present, but Victorian British art critics were inaccurate to insist that such vital female dimensions were "obviously exaggerated idealized fertility cult figurines," as those who never visited an Indian village argued. The vital strength of Indian figurine art is in part its accurate translation of the plasticity and fullness of youthful flesh into highly polished smoothness of sandstone and marble. But it is also much more than that, for animating, inspiring Indian plastic art is Hindu faith in the re-creation of beautiful bodies locked in eternal embrace where "each is both" as the highest form of spiritual as well as sensual bliss.

To higher Hinduism and its most sophisticated devotees the "profane" is indeed sacred, even as "extinction" is the key to immortal salvation. Love is God, after all, and the union of one's soul with God, an abstraction always sought but impossible to imagine, can most nearly be experienced only in "deep dreamless sleep" or at the instant of total "extinction" reached at mutual climax in coitus. Nothing is more beautiful, more satisfying, more complete, nor closer to release. What then is more worthy of adorning a Hindu temple? How better to celebrate the perfection of God on earth, the Divine within each of us? That bliss of extinction is perhaps closest to Moksha, when one's being is momentarily transported, one's invisible self hurled to merge with that Other, whose joy reflects and responds to one's own. Art of mundane human pleasures enhances the spirituality of a Hindu temple, where all "profane" objects are part of the home of gods, and Western dualities dissolve in the river of Indian unity.

Hindu artistic celebration of human beauty and love visually depicts literary eroticism like Jayadeva's twelfth-century *Gita Govinda*, which poetically recounts tales of Krishna and his consorts. Krishna in that poem was called "*Hari*," the most common name of multifaceted sun-god Vishnu:

One cowherdess with heavy breasts embraces Hari lovingly
And celebrates him in a melody of love.
Hari revels here as the crowd of charming girls
Revels in seducing him to play.

Another simple girl, lured by his wanton quivering look,
Meditates intently on the lotus face of Madhu's killer.
Hari revels here as the crowd of charming girls . . .

A girl with curving hips, bending to whisper in his ear,
Cherishes her kiss on her lover's tingling cheek.
Hari revels here . . .

Eager for the art of his love on the Jumna riverbank, a girl
Pulls his silk cloth toward a thicket of reeds with her hand.
Hari revels here . . .

He hugs one, he kisses another, he caresses another dark beauty.
He stares at one's suggestive smiles, he mimics a willful girl.
Hari revels here as the crowd of charming girls
Revels in seducing him to play.

The wondrous mystery of Krishna's sexual play in Brindaban forest
Is Jayadeva's song. Let its celebration spread Krishna's favors![2]

Such paeans to the pleasures of erotic passion have been translated in voluptuous detail onto many a stone facade of the towering temples that still stand in tranquil beauty and isolation in a park outside Central India's Khajuraho, nine centuries ago the home of a mighty dynasty, the Chandellas, now but a village and tourist attraction. Some of the statues on those Khajuraho temples also appear to be graphic re-creations of contortionist positions of love-making described in India's earliest textbook of eros, the *Kama Sutra*,[3] attributed to Vatsyayana, who probably wrote during the fourth century of the Christian era. That sophisticated guide to mutual sexual satisfaction for women as well as men, for married as well as single lovers, has enjoyed global renown and singular sales more for its pictures perhaps than the rote listing of categories of passion and techniques of pleasure. Medieval Hindu temple art at Central India's Khajuraho and Orissa's Konarak provide outdoor visual museums on that subject for those who never read the handbooks. Many Brahmans, however, who read perfectly well also went regularly to such temples, insisting that they provide the true test of one's undeviating religious faith and inner discipline. Whoever viewed such figures without either excitement or distraction was said to be a truly devout Hindu. The "disinterested" method of action, *ḳarma yoga*, offered its practitioners still another way of viewing and appreciating such art. Hinduism embraces all opposites!

Indian artists traditionally labored anonymously, supported by temple, palace, or monastic orders, rewarded in their faith that by carving images of gods they would themselves attain merit in later lives, and perhaps, if good enough at their labors, Moksha. Nowadays, fashionable artists in New Delhi, Bombay, and Calcutta have become as famous and wealthy as their counterparts in London, New York, or Los Angeles. A Jaimani Roy or Satish Gujral are as well known and richly rewarded outside of India as within their homeland. We don't, however, know the name of a single genius among the many who created early Chola *Natarajas* as magnificent as any work by Benvenuto Cellini, or of those Indian Michelangelos who lured gods to life out of dismal mountain rock at Ellora, Ajanta, Elephanta, and Karli. Each god's icon acquired recognizable attributes to help worshipers identify him, a trident and crescent moon for Shiva, a conch and discus for Vishnu, a necklace of skulls for Goddess Kali, the flute for Krishna, a tall bow for Rama. Even the number of excess limbs or heads, over time, became iconographic clues—Brahma usually depicted with four heads, Shiva with three, and his war-god son Kartikeya with ten. The reason that India's most powerful gods required so many arms, legs, and eyes was that they all had so much to do, so many problems to resolve, so many devotees to see and care about, so many adversaries to defeat in battle. Nothing Indian is simple.

The most intricate and serenely symbolic of all Indic figures of divinity was the Buddha image, which first appeared after the dawn of the Christian era, with the development of Mahayana Buddhism and the emergence of the Bodhisattva "Savior." Dozens of major and minor symbolic "signs" (*lakshanas*) depict the Buddha's great wisdom, serenity, and enlightened power, from the raised mound of "snail-curled" hair atop his head where his "Soul" can be seen symbolically rising out of his body, to the dot of enlightened wisdom emerging from his forehead between his eyes, or the elongated lobes of his "elephant" ears and the mighty smoothness of his elephant shoulders. His hands and fingers are most carefully carved and positioned to convey the appropriate *mudra*-message, whether of Peace or "setting in motion the wheel of the Law" or to encourage his viewer to "forget fear," or remember prayer. The standing, seated, or reclining Buddha image was thus to become a visual educator of all who observed his wise and placid countenance in stone, bronze, silver, or sand, the most luminously didactic of India's many icons, with a message of peace and love destined to be noted worldwide.

Lord Shiva as Nataraja[4] rivals the Buddha image in its complex symbolism, depicting as it does the dance of life (*Nadanta*) that Maheshvira performed in the great hall of the Chola temple at Chidambaram in modern Tamil Nadu. The demon dwarf Muyalaka lies crushed under the Great God's right toe, the fire tiger's skin that he stripped with his smallest finger drapes his loins like a silk dhoti, the serpent garlands his neck that was blackened by poison nectar of the universe which he swallowed and survived. Shiva dances upon a lotus petal, symbol of Lord Vishnu's creative powers, from which springs the mandala of fire that encircles Shiva like a ring of solar energy, thus integrating in a single masterpiece of bronze art the two mainstreams of Hindu divinity, Vaishnavism and Shaivism. The Indian impulse toward reconciliation, unity, and consensus once again triumphs over its multiplicity of forms and beliefs, harmonizing polar differences, stretching its umbrella or fiery mandala over all pluralism.

The dance itself symbolizes destruction as well as creation, the end as well as beginning of the universal cycle of life, and the same Lord Shiva, in his darker aspect as Bhairava, performed what was called the *Tandava* dance of death. So we speak of Shiva as the "Destroyer" as well as the "Creator," and the Great God reconciler of universal opposites, all three of his "faces" immortalized in monumental stone, as a mighty *tri-murti* ("three-faces") masterpiece on the island of Elephanta. There are nine other enormous stone statues of Shiva and his beautiful consort Parvati carved inside that cave-temple on the museumlike island off Bombay. The trimurti alone has survived the ravages of time and conquering iconoclasts. That insular treasure temple of art dates back to the seventh century and contains one of the best preserved early examples of Shiva and Parvati integrated into a single sculpted body (*Ardhanarishvara*), the ultimate artistic unity of sexual diversity.

Perhaps the most delightful of all Indian icons is elephant-headed Ganesh, divine son of Shiva and Parvati, worshiped throughout India as the patron god of scholars, authors, and thieves. Why the first two categories should be under the same divinity as the last remains a mystery! Or is this another example of Hinduism's integration of opposites? As "Lord of Obstacles" Sri Ganesh is also the special guardian of newlyweds and should receive the first invitation to a wedding, thus ensuring that no obstacle will stand in the way of marital bliss. He has, like his father, four arms, and a trunk as well to help him accomplish his many tasks. Merely rubbing Ganesh's trunk is said to be enough to ensure good luck, while leaving flowers or fruit puja for him could bring even greater merit to the donor. Ganesh usually holds his trunk in his lower left hand, but some icons have "more powerful" right-handed trunks. Indian Civilization, like most others, seems prejudiced in a right-handed direction. Ganesh is appropriately portly, but lost one of his tusks in a terrible battle with *Parashurama* ("Rama with the Axe"), the Kshatriya-destroying avatara of Vishnu preceding Rama, who wielded his powerful weapon so indiscriminately that he was finally stripped of his divine status.

Strange as it may seem, bulky Ganesh's mount (*vahana*) is a rat, the tiny rodent generally carved or depicted somewhere around Ganesh's image. Every Hindu god and goddess has a personal vahana; Nandi the bull bearing Shiva, Garuda a golden goose-like bird holding Vishnu, Durga riding her lion, Kartikeya his peacock. The most beautiful ancient stone work was rose and white-spotted Mathuran and Guptan sculpture, and the polished black stone of Bengal. On Orissa's eastern coast, the great temples of Konarak and Bhubaneshwar were carved with figures of beauty and power worthy of sacred palaces to the sun God. To the south of those temples, the Pallava art of ancient Mahabalipuram liberated divine "chariots" from free-standing outcrops of rock along the seashore of Tamil Nadu. One rock-wall bas-relief, known as "Arjuna's penance," which shows mermaid goddess Ganga descending a natural break in the wall, has some of India's finest ancient elephants and clever cats so vividly depicted that they seem poised and ready to step from their stone facade onto an adjacent road to march toward Madras.

In the Southern heartland of Tamil Nadu are Chola bronzes from the tenth through fourteenth centuries that mark the high point of Indian art. The best of these bronzes can be seen in Madurai and Thanjanur temple museums and in Madras and Chidambaram, where priceless green-patinaed Natarajas and Parvatis, each animated with inner "breath" that makes them seem more alive than most of their lethargic guards, are preserved in awesome profusion. Many Natarajas are life-size, and appear quite prepared to whirl from their pedestals.

Pala artists of Bengal also used bronze to create lovely Buddha images, and in Nepal gold and silver were employed for the same sacred purpose in miniatures. Few of those Northern works, however, matched the graceful vital splendor and remarkable lightness, considering their size, of the Chola bronzes. Tamil artists and craftsmen have of late once again started to reproduce giant Natarajas modeled on those brilliant ancient forms, for display in modern Indian homes and export.

Caves, Temple and Regal Art, and Architecture

Buddhist and Jain monks started to carve their simple cells (*vihara*s) and meeting halls (*chaitya*s) out of mountain faces in Eastern and Central India over 1,500 years ago. By the Christian era, India's stone carvers were among her greatest artists. In Maharashtra's Deccan, at Ajanta and Ellora, they excavated almost sixty caves and turned several of them into temple worlds and museums of early Indian painting. The paintings at Ajanṭa remain the finest examples of classical Indian art. Although time has ravaged the priceless murals of every cave, vivid patches of classical Indian court life and haunting portraits of men and women, whose individuality and beauty have never faded, survive as tributes to the durability of such works of genius. The interior ceilings and walls of half a dozen caves at Ajanta were prepared with coats of cow dung and rice-husk clay covered with gypsum, and painted upon only after most of that surface dried, so we cannot call those murals true frescoes. Much of the eggshell-thick layer of paint flaked off over time, leaving a sea of blank wall around vivid islands of brilliant color and beauty.

Since the caves were primarily Buddhist, Ajanta mural scenes are for the most part depictions of stories from the Buddha's past lives, which in literary form are called *Jataka* ("Birth") stories. Mahayanists believe that for hundreds of lives prior to his attainment of enlightenment, the Buddha went through various stages of evolution and development, as an animal as well as a prince, and in each of those incarnations he learned and did things that are still useful guidelines for others. The Jataka tales are much like Aesop's fables, and must have drawn upon the same universal pool of folklore, wisdom, and experience that was passed on to Hindu children, initially reserved for royalty, in works like the *Panchatantra* ("Five Texts") and its later Sanskrit version, called *Hitopadesha* ("Instruction in Well-being"). These tales include lessons in practical behavior epitomized by such clever creatures as "Forethought" and "Readywit," whose names explain how they avoid hazards that entrap and destroy less intelligent beings like "What will be will be."

Floral and foliage motifs in rich color are found in profusion inside the painted Ajanta caves, together with palace figures and faces of merchant visitors from afar as well as Indian harem beauties and noble princes. There are also many Buddha figures and Bodhisattvas, especially *Avalokiteshvara*, "The Lord Who Looks Down with Compassion." It is impossible to photograph adequately Ajanta paintings, since part of their impact comes from the environment of the interiors of the caves themselves, generating feelings of mystery and claustrophobia literarily captured by E. M. Forster in *A Passage to India*'s "Caves" section. One of the most beautiful murals at Ajanta is in Cave X, where the Jataka tale of how the Buddha sacrificed his tusks during his previous incarnation as a white elephant is visually depicted by a splendid herd of elephants enmeshed in forest decor. Unfortunately, this cave had to be closed for many years, while the Indian Archeological Survey team photographed the walls, and sought ways to prevent further flaking of its uniquely designed surface.

The transition from cave excavation and carving to the creation of Hindu temples is most dramatically and powerfully depicted at Ellora, where an entire mountain has literally been scooped out over several centuries by patient devoted artists and architectural geniuses, who envisioned and "extracted" Lord Shiva's Mount Kailasa temple inside that enormous rock dome. Completed during the eighth century, Ellora's *Kailasantha* cave-temple remains one of the true "wonders" of the world of art and a unique monument to Shaivite devotion. The multistoried "chariot" of stone in which Shiva is worshiped rises inside the hollowed-out mountain shell, whose inner wall is also brilliantly adorned with excavated carvings of gods and goddesses. Their glacial mythical "home" atop Kailasa in the North has thus permanently been transported by art to India's torrid Deccan. There are free-standing Shaivite pillars and elephants as well as the kneeling vahana bull, Nandi, just inside the small entranceway that admits each visitor to this universe of artistic devotion, never seen from the road, only from within the shell of stone or from the sky above the opened mountaintop.

The Pandava brothers' "chariots" (*ratha*s), carved out of free-standing rocks on the Coromandal seacoast at Mahabalipuram, similarly reflect the earliest stage of Hindu temple architecture, which, like earlier cave-art, first used natural outcroppings of stone as sites of "houses" for the gods that would then become places of Hindu pilgrimage and worship. Pallava Rajas, who supported the great stonemasons of fifth- to ninth-century South India, never actually used the Mahabalipuram rathas as temples, which is why they have remained so clean and unsoiled inside. The only remaining one of the "seven" temples at the seashore at Mahabalipuram was, however, used for worship, and represents the earliest temple created out of many stone blocks, brought by its builders to the desired spot chosen for worship, where devotees could come each morning to wash away their impurities in the sea, chanting sacred mantras as Ushas sent her first blushing rays above the eastern horizon.

The Hindu temple is a microcosm and evolved over time as much more than a simple place of worship, or museum of divine art. As the palace of gods and goddesses, it became the home of their attending Brahmans as well, visited daily by devotees. Temple "cities" like Kanchipuram and Madurai in Tamil Nadu are still self-contained worlds devoted to worshiping and nurturing the gods and their caretakers. Dravidian temples were surrounded with high walls and encompassed hundreds of acres of land, their towering gilded *Gopuram* ("Cow-gate") pyramids over each major entranceway visible for miles in every direction. Temple grounds were like Mughal imperial palaces, with living quarters not only for gods and goddesses but also for their Brahmans and Devadasis, with storage areas for grain, shelter for temple elephants and tanks for bathing and washing clothes, areas for study as well as worship, and stalls for craftsmen and merchants and astrologers and artists of every variety. Beautifully painted and carved chariots for the gods were constructed and kept inside temples so that on festival days, divine birthdays, or other special occasions, the gods could be rolled out for general viewing, dragged around town and village for all to see, worship, and follow. Traditional Hindu life was temple-oriented, and most leisure time was spent in admiring, feeding, or talking about gods, who provided periodic entertainments as well as the major impetus for artistic creation.

North Indian free-standing rock and brick temples were begun during the Guptan era and have proliferated ever since. A distinctive shikara-tower rises high over the "womb house," inside which an icon of the temple's major deity is found, and to which each suppliant goes alone with puja-offerings. The Ganga is lined with temple cities, the most sacred of which is Varanasi, and each temple usually has steps leading up to its open porch, thence into a pillared hall and from there to the sanctorium of the god, where a Shiva lingam may be found waiting, or a goddess, for whom fruit or flowers or ghi are brought and left, or else coins are handed to the Brahman who circles his wick lamp and rings the temple bell to catch his icon's eye and arrest divine attention.

The modern Birla temple to Lord Vishnu in New Delhi is one of the more recent examples of North Indian Hindu architecture, garishly painted and with ornate gods and goddesses that lack the classical austerity that time and erosion have given to Khajuraho and Mahabalipuram art. Pristine Hindu temples, like ancient Greco-Roman art when first produced, appealed to popular taste. Brightly painted gods lived in overdecorated houses of stone and marble. Hindu temples vary greatly in size and quality. Some are almost ethereal in their classic simplicity, others so Baroque as to seem grotesquely ornate. But Hinduism is "alive," and its worshipers treat their gods as true royalty, begrudging them nothing, bringing them all manner of sweetmeats, jewels, flowers, and silks to their shrine-homes, celebrating their eternal and daily "victories" over demon forces of "darkness" or "untruth" that must constantly be kept at bay. In a land where so many people live in penury and pain from which there is no relief or escape, the gods enjoy eternal pleasure and plenty.

India's Rajas, and later Sultans and Padishahs, were the secular gods of this land of idols and worshipers. Even Islamic monarchs were deified once they became Indian, adorned with all the silks and jewels, idolized with floral adulation hitherto heaped upon Hindu Chakravartins and Maharajas. Muslim iconoclasm survived in theory, but virtually every Sultan of Delhi and the Deccan, and all the Mughal Emperors, including that "prayer-monger" Caliph Aurangzeb himself, were worshiped by their courtiers and soldiers and the Indian peasant mass who glimpsed their glittering entourage and golden raiment atop bejeweled elephants. "Ah, behold, His high-and-mightiness! Wonder, wonder!" Distant darshan was satisfying enough for most, a glimpse of greatness carrying one out of daily wretched reality to a higher plain of hope.

Rajput and Mughal palaces that continue to fascinate visitors to this day were built as mighty fortresses, their crenellated stone walls extending many miles round bastions of iron, stone, and marble in Delhi, Agra, Jaipur, and Jodhpur. Palaces, like temples, were self-contained cities. Under siege they had at times to support residential human and animal populations for months, possibly years. The Red Fort in Old Delhi is the best preserved example of the Mughal Empire in miniature, a bastion of martial extravagance with its marble-topped pearl mosque, harem quarters for hundreds, handsomely pillared halls of public and private audience, stables, artisan stalls, and pure-white marble private quarters for "Kings of the Universe," who showed themselves twice daily to crowds gathered along the then-uncluttered bank of the River Jumna. Slum-bustees now proliferate along rusting railroad tracks, beside red brick smokestacks of a municipal power plant in that cluttered quarter of the old city, whose ancient walls serve as foundation stones for modern middle-class homes.

Some of the most beautiful old Rajput palaces, the *Rambagh* ("Rama's Garden") in Jaipur and Lake Palace in Udaipur, are among the best of modern India's luxury hotels. The hearty sumptuous elegance of Rajput royal life, preoccupied as it was with harem and hunt, can best be glimpsed in those two capitals of leading Rajput clans, while the formidable power of that Hindu martial arm of the Mughals may best be seen from the mountaintop fortress of rugged Amber. Jaipur's city palace is another superb example of Rajput architecture at its handsomest, and houses the finest collection of Rajput and Mughal paintings in its palace museum. As one of the sixty-four "Arts" (*Kalas*) of ancient India, painting was enriched by Persian miniature artists lured to Delhi by early Sultans before the end of the thirteenth century. The blend of indigenous Indian and Persian arts is most brilliant in Mughal miniature painting, but also affected various Rajput schools

First Indian National Congress, Bombay, 1885.

M. A. Jinnah and daughter, Hampstead, London. Courtesy: National Archives, Pakistan.

Lord Louis Mountbatten and Mrs. Indira Gandhi. Courtesy: India Office Library and Records, London.

Sardar Vallabhbhai Patel with Maulana A. K. Azad. Courtesy: India Office Library and Records, London.

Prime Minister Jawaharlal Nehru. Courtesy: Nehru Museum and Library, New Delhi.

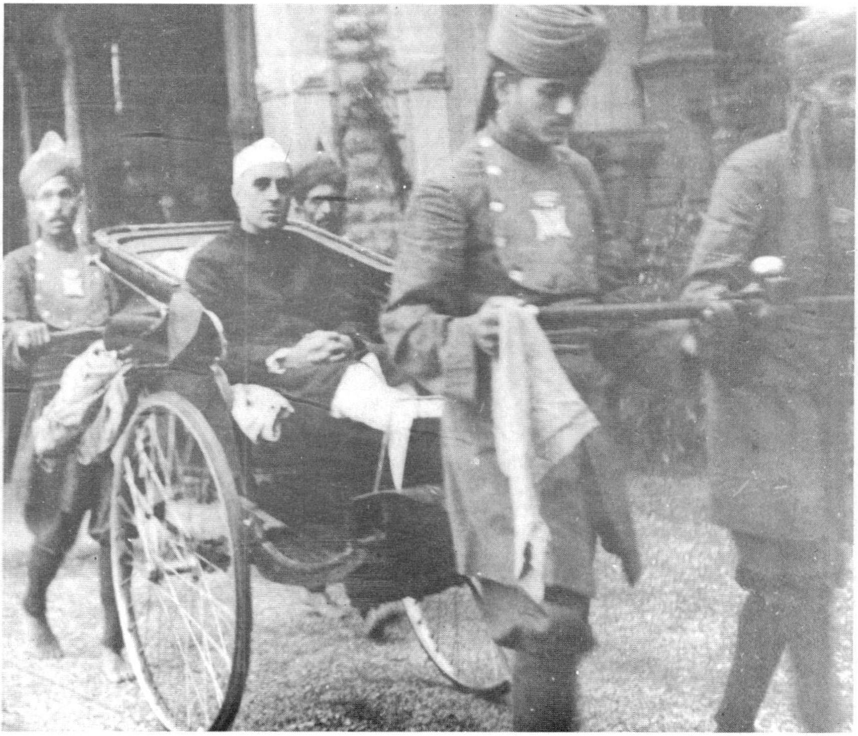

Pandit J. Nehru (Simla Summit), 1946.

J. Nehru and M. A. Jinnah. Courtesy: India Office Library and Records, London.

Lord Pethick-Lawrence and Mahatma Gandhi. Courtesy: India Office Library and Records, London.

Faces of Young India. Courtesy: Seymour M. Greenstone, M.D.

Young woman of Rajasthan. Courtesy: Seymour M. Greenstone, M.D.

South Indian Sadhu. Courtesy: Seymour M. Greenstone, M.D.

Vegetable seller with her produce. Courtesy: Seymour M. Greenstone, M.D.

Reception Committee at boat landing of the Lake Palace Hotel, Udaipur. Courtesy: Seymour M. Greenstone, M.D.

Shaivite Sadhu with beads and trident. Courtesy: Seymour M. Greenstone, M.D.

from the sixteenth through the nineteenth century. Vivid scenes of bustling palace life and the hunt dominate Mughal painting, while Rajput art is preoccupied with the loves of Krishna, portrayed as the Raja in a Rajput palace, or fluting in pastoral fields of idyllic rural life. Luminosity of color, including lavish use of gold, minute detail in every feature of human, animal, vegetative, and floral life, and harmonious balance in design rank the best of Mughal and Rajput painting among the world's finest art. Mughal and Rajput workshops, housed within palace grounds, permanently employed hundreds of artists, some of whom specialized in portraiture, others in birds, others in flowers, each contributing his special artistic talent to a composite miniature that often embodies the genius of no fewer than twenty fine artists. Although most of the artists remain unknown, and virtually all of the works that have been preserved were the product of many hands, master painters of Mughal times, Akbar's Basavan and Dasavant and Jahangir's Govardhan, prevailed over Indian anonymity. Several of Dasavant's most luminous illustrations of the Persian translation of the *Mahabharata* can be seen in Jaipur's City Palace museum.

Each of the princely states of Rajasthan patronized its own court artists; hence each developed a distinctive style or "school," Jaipur and Amber painting emerging by the late seventeenth century as quite different from that of Bikaner or Bundi, Mewar or Kishangarh. The subject matter of most Rajastani painting remained focused around Krishna and his legendary life and loves, but regional palettes and figure styles as well as general design varied so greatly that it is quite simple to distinguish one school from another. Such local variations continue in the production of regional folk arts and of modern-day reproductions of artistic classics, part of the pattern of Indian fascination with continuity and the reincarnation of works as well as people. Virtually every fine-art gallery in Jaipur or Udaipur will thus have a pool of artists in its employ currently devoting their lives to copying the masterpieces of their heritage. Even as India's Brahmans have preserved Vedic chants for thousands of years by oral tradition, her young artists today continue to preserve the beauty of her many streams of palatial painting on silk and ivory, parchment and paper, for sale in countless secular bazaars and palatially priced luxury-hotel shops.

The most majestic monuments to Islam in India are tombs. Islamic preoccupation with a Last Judgment may help account for the inordinate size of Mughal and even Sultanate burial places and the lavish expenditure of resources on houses for dead monarchs and their brides that exceed the budgets of entire cities for the living. The most famous, hauntingly beautiful of those temples to the dead, of course, is the Taj Mahal at Agra. No photograph truly captures it, since it changes in every light and from every angle, almost floating at times, glowing at others, inspiring awestruck silence or involuntary exclamation from those fortunate enough to view it with their own eyes. Yet the Taj is but one of many mausoleums that mark the final resting places of Perso-Afghan-Mughal monarchs and their wives, who once commanded India's millions and may have believed, as Egyptian Pharaohs did, that they deserved as much eternal adulation lying immured as they had enjoyed while ambulatory. Humayun's Tomb in Delhi and Akbar's at Sikandra are larger and in some details more beautiful, as is Itimad-ud-daula's smaller tomb at Agra; yet none matches the overall perfection of proportion or purity of white marble that make the Taj so unique a world monument of art. The grounds on which the Lodi Sultans of Delhi erected their uglier, heavier, oppressive stone tombs have recently been converted into a "park" for Indian joggers and strollers, thanks to a grant from the Ford Foundation and the far-sighted planning by Prime Minister Nehru. The grounds at Lodi Estates are at least used by the public, surely the best legacy to India of that otherwise oppressive, hardly memorable Afghan dynasty.

India's oldest reliquary monuments are stupas, built to hold some portion of the Buddha's ashes. The largest, most famous stupas are at Sanchi, near Central India's Bhopal, dating from the second century B.C. The great egg-shaped hemisphere over 100 feet in diameter is a pile of cut stones set over a solid mound of earth that covers the reliquary urn. Buddhist monks circumambulate the stupa in a clockwise direction, chanting mantras and turning prayer wheels as they walk, counting off each full turn on their beads, accruing merits to help them attain Nirvana. The "little square house" at the top of the stupa-egg symbolizes four-quartered heaven to which the Buddha's "soul" could escape after rising through an air shaft left inside the mound. Atop the heavenly-*harmika* were several tapering umbrellas that may have inspired the architecture of the Chinese pagoda, after Buddhism migrated over the diamond path–silk route to East Asia. The Dharmek stupa in Sarnath, Varanasi's archaeologically rich suburb, is another fine example of this type of monument, and dates from about the first century of the Christian era. There are many stupas in Kashmir and Nepal, as well as

Bhutan and Sikkim. Buddhists the world over visit India to view and circumambulate them.

Islamic mosques are found throughout most of India, from Kashmir to Mysore. The largest, most famous of those magnets for Muslim worship is Jama Masjid in Old Delhi, the vast courtyard of which fills with devout Muslims every Friday at noon. Minarets on either side of the great screen rise above Old Delhi's crowded bazaar and an army of vultures hover in trees near the meat market outside. The piercing cry of the prayer leader's voice amplified as he recites verses from the *Qur'an* echoes across the old city, reverberating over the road that separates Jama Masjid from the Red Fort and its now filled-in moat. In Pakistan's Lahore, capital of the Punjab, a twin Masjid attracts Pakistani thousands to Friday prayers. All who thus gather to bow and rise in unison face Saudi Arabia's Makka (Mecca) with its precious Black Stone, reciting: "*La Illaha'Ullah'ilaho. . . .*"

The Sikh Golden Temple at Amritsar has been the center of Sikh worship since its completion by Guru Arjun late in the sixteenth century. *Guru Granth Sahib*, the Sikh bible, is draped in white linen and sits on a golden pedestal inside the Golden Temple sanctuary, Harmandir Sahib, set like a jewel in the middle of the sacred pool within the huge square temple wall with its golden towers over each entranceway. Since the early eighteenth century that *Granth Sahib*, the compiled wisdom of the Gurus, written in their cursive script, has been worshiped by Sikhs the world over as their most sacred treasure. It is the Islamic *Qur'an* and Black Stone of the Sikh faith, and the Golden Temple is the Sikh equivalent of the Catholic Vatican. Harmandir Sahib must only be approached by Sikhs in bare feet, and the marble pathway on which they walk is generally washed with cool water by employees of the Temple complex. In June 1984, however, it was drenched in blood.

The Art of Literature

Indians have always worshiped "sacred utterances" (*Brih*) as divinities incarnate, Brahmans. Story-telling has, moreover, been a fine Indian art since the creation of Epics *Mahabharata* and *Ramayana*,[5] some 3,000 years ago.

Indians love a good story, and thanks to their prodigious powers of memory Brahman bards have captivated countless attentive ears with tales of gods and demons, heroes and villains, enrapturing village audiences of every age and stage of life to this day. Valmiki, author of the *Ramayana*, was a wandering bard inspired to recite his great Epic when he saw a hunter shoot down a dove, and watched its heartbroken mate fly in anguished circles over that corpse. Valmiki was so moved by what he saw that he sat pondering the cruelty and poignant beauty of life until his body was covered by an anthill. Luckily, before the ants could destroy him, Valmiki started to move reciting his inspired story of love and devotion, pain-filled separation and loyalty, heroism and treachery, war and death, and the ultimate victory of Righteousness.

Kalidasa, whose name means "Slave of the Goddess Kali," was the greatest secular author of classical India, a poet-dramatist, of whose life we know virtually nothing more than that he lived at the time and under the patronage of a Raja "whose effulgence was like the Sun's," presumably Chandra Gupta II, around the turn of the fourth century. Rightly renowned for the "sweetness" of his work, Kalidasa must have traveled widely throughout India and was sensitive to all the beauties of nature and of India's women. One of his poems, "Cloud-Messenger," is a panegyric to both. A forlorn lover, anticipating the wireless by many centuries, sends his message of longing from his Vindhya mountaintop exile on a cloud's wings to his bride on distant Himalayan heights.

"The lonely lover's pain . . . choking down his tears . . . poor wretch. . . . Longing to save his beloved's life, With joyous tidings, through the rainy days, He plucks fresh blossoms for his cloudy guest. . . . And bravely utters words of greetings and of praise. . . . 'O cloud. . . . My bride is far away. . . . Bring her my message. . . . Yet hasten, brother, till you see. . . . The faithful wife who only lives for me: A drooping flower is woman's loving heart, Upheld by a stem of hope when two true lovers part."[6] For all his singular sensitivity, Kalidasa reflected chauvinist Indian male beliefs about female "drooping flowers."

In his shorter poem, "Seasons," Kalidasa matched weather conditions to lovers' feelings, starting with summer's "Pitiless heat. . . . When love that never knows its fill, Is less demanding, dear."[7] Rain, on the other hand, "advances like a Raja . . . his thunder like the ring of royal kettle drums. . . .

The clouds, a mighty army. . . . To you, my dear, may this cloudy time bring all your heart's desire . . . every pleasure perfect, To set my bride on fire."

Only three of Kalidasa's plays have survived the perils of time. The earliest of that trio, *Malavikagnimitra*, is a court comedy about two lovers, Malavika and Agnimitra, rather reminiscent of Shakespeare's *Much Ado About Nothing*. His other less well-known play, *Vikramorvashiya*, "Urvashi won by Valor," is a re-creation of an Epic myth about valiant Pururavas who falls hopelessly in love with the divine nymph Urvashi. She marries him only on condition that she must never see him naked. Of course, when she does, Urvashi leaves her poor husband and returns to high heaven. He is never happy again till their reunion, which follows his death.

Kalidasa's greatest work is named for its heroine, *Shakuntala*.[7] The best Sanskrit work of dramatic art, this tragic-comic love story has been translated into every major language and is almost as well known outside of India as the *Mahabharata*, from whose inexhaustible Epic forest the original dramatic seed was borrowed. The virginal heroine, captured by King Dushyanta on his "hunt," is left with only his "token" ring and his embryonic son. Abandoned by her husband-lover, the distracted Shakuntala fails to heed a pious Brahman's appeal for a drink on a hot day, and the curse he hurls at her is that he with whom her mind was so preoccupied (King Dushyanta) as to ignore the cry of a stranger in need, would forget her when next she called out to him. Karmic retribution! So on her way to visit her husband-king in his palace, the much-pregnant Shakuntala stops to wash her hands in a stream, and thus loses his ring, without which King Dushyanta fails to remember her. The story sounds trite, but Kalidasa animates his characters with passion-blinding love and the all-too-human foibles that bring more pain than pleasure as the aftermath of their bliss. As great Goethe himself put it after first reading *Shakuntala*: "Willst du den Himmel, die Erde, mit einem Namen begreifen; Nenn'ich, Shakuntala, Dich, und so ist Alles gesagt." ("Would you capture heaven and earth with a single name? I say to you then, *Shakuntala*, and all is said!")

Many other classical Sanskrit plays have endured the test of time, but none has the universal appeal of Kalidasa's best work. Shudraka's fifth-century "Little Clay Cart" (*Mrichakatika*) offers interesting insights into Guptan society and ancient Indian legal procedures, and its poor hero, Charudatta, is human enough, a married merchant who falls hopelessly in love with a courtesan. That same theme is as common in later Indian literature as it was to become in the West. Unlike married women, Indian courtesans were trained in all sixty-four classic arts, singing and dancing as well as painting and playing. A picaresque "Ocean of Stories" (*Katha Saritsagara*) dates back at least 2,000 years into the fabled ancient jungle of Indian legend, but was first rendered in abridged Sanskrit by Budhasvamin in the seventh century, and later by Somadeva in the eleventh. The novel, then, is hardly a new genre in Indian literature. Its full flowering, however, comes only after the growth of popular Indo-Aryan and Dravidian regional languages during the nineteenth and twentieth centuries.

Classical Dravidian Tamil literature dates back to the dawn of the Christian era, and is to South Indian culture almost as sacrosanct as ancient Sanskrit works remain to the Hindu North. The ancient Tamil grammar, *Tolkappiyam*, is prerequisite to translating the several thousand ancient Tamil devotional and love poems, composed around Madurai in Tamil Nadu during the first five centuries of the Christian era. These poems, both sacred and secular in content, are still memorized by Tamil Nadu students today and help impart to South India's more than 50 million Tamils a deep sense of cultural identity and unity rarely matched in any other region of India. There are even two epic poems in Tamil, dating from the sixth century, the first called *Shilappadigaram* ("Jeweled Anklet"), followed by its sequel, *Manimegalai*, the heroine's name. The first epic is the tale of a weak merchant, Kovalan, and his singularly powerful wife, Kannagi, the prototypical Tamil Nadu matriarch. Infatuated Kovalan falls so desperately in love with a dancing-girl prostitute that he gives her all his wealth, including one of his wife's jeweled anklets. The latter looked exactly like anklets owned by the Pandyan queen, which had just been stolen; thus poor Kovalan is arrested and killed by royal guards. When Kannagi learns of her husband's death, her wrath is so fierce as to bring divine fires of retribution down upon the king himself, and his entire royal city is consumed by flames of righteous fury. Kannagi herself dies, but then is reunited with her husband in heaven, and subsequently worshiped as the Mother Goddess throughout Tamil Nadu, where women are generally viewed as much stronger and wiser than men.

Bhakti devotional poetry in the Dravidian tongues Tamil, Telugu, and Kannada merged after the twelfth century with similar northern Indo-Aryan mainstreams that flowed from Bengal to Kashmir, from Rajasthan to

Maharashtra. Almost equally divided among Shaivite and Vaishnavite sects, these religiously inspired poetic artists of "medieval" Indian literature addressed countless *shlokas* (Sanskrit verses) of love to the divine forms of Krishna and Rama, Shiva and Parvati. Persian Sufi poets added a current of Islamic mystic worship to waves of devotional verse that mounted from every corner of the continent. Sultans of Delhi and later Mughal Emperors of Agra spread Perso-Arabic poetry and prose with their swords of Islamic conquest and conversion. One of the great early poets of modern Hindi was, in fact, a Persian Muslim, Amir Khusrau, who lived in North India in the late thirteenth and early fourteenth century. Khusrau, a disciple of the Sufi saint Nizam ud-din Auliya, is credited with having composed over 200,000 couplets in Hindi, Urdu, and Persian.

India's national language, Hindi, has evolved since the twelfth century as a blend of many North Indian dialects, from Rajasthan to the borders of Bengal. In spoken form, Hindi is much the same tongue as Pakistan's national language, *Urdu*, the language of the "camp" or "army." Urdu, however, is written in Perso-Arabic script from right to left, whereas Hindi is the *Devanagari* ("City of the Gods") script used for Sanskrit, written from left to right. Although most Indians and Pakistanis speak the same language, very few of them can read anything written in the national script of the other, adding walls of linguistic isolation to barriers of religious difference and distrust that divide those neighbors. The most popular early themes for books written in modern Indian languages, no less than fifteen of which have been granted official recognition in India's Constitution, were drawn from the Epics. Most highly acclaimed of all Hindi authors, Tulsidas (d. 1623), is best known for his "Mountain Pool of Rama's Deeds," *Ramacharitmanas*. Similar translations, abridgements, and in some respects rewriting of that Epic tale are found in modern Tamil and other Dravidian languages, where the "demon" king of Lanka, Ravana, is depicted in a far more sympathetic, brighter light.

Modern Bengali literature antedates Hindi and Urdu, and emerged by the nineteenth century as the first regional literary language of India in which popular works of fiction as well as newspapers were published. The latter were inspired by English, injected most vigorously into the intellectual life of Bengal after the East India Company established its headquarters in Calcutta in the late eighteenth century. Young Bengali intellectuals, like Ram Mohan Roy, learned English in the service of the Company Raj, and communicated with their elite peers in that language as well as their native tongue. Roy's *Brahmo* "Society" (*Samaj*) became the premier cross-cultural seedbed of ideas that helped transform Calcutta after 1830 into the center of Anglo-Indian culture as well as the capital of a bustling mercantile empire. Young Bengali writers and social reformers such as Ishvara Chandra Vidyasagar (1820–1891) and Bankim Chandra Chatterji (1838–1894) followed in Roy's trail-blazing path, awakening Bengali readers to reborn pride in their own culture and nascent nation.

The passionate novels of Bankim Chandra, especially *Anandamath* ("Abbey of Bliss"), published in 1892, became thinly veiled battle-cries in prose extolling freedom. India's first National Congress anthem, *Bande Mataram* ("Hail to Thee, Mother") was, in fact, a poem from Bankim Chandra's most famous novel, set to music by Rabindranath Tagore. Tagore himself wrote many novels, plays, and short stories, several of which have been filmed by India's greatest film-maker, Bengali Satyajit Ray. Ray's 1985 film, *The House and the World*, about a young Bengali couple at the turn of the century caught between the two cultures that alienate them from their roots and each other, is based on a Tagore novel.

The first Partition of Bengal, from 1905–1910, stimulated a flood of revolutionary literature that poured from young Bengali revolutionaries like Bipin Chandra Pal (1858–1932) and Arabinda Ghosh, who dedicated their lives to the struggle against British rule, fighting for their motherland. Passionate poetry, ardent political pamphlets, religious treatises poured forth, flooding "golden" Bengal with their whispered cries and secret messages channeled through 10,000 underground streams of political activism. "Our opposition to the division of Bengal was fierce," recalled Nirad C. Chaudhuri in his brilliant *Autobiography of an Unknown Indian*. "The Press, that kept woman of Demos, egged us on against partition. . . . I still remember a cartoon in a Bengali newspaper . . . which showed Lord Curzon sawing a live woman."[8]

"S. N." ("Surrender-Not") Banerjea, venerable leader of the Bengali opposition to the first Partition, had told India's National Congress a decade earlier, when he presided over its 1895 session: "To England we look for inspiration and guidance. To England we look for sympathy in the struggle. . . . England is our political guide and our moral preceptor in the exalted sphere of political duty. English history has taught us those principles of freedom which we cherish with our lifeblood." Congress's first President in 1885 was another English-educated Bengali, W.C. Bonnerji, who reminded that inaugural session of the movement that would lead to India's independence: "Much has been done by Great Britain for the benefit of India, and the whole country is truly grateful to her for it. She has given them order, she has given them railways, and, above all, she has given them the inestimable blessing of Western education." It was the English language that young India cherished most ardently and adopted most passionately as its very own. Students of Burke, Mill, and Morley emerged from Bengal's best schools and colleges as Shakespeare-wallahs as well as ardent revolutionaries.

Young India's intellectuals emerged by the twentieth century as bilingual, but many of them focused on their native languages as the primary medium for their literary creativity. Yet, as Bankim Chandra Chatterji himself warned: "There is no hope for India until the Bengali and the Panjabi understand and influence each other, and can bring their joint influence to bear upon the Englishman. This can be done only through the medium of English."[9]

Of the many English authors who wrote poetry and prose about India, two tower over the rest, Rudyard Kipling (1865–1939) and E.M. Forster (1879–1970). Kipling was the poet of the Raj at its strongest; Forster, the prophet of its demise. Kipling's experience of India, like his literary output, was much greater, in years and number of works at least, than Forster's, who visited India only three times, twice briefly, and has left us only two books about those insightful passages. Most of Kipling's works illuminate the life of English Tommies in their "barracks" on the Frontier, or of British bureaucrats and their interminable "files," or are plain "tales" from the Punjab or fascinating yarns like "The Man Who Would Be King." *Kim*, however, proves that Kipling knew not only the British in India, but India's India as well. His "White Man's Burden" remains, however, the epitaph for an Empire on which the sun was to set far faster than either Kipling or his Col. Blimp brothers of the White Man's Club ever dreamed it would. Kipling's love–hate relationship with India epitomized more of the post-Mutiny mentality of British paternalistic feelings toward their "Native-children" than did any other poem of the Raj-that-failed. As he so trenchantly put it:

Take up the White Man's burden
The savage wars of peace
Fill full the mouth of Famine

And bid the sickness cease;
And when your goal is nearest
The end for others sought,.
Watch Sloth and heathen Folly
Bring all your hope to nought.[10]

Kipling and his cohorts truly believed that it was "heathen Folly" more than British arrogance or greed that brought the early demise of their comrades in Empire, who were often "fools" enough to try to get Natives to "hustle" and work a bit harder even in the "noon-day Sun." As another Kipling gem put it:

And the end of the fight is a tombstone white,
with the name of the late deceased,
And the epitaph drear: "A fool lies here
who tried to hustle the East."

Forster's *Passage* was, of course, quite another cup of tea. He viewed Anglo-India as an "outsider," falling in love with a young Indian Muslim, Syed Ross Masood, rather than any British Regiment or romantic idea of Imperial Raj. Forster's passionate devotion to his Indian friend started in 1906, when he was hired by Theodore Morison to tutor Ross in Latin, to help prepare the grandson of Sir Sayyid Ahmad Khan, founder of Aligarh, for Oxford. Ross would become E. M.'s inspiration for the Dr. Aziz character in his great novel about Anglo-India that was published in 1924, and dedicated to his dearest Indian friend. Forster first visited India for a few months in 1912, and met the young Maharaja of Dewas Senior, Tukoji Rao III, at that time. He returned to serve the Maharaja as his Private Secretary after World War I, and that second and longest of his visits inspired him to finish *A Passage to India* shortly after he went home. His diary and letters to the Maharaja were published as *The Hill of Devi*.[11]

His last visit, in 1945, was to address a PEN (International Association of Poets, Playwrights, Editors, Essayists and Novelists) Congress. He never returned to India, wrote no more of any importance about it, yet the luminous insights his finest novel provide into Anglo-Indian relations and mutual misperceptions are undimmed by time. In the characters of Cyril Fielding and Mrs. Moore, Forster created twin sounding-boards for his own personal humanistic and religious feelings of love, empathy, and attraction toward Indian Civilization. In Aziz, moreover, he developed another part of himself, and Ross. As Ross often said of him, E. M. was "Oriental" at heart. He dressed in the silks and jewels of his friend, the Maharaja, and shared the smoke of his hubbly-bubbly together with his Dewas Senior palace. To Forster, moreover, India remained a "mystery"—"ou-boum" its insoluble echo-equation. The final cry of Aziz at the end of *Passage* is "Clear out, all you Turtons and Burtons . . . India shall be a nation!" But Forster and Fielding know better: "India a nation! What an apotheosis! Last comer to the drab nineteenth century sisterhood! Waddling in at this hour of the world to take her seat!"

> Aziz replied: "'Down with the English anyhow. That's certain. Clear out, you fellows, double quick, I say. We may hate one another, but we hate you most . . . we shall get rid of you, yes, we shall drive every blasted Englishman into the sea, and then'—he rode against him furiously—'and then,' he concluded, half kissing him, 'you and I shall be friends.'"
>
> "'Why can't we be friends now?' said the other [Fielding], holding him affectionately. 'It's what I want. It's what you want.'"
>
> "But the horses didn't want it—they swerved apart; the earth didn't want it, sending up rocks through which riders must pass single file; the temple, the tank, the jail, the palace, the birds, the carrion, the Guest House, that came into view as they issued from the gap . . . didn't want it, they said in their hundred voices, 'No, not yet,' and the sky said, 'No, not there.'"[12]

Forster's last word on India, then, seems to reiterate the iron law of Kipling's "East is East, and West is West, and never the twain shall meet!" For E. M., the gap, however, was both more universal and more personal. Ross had married and was surrounded by friends and family. What proved unbridgeable for him and E. M. was their love, man to man. Yet to generations of young Indian intellectuals, like novelist Mulk Raj Anand, the final message of *Passage* was political, "that there could be no friendship between Indians and Englishmen until Indians were free." For them, Forster's greatest work exposed all the pretentiousness, all the sham and hollowness of British bureaucrats and their shallow ladies of the Club, the "Burra Sahibs" and the "Mems," who grew stiffer each year they spent among the "Natives," desperately seeking to drown their fears and inadequacies with gins and tonics and "bridge parties."

Mulk Raj Anand's first great novel, *Untouchable*, was published a decade after *Passage*, and the author credited E. M.'s "sympathy" (Forster wrote the preface) with inspiring him to finish that fine book about a single day in the life of an "outcaste" young sweeper, named Bakha, who cleaned the latrines of his town. Before the end of this book, Mahatma Gandhi comes to Bakha's town and the young Untouchable sits perched on the branch of a tree close enough to see the Mahatma and think, "He is black like me." Gandhi prays, then speaks, and Bakha is all ears and he hears:

> If there are any Untouchables here . . . they should realise that they are cleaning Hindu society. . . . They have, therefore, to purify their lives. They should cultivate the habits of cleanliness, so that no one shall point his finger at them. . . . In order to emancipate themselves they have to purify themselves. They have to rid themselves of evil habits, like drinking liquor or eating carrion. . . . If they are able to do all that I have asked them to do, they will secure their emancipation.[13]

For young Bakha those words prove a powerful incentive. He derived "a queer kind of strength" from just thinking about the Mahatma's face. He goes to tell his father all he has heard, all that has started him thinking about ways to change his life. The next year, Mulk Raj Anand published his equally powerful and much longer *Coolie*,[14] a tragic story of the life of Munoo, a rickshaw coolie, who worked like a horse without enough rest, food, or shelter, and died prematurely of tuberculosis.

India's greatest modern novelist, R. K. Narayan of Madras and Mysore, published his first work, *Swami and Friends*,[15] in 1935. Set in his fictional world of Malgudi, a South Indian town that greatly resembles his home in Mysore, Narayan's gentle, subdued characters lead unobtrusive lives like those of his own family and friends. Indeed, in many ways, his *Bachelor of Arts* and *English Teacher* are stories from R. K.'s own quiet life and human experiences, as his later autobiography, *My Days*, confirms. Narayan's most famous and widely acclaimed novels, *The Financial Expert* (1952) and *The*

Guide, led to his well-deserved nomination for a Nobel Prize. The heroes of both stories are, each in his own way, "charlatans," who win fame and fortune by the "magic" of their "artistry," much to their own amazement as well as amusement of others, until the bubble of life's Maya-world bursts for each of them, as it must for all of us. But believing in reincarnation, R. K. Narayan never leaves his characters or audience in the depth of penury, or despair, for the wheel moves on and up again, even as Brahma's day follows the darkest night, and Shiva's creative dance comes in the wake of universal destruction, stirring the very cinders of death back to vibrant life.

Some of India's most brilliant modern authors emigrated from that country as children and have spent most of their lives abroad, yet write poignantly and with deep insight about Indian Civilization. Ved Mehta's first autobiography, *Face to Face*, was finished in 1956 before that remarkable young author headed for Oxford. Although blinded at the age of three, following a long bout with meningitis, Ved's creative sensitivity to color, form, and every facet of light has remained far clearer and brighter than that of most people with perfect vision. His courage was clear from the first page of his first book, where he noted: "It was good that I lost my sight when I did, because having no memories of seeing, there was nothing to look back to, nothing to miss."[16]

V. S. Naipaul was not even born in India, but in Trinidad of Indian parents, yet the powers of Indian Civilization remain potent for generations, as Naipaul's perceptive *India: A Wounded Civilization* proves. "The customs of my childhood were sometimes mysterious," Naipaul noted. "I didn't know it at the time but the smooth pebbles in the shrine in my grandmother's house, pebbles brought by my grandfather all the way from India with his other household gods, were phallic emblems. . . . In India I know I am a stranger; but increasingly I understand that my Indian memories . . . are like trapdoors into a bottomless pit."[17] Similar trapdoors open as well for the characters in Salmon Rushdie's brilliant *Midnight's Children*,[18] and for Anglo-Indians in Paul Scott's remarkable Raj Quartet, from *The Jewel in the Crown*[19] to *The Day of the Scorpion*, through *The Towers of Silence* to *A Division of the Spoils*. For there is no fathoming India, no plumb line long enough to touch solid soil under her dark, deepest waters. Only the silence—or the echoing *o-boum*.

Scientific Contributions

India's contributions to the sciences of mathematics and medicine have been unique. In other sciences, especially linguistics, metallurgy, and chemistry, Indians made trail-blazing discoveries. Several Indian scientists, mostly physicists and mathematicians, have been honored with Nobel Prizes or made Fellows of the Royal Society, among them Sir C. V. Raman, Dr. Homi Bhabha, Sir J. C. Bose, and Dr. M. N. Saha.

Medicine appears to have been the oldest Indian science, its roots going back to Yoga practices, which stress a holistic approach to health, based primarily on proper diet and exercise. Ancient Indian texts on physiology, much like those of Galen and others in ancient Greece, identified three body "humours"—wind, gall, and mucus—with which were associated the *sattva* ("true" or "good"), *rajas* ("strong"), and *tamas* ("dark" or "evil") "strands" of behavior, as primary causal factors in determining good or ill health. Six "tastes" (*rasas*) were associated with different foods, some good for certain illnesses, others for others. Meats of every sort, viewed as *tamas*, were to be avoided. Honey was identified as *amrita*, the elixir of "immortality." Garlic was believed to have special powers capable of prolonging life as well, and since traditional ancient Indian medicine, *Ayurveda*, focused on longevity, honey and garlic were often prescribed. Gold, silver, and mercury were also believed to have specially potent powers, as were a wide variety of herbs listed in ancient India's pharmacopoeia. Some of these medicinal herbs or plant oils have indeed proved to be cures for specific diseases. Oil from the bark of chaulmugra trees remains the most effective treatment for leprosy. Indian yogis emphasized the importance of the spine to the body, but knew nothing about the powers of the brain, believing that the "seat of intelligence" was in the heart.

India's oldest scientific medical text is attributed to Caraka (*Caraka Samhita*), court physician to King Kanishka in the first century of the Christian era. This treatise includes material dating from at least the second century B.C. and may incorporate the work of a much older physician, named Atreya, who according to Buddhist texts taught medicine in Taxila, near Pakistan's present capital, Islamabad, during the age of the Buddha. Caraka is credited with having saved Kanishka's wife by attending her during the difficult delivery of her first child. His treatise consists of eight chapters, starting with a section on pharmacology, diet, and the ethics of a good doctor, where he warns: "You must not betray your patient, even at the cost of your life. . . . Nothing that happens in the house of a patient can be recounted outside, nor may you report your patient's condition to anyone who might do him any harm by virtue of that knowledge, which is your sacred trust." His second section deals with eight major diseases: diarrhea, fever, dropsy, consumption, tumor, abscess, leprosy, and skin diseases. In his sixth chapter on special treatments, Caraka diagnoses and prescribes treatment for jaundice. He also wrote chapters on general pathology, general therapy, anatomy, embryology, and special nourishment for patients. The one major modern medical subject totally ignored by Caraka is surgery, of which he was obviously innocent.

The fourth-century *Sushruta Samhita*, "Treatise of Sushruta," is India's first medical text to include surgery, with two chapters on surgical instruments and one on modes of operation. Sushruta, an ingenious court physician in Guptan Imperial times, used Caesarean section for difficult deliveries and performed cataract operations and plastic surgery, including rhinoplasty and such complex operations as the reconnection of severed ears and noses as well as fingers and limbs. Sushruta lists no fewer than 125 different surgical instruments that he used for his varied operations. Indian surgeons were the first to develop effective techniques for transplanting skin flaps, still used the world over as basic plastic surgical procedure. By Sushruta's era, amputations and abdominal sections were commonly performed, compound fractures set, and sophisticated puncturing, probing, extraction, drainage, and suturing techniques for surgical operations were all described. Surgeons were required to learn anatomy by dissecting corpses. In preparing for operations, patients were urged not to eat, and "refreshed" with cool water after surgery was completed. Sushruta noted fourteen different kinds of bandages, applicable to different parts of the body, used for various operations. Tight bandages could be tied on a patient's buttocks, thighs, and head; "medium tight" bandages on the face, arms, legs, and belly; "loose" bandages on eyes and joints, and no bandage at all on wounds caused by burning or cauterization or poison. By Sushruta's era, Indians had hospitals, where, according to visiting Buddhist Chinese testimony, anyone who required medical treatment would be admitted freely.

Veterinary science had developed into an Indian medical specialty by that early era, and India's monarchs seem to have supported special hosptials for their horses as well as their elephants. Hindu faith in the sacrosanctity of animal as well as human souls, and belief in the partial divinity of cows and elephants helps explain perhaps what seems to be far better care lavished on such animals than on so many of India's poorest people. Elephants, cows, and horses remain, moreover, extremely valuable and generally very useful to their owners. A uniquely specialized branch of Indian medicine was called *Hastyayurveda* ("The Science of Prolonging Elephant Life"). Special treatments were prescribed for various elephantine illnesses, and to this day Indians continue to pride themselves on their care for and knowledge of elephants, as well as cows.

India's oldest medical texts were far superior to most subsequent works in that field. Increasing Hindu preoccupation with religiophilosophic idealism inhibited scientific studies of anatomy, and lack of sterilization or antisepsis soon diminished the effectiveness of Indian surgery and hospitals. Herbal and holistic medical treatments have, however, remained valuable contributions of Indian medicine, and the utility of Yoga in helping to keep bodies sufficiently strong and fit to ward off infectious diseases is now much more generally recognized throughout the West.

Mathematics is the science to which Indians have contributed most. Our decimal system, place notation, numbers 1 through 9, and the ubiquitous 0, are all major Indian contributions to world science. Without them, our modern world of computer sciences, earth-launched satellites, microchips, and artificial intelligence would all have been impossible. Thus Indians have not only taught us how to count but have also endowed us with the capability, thanks to high-speed calculators and computers on new weapons-systems, to destroy our entire world and all of its civilized achievements unless we first manage to control ourselves and one another's rapacious greed.

Like many ancient peoples, Indians initially focused mathematical attention on the stars and developed geometric techniques for squaring the circle and circling the square, allowing them to construct sacrificial altars, designed to propitiate the gods. Indians thus early became proficient at astronomy and remain addicted to astrology. But they went much beyond all that, probing the study of pure numbers for its own sake, devising algebra with their simple numerical notation system. Before the end of the fifth century, a remarkable Indian mathematician named Aryabhata compiled his great treatise, called simply *Aryabhatiya*, in which he calculated Pi (π) at 3.1416, and discussed for the first time subjects such as numerical square and cube roots, sines, arithmetical progressions, factors, and algebraic identities.

This important early work also discussed spherical astronomy, leading to the emergence much later of spherical trigonometry, even as Aryabhata's quest for more abstract methods of reckoning than Ptolomy's chords of a circle led to the emergence of trigonometry, through sines. Ingenius Aryabhata also noted that earth's shadow was responsible for the waxing and waning of our moon, and concluded that our planet must constantly rotate around its own axis, while the moon was rotating around us.

For at least 1,500 years Indians have led the world in understanding pure numbers and their characteristics. An untutored Kerala mathematician named Madhava developed his own system of calculus, based on his knowledge of trigonometry around A.D. 1500, more than a century before either Newton or Liebnitz. More recently, intuitive Indian mathematical genius Srinivas Ramanujan (1887–1920), a friend to all numbers, was invited to Cambridge by Professor G. H. Hardy, who recognized his brilliance at the sight of his first equation solution. Julian Huxley called Ramanujan "the greatest mathematician of the century." At the age of thirty he developed a formula for partitioning any natural number, which led to the solving of the Waring problem, expressing an integer as the sum of squares, cubes, or higher powers of a few integers. As Ramanujan lay dying of tuberculosis, Hardy, who was so depressed at seeing his young friend when he came to visit him in the hospital, remarked morosely, "It's such a dull day! Even the number on the cab that brought me here was dull—1729." Ramanujan responded instantly, "No, Hardy, 1729 is a *wonderful* number! That is the only number which is the sum of two different sets of cubes, 1 and 12, and 9 and 10."

The science of linguistics owes much to the brilliant ancient Sanskrit grammarian, Panini, whose fourth-century-B.C. *Ashtadhyayi* ("Eight Chapters") was the first scientific analysis of any alphabet. Panini's letters are arranged according to the places within the head and neck from which each sound originates, from vocatives to dentals and plosives. His grammar was the world's first morphological analysis of words. Brahmanic powers in committing entire Vedas to memory focused Indian attention upon the anatomy of language. Panini was surely not the first brilliant Indian to dissect his Sanskrit compounds, breaking down those often lengthy words to bare roots, studying changes in each case, mood, person, tense, and number, analyzing prefixes and suffixes. He did, however, devise over 4,000 rules to teach others what he had learned. Until the midnineteenth century, in fact, Panini's great grammar remained the best standard guide to the study of Sanskrit, an inspiration to students of language everywhere. Even Otto Bohtlingk and Rudolf Roth, whose monumental Sanskrit-German Dictionary, called the "St. Petersburg Lexicon" because it was published by the Russian Imperial Academy of Sciences from 1852 to 1875, owed a great debt to Panini's remarkable "Eight Chapters."

Sir William Jones (1746–1794), who went to India as chief British justice of the Supreme Court of Calcutta, was also founding-father of the Asiatic Society of Bengal in 1784. That premier organization stimulated the renaissance of scientific studies in India. Its most distinguished Indian Fellows included Sir Jagdish Chandra Bose (1858–1937) of Calcutta, who studied natural science at Cambridge and returned to teach physics in Calcutta, and was one of the first scientists to link up the botanical and physical sciences. Bose's electric radiator and high-magnification Crescograph polarized electromagnetic waves through double refracting crystals, and could actually detect a change in plant growth rate of one millionth of a millimeter per second, induced by the opening or closing of a single window in his laboratory.

Sir Chandrasekhar Venkata Raman (1888–1970) was elected to the Royal Society in 1924 for his original research in physics, focusing on the molecular scattering of light, a subject with which Albert Einstein was also preoccupied. Raman's experiments with differing diffusions of light through transparent bodies led to his conclusion that scattered light changed wavelengths, the exact dimensions of which depended on the molecular structure of the substance doing the scattering. This phenomenon has come to be known as the *Raman effect*, and merited a Nobel Prize in Physics in 1930, the first ever won by an Asian. Raman directed the Indian Institute of Science at Bangalore from 1933 to 1943, after which he started his own Raman Research Institute in the same city. He received India's highest honor, *Bharat Ratna* ("Jewel of India"), from the President of India in 1954.

Bombay Parsi Homi J. Bhabha (1910–1966), founder of the "Cascade" theory of cosmic-ray showers, was elected a Fellow of the Royal Society in 1941 and appointed Director of the Tata Institute of Fundamental Research four years later. Much like our Bell Laboratories, the Tata Institute is India's premier center of scientific research, so it was hardly surprising when Prime Minister Nehru chose Dr. Bhabha to chair India's Atomic Energy Commission and to serve directly under him as Secretary to the Government of India's Atomic Energy Department, from 1954 until Nehru's death a decade later. Bhabha himself died in a plane crash in Switzerland in 1966. Dr. M. N. Saha (1893–1956) of Bengal was another great Indian nuclear scientist, whose study of stellar atomic truncation or ionization helped clarify our understanding of outer space. Dr. Saha's equation proved most important in the transmission of radio waves and formation of arcs. He was the first Indian scientist of international reputation ever elected to the Lok Sabha and took an active role until his death in supporting India's economic development, vigorously advocating more scientific use of wasted resources, especially hydroelectric power, to tackle the scourge of poverty.

In 1958 Prime Minister Nehru's Government adopted a "Science Policy Resolution" that affirmed "an inherent obligation of a great country like India . . . to participate fully in the march of science, which is probably mankind's greatest enterprise." More than a decade later, Dr. Vikram Sarabhai (1919–1971), Ahmedabad's leading industrialist-scientist and Prime Minister Indira Gandhi's Chairman of Atomic Energy, confessed that "most of us are largely dissatisfied with the role that science is currently playing in promoting national goals." Sarabhai himself had organized India's space research program, setting up her Thumba Rocket Launching Station and Experimental Satellite Communication Station at Ahmedabad, advising India's Cabinet on things scientific. "The social culture of an organisation is influenced mainly by the men who are in it," Sarabhai warned shortly before his death. He continued:

> It is because of this that one despairs. . . . There is a need for a constant interplay between the basic sciences, technology and industrial practice if economic progress is to result. . . . We have today in India an excellent infrastructure for undertaking complex tasks involving science and technology. . . . It is now clearly necessary to translate the broad national goals into precise objectives to be realised in two, five and ten years.

Twenty years after his death, however, many such precise objectives appeared to remain ever-receding goals. What had gone wrong? Why were Indians, so ingenious in scientific theory, so deficient in the practical and technological applications of such ideas toward alleviating their own most urgent social, political, and economic problems?

Polity and Foreign Policy

Long years ago we made a tryst with destiny, and now the time comes when we shall redeem our pledge. . . . At the stroke of the midnight hour, when the world sleeps, India will awake to life and freedom. A moment comes, which comes but rarely in history, when we step out from the old to the new, when an age ends, and when the soul of a nation, long suppressed, finds utterance.

—Jawaharlal Nehru to India's Constituent Assembly, New Delhi, August 14, 1947

With over 400 million eligible voters, India is the world's largest democracy. It is also a federal republic of twenty-five states and several centrally administered Union Territories. The Center (Central Government), ruled from New Delhi, has full control over almost 100 of India's most important matters, including defense and foreign affairs, and shares a "Concurrent List" of almost fifty subjects with state governments, retaining residual powers for matters unlisted in the Constitution. State administrations control agriculture and land revenue as well as police and public welfare, some sixty items in all, but remain clearly subordinate to New Delhi's authority in most areas and during any emergency interlude.

In emulation of Great Britain's model, New Delhi's Government of India is led by a prime minister and cabinet responsible to the *Lok Sabha* ("House of the People"), equivalent to Britain's House of Commons, whose approximately 550 members each represent more than a million constituents and belong to one of India's some two dozen political parties. The nominal head of state is India's President, but he is a virtual figurehead, except during rare intervals of emergency or change of government, elected indirectly by elected members of Parliament and state assemblies. The prime minister usually has power enough to choose a specific candidate for presidential office, as Mrs. Gandhi did in 1969, when she backed Vice-President V. V. Giri against her own party's candidate and again in 1982, when she chose her loyal Home Minister, Sikh Giani Zail Singh, to stand for President.

India's ninth general election since adoption of her Constitution in 1950 was held in November 1989. Over 5,000 candidates competed for the more than 500 Lok Sabha seats in the nation's most hard-fought, violent election, which left more than 100 people dead, wounding several candidates. Rajiv's government seemed determined to hang onto power at any cost. But the man whose political rise came with his reputation as "Mr. Clean" ended his half decade in premier office tarnished with the label "Mr. Kickback," leading his party to lose more than half its coveted seats in the Lok Sabha. V. P. Singh's Janata Dal ("People's Party") led a "National Front" against Rajiv's corrupt dynastic rule, rallying most of the splintered opposition from the Hindu-communal Bharatiya Janata party (BJP) on the right to the major Communist parties of the left to agree to field a single candidate in each Lok Sabha constituency against Congress incumbents. India's electorate, thus offered the choice of retaining Rajiv and his cohort for another five years of empty promises or opting for change, chose to try the new broom. V. P.'s courage and integrity appealed to India's masses, for, like ancient Rama, he was a "Raja" who did not hesitate to abandon power and enter the wilderness to wage war against demons of corruption and waste as evil as Ravana. India's Epic conflicts were replayed in every generation. What better arena for the struggle of good against evil, moreover, than the national stage of elections? Rajiv's fall ended the Nehru-Gandhi "Dynasty" that had managed quite remarkably to retain premier power in the hands of a single family of Kashmiri Brahman Pundits for no less than thirty-eight of independent India's forty-two years of freedom.

Congress was once again displaced by Janata as the name of the new ruling party in the new National Front, for *Janata* means "People," after all, and in modern India the people are sovereign. Yet V. P. himself had long served within the Congress party, as had several of his most important and trusted cabinet colleagues. Inder K. Gujral, the brilliant new Foreign Minister, had served as Indira Gandhi's Minister of Information and Broadcasting, Housing, Planning, Communications, and Parliamentary Affairs, before he resigned from her cabinet in the wake of her declaration of "Emergency Raj" in 1975. Arun Nehru, the new Minister of Commerce and Tourism, was also an old Congress hand, as well as Indira's cousin, who had been both in her cabinet and in Rajiv's, before he quit the latter to join V. P.'s crusade. Maneka Gandhi (b. 1956), the new Minister of Environment and Forests, had challenged her brother-in-law Rajiv unsuccessfully in the previous elections, feeling herself to be better qualified to inherit her husband Sanjay's political mantle after his fatal plane crash, as she may indeed soon prove to be.

So the more India's central government changes, the more some may say it appears to stay the same, but every round in the struggle of the forces of Good against Evil does seem to release vital energies that make some things better, if not sufficing to solve overwhelming problems. Nor would India's vast population know how to deal with too dramatic a change, for continuity itself is considered a virtue, and lineage, antiquity, inherited rank, the right family, are all traditional assets. V. P.'s fearless principled exposure of Rajiv's incompetence or corruption won him considerable support among urban intellectuals, but his inherited title of Raja probably helped secure more votes from the peasant majority of his own constituency. The past-perfect remains modern India's most popular tense, as the happy producers of Delhi's endless Epic TV replay of the *Ramayana* well know!

Kingship and Democracy

"Man should first select a King," one ancient Indian text advised, "and only after that should he select a wife, and earn wealth. For if he has no King to protect them, what would become of his wife and wealth?" Rajas were required both for protection and to enforce punishment. "The whole world is kept in order by punishment," Manu's sacred law code noted, "for a guiltless man is hard to find."

For 2,000 years, possibly twice as long, Indian polity has thus been primarily monarchic. The Sanskrit word for king, *Raja*, came to mean "Government" as a whole. Even under the British, the word *Raj* was used for Imperial "Rule." Modern India's Hindi word for "Politics," *Rajaniti*, literally means "leadership of Kings." Rajas were considered at least partially divine, and even great Mughals, like Akbar, continued that tradition, being "worshiped" by their people. Raja Rama, of course, was the Epic prototype of the perfect Hindu King. "Even an infant Raja must never be despised," one ancient text warned, "for he is a great deity in human form." Traditionally, a bad king was considered better than none, since without monarchic rule chaos could reign, then the "law of fishes" might prevail on earth, much to the sorrow of all the little ones.

Despite the primacy and antiquity of monarchic power, Indian Rajas and Maharajas were urged to heed advice of "wise Brahmans," and wield their "Rod" (*Danda*) of punishment with restraint, in accord with religious "Law" (*Dharma*). Even Chanakya cautioned ancient Rajas against the pitfalls of totally autocratic rule. "A single wheel cannot turn," he warned, "therefore, a Raja should appoint advisors and listen to them." His *mantriparishad* was more a "privy council" than a modern cabinet; still, the most autocratic of monarchs was expected to listen to others and restrain his passions as well as appetites:

> By conquering the six enemies—lust, anger, greed, vanity, haughtiness and exuberance—a Raja acquires balanced wisdom. He should keep the company of wise Brahmans. . . . He should exercise control over himself, learning sciences. He should help his subjects acquire wealth and be good to them. By controlling his impulses, a wise Raja will abstain from taking the women or the property of his people.

From earlier Vedic times, Rajas at least had two "bodies" of advisers, one called *Sabha*, a "Chamber" or "House," as in Lok Sabha; the other called *Samiti*, another sort of "Council." Buddhist sources state that tribal "republics" were common in northeastern India during early Buddhist times, although the nature of such presumptive "democracies" remains unclear. Indian villages have long enjoyed *Panchayat* ("Council of Five") rule together with Headman leadership, but traditional Panchayats were certainly most conservative.

Liberal ideals of representative government and concepts of social and economic democracy were introduced to India by British Utilitarians, Positivists, and Evangelical missionaries during the early nineteenth century. Tides of nationalism rose in the final decades of that century, and half a century of annual meetings of the Indian National Congress resounded with countless cries for freedom, equality, and the entire lexicon of democratic rights, civil liberties, and social and economic justice. Many eloquent leaders preceded Jawaharlal Nehru at the helm of Congress, but none was more outspoken in advocacy of democratic rights and freedoms. Jawaharlal first became President of Congress in 1929, succeeding his ambitious father, Motilal. As a barrister of the Inner Temple and graduate of Harrow and Trinity College, Cambridge, Jawaharlal felt no reticence about telling British viceroys and ministers exactly what he thought of them. As a Fabian Socialist and Indian Nationalist, what he thought and demanded were usually opposed to what they did and were ready to grant to India. Nehru presided over the All-India Trade Union Congress in 1929, a month before he delivered his presidential address to Congress. Jawaharlal told his Trade Union fellows:

> It is the system that is wrong, the system that is based on the exploitation of the few and the prostitution of labour . . . which is the natural outcome of capitalism and imperialism and if you would do away with this system you will have to root out both capitalism and imperialism and substitute a saner and healthier order. . . . It will not profit you much if there is a change in your masters and your miseries continue. You will not rejoice if a handful of Indians become high officers of the State or draw bigger dividends, and your miserable conditions remain. . . . You want a living wage and not a dying wage.

Jawaharlal had charisma. He was handsome, eloquent, brilliant, idealistic, romantic, dynamic, yet always a very private person. He had countless followers, admirers, courtiers, but few friends, no confidants, other than his daughter, Indira, during the last lonely decade of his life. In 1937 he wrote an interesting "anonymous" letter about himself, on the eve of his third re-election to preside over Congress, cautioning:

> Men like Jawaharlal . . . are unsafe in a democracy. He calls himself a democrat and a socialist . . . but a little twist and he might turn into a dictator . . . he has all the makings of a dictator in him—vast popu-

> larity, a strong will, energy, pride. . . . His conceit is already formidable. It must be checked. We want no Caesars.

He quickly admitted authorship, and the letter was seen as nothing more than a clever joke.

Jawaharlal also authored the *Purna Swaraj* ("Complete Independence") resolution that was enthusiastically adopted by his Congress followers at Lahore in December 1929, and became the first plank of the Congress platform on January 26, 1930, subsequently celebrated as Independence Day and, after 1950, as Republic Day:

> We believe that it is the inalienable right of the Indian people, as of any other people, to have freedom and to enjoy the fruits of their toil and have the necessities of life, so that they may have full opportunities of growth. We believe also that if any government deprives a people of these rights and oppresses them the people have a further right to alter it or to abolish it. The British government in India has not only deprived the Indian people of their freedom but has based itself on the exploitation of the masses, and has ruined India economically, politically, culturally, and spiritually. We believe, therefore, that India must sever the British connection and attain *Purna Swaraj* or complete independence.

The following year Congress met in Karachi, and Nehru once again drafted the most important and popular historic resolution on Fundamental Rights and Economic Policy, carried by acclamation in August 1931. It assured "Every citizen of India . . . the right of free expression of opinion, the right of free association and combination, and the right to assemble peacefully and without arms." It further promised that "Every citizen shall enjoy freedom of conscience and the right freely to profess and practice his religion, subject to public order and morality," and that "All citizens are equal before the law, irrespective of religion, caste, creed or sex." In that 1931 Resolution "universal adult suffrage" was promised, and two decades later became the basis for choosing India's first administration. Other noble promises were made by Congress in 1931, including that "The State shall safeguard the interests of industrial workers and shall secure for them . . . a living wage, healthy conditions of work, limited hours . . . and protection against the economic consequences of old age, sickness, and unemployment." Women and children workers were promised special protection; "an equitable adjustment" was promised in the land tenure and revenue systems to provide "relief to the small peasantry" and an end to "serfdom" and relief of "agricultural indebtedness" and protection for "indigenous industries." All those promises were made in that single resolution, summing up Nehru's and Congress' ambitions and aspirations for a "free" India that was to eliminate all wrongs and hardships inflicted on the land and its people by alien British rule.

Nehru's words and dreams, Nehru's leadership and personal example of courage and long-suffering incarceration, inspired millions of youthful followers in the struggle that brought Freedom with Partition, India's "wooden loaf," as Mahatma Gandhi called it shortly before his own death. Jawaharlal Nehru took charge of India's government that midnight hour in mid-August 1947, and Sardar Patel was his deputy. Nehru's voice remained resonant, his words as full of promises as ever before. The first prime minister of free India told his followers in Delhi's Constituent Assembly that evening:

> A moment comes, which comes but rarely in history, when we step out from the old to the new, when an age ends, and when the soul of a nation, long suppressed, finds utterance. It is fitting that at this solemn moment we take the pledge of dedication to the service of India and her people. . . . The service of India means the service of the millions who suffer. It means the ending of poverty and ignorance and disease and inequality of opportunity.

First, however, there was an undeclared war to be fought against Pakistan for Kashmir, from whose mostly Muslim state Nehru's family traced their ancestry, whose Himalayan vale would soon be invaded and ravaged by plundering Pathan tribals. There were also five million or more refugees to be resettled, and a marginal economy depressed by Partition to be rebuilt.

Still, "Democracy" was promised by Congress, and universal adult suffrage was written into the Constitution of the Republic of India adopted in January 1950, by "We, The People of India" who "resolved to constitute India into a Sovereign, Democratic Republic and to secure to all its citizens: Justice, social, economic and political; Liberty of thought, expression, belief, faith and worship; Equality of status and opportunity; and to promote among them all Fraternity assuring the dignity of the individual and the unity of the Nation." India's first general election took four months to complete, starting in December 1951. Merely preparing lists of the names of 173 million Indians, who were qualified to vote, was a monumental task, especially since over 80 percent were illiterate. More than 17,000 candidates from fifty-nine parties filed for the 3,800 seats in state assemblies and central Parliament to be filled by democratic choice. Nearly 200,000 polling booths had to be built, 600 million ballots printed, most of which were eventually stuffed into over two million ballot boxes, since each candidate then had a box of his own. Millions of women voters refused to identify themselves other than as someone else's "wife" or "daughter." Each party used a visual symbol—Congress, yoked bullocks; the Communists, a sickle and grain—so that illiterate voters, whose fingerprints were taken, would know where to make their mark.

Nehru led his party to victory, Congress securing some three-quarters of the seats in the Lok Sabha, though only forty-five percent of the total votes cast. The majority of votes nationwide were dissipated among many competing smaller national and provincial parties. The Congress manifesto reflected Nehru's Socialist ideals, and Jawaharlal himself was his party's major campaigner, covering more than 30,000 miles in only 43 days, personally addressing an estimated 30 million Indians in that pre-TV era. His goal and that of his party and government, Nehru insisted, was "freedom of the masses of India from want." Nehru was Congress' leading asset. Other than Mahatma Gandhi, his was the only name recognized by most Indians. Millions called him "*Panditji*," Nehru's honorific Brahman jati-title, or *Chacha* ("Uncle") Nehru. He was idolized, adored by tens of millions, whose first question when they arrived at polling stations was, "Which is Panditji's party?" He was, after all, Mahatma Gandhi's chosen heir. His appeal to most Indian intellectuals was also great. Only a small group of doctrinaire Marxists or ideological Capitalists rejected Nehru's humanistic socialism, which advocated a "leveling-up" of incomes, rather than a class-conflict–based leveling-down or laissez-faire policy. His political dhoti tails proved powerful enough to carry 362 Congressmen into the Lok Sabha on that first round of voting.

Congress candidates, of course, were chosen by central party and state machines, rarely reflecting Nehru's idealism, intelligence, or nobility of heart and mind. They were politicians who belonged to the right jatis and paid their dues to the right local and central committee bosses of Congress.

They had tilled the soil of political wards well, labored in provincial vineyards until they proved their loyalty and worth, or spent the requisite time in British jails, or married into the right family, as Feroze Gandhi, Nehru's son-in-law, did when he married Indira in 1942, later to be elected to the Nehru Family Lok Sabha seat of Rae Bareilly, as was his son Rajiv. India's democracy, like most, was thus subject to private pressures and purchases, favoritism and nepotism, bossism and corruption of every political variety.

Nehru himself was incorruptible. He had more power than he could possibly use and the wisdom to realize that power and impotence went hand in hand. In a radio-broadcast speech on December 31, 1952, Nehru wondered aloud:

> Ours is a wonderful inheritance, but how shall we keep it? How shall we serve the country which has given us so much and make her great and strong? We should adhere to the high principles which have always formed the background of Indian thought from the days of the Buddha to our own day when Gandhiji showed us. . . . In India, the first essential is the maintenance of the unity of the country, not merely a political unity but a unity of the mind and the heart, which precludes the narrow urges that make for disunity . . . in the name of religion or those between States. . . . Our economy and social structure have outlived their day and it has become a matter of urgent necessity for us to refashion them so that they may promote the happiness of all our people in things material and spiritual. . . . We must aim at a classless society, based on co-operative effort, with opportunities for all.

Jawaharlal led his Congress party to victories in two more national elections. His charisma barely faded. In 1957 Congress won 371 Lok Sabha seats when their standard-bearing prime minister was sixty-eight years old. Five years later his majority slipped by only ten seats. By 1962, however, Nehru was starting to look and feel his age, yet remained bolstered by his bright, attractive daughter, leader of Congress' "ginger group" youth movement, and her nation's official "hostess." Since 1958, Nehru had begun to talk publicly of a "a deep malaise" in Congress, which reflected perhaps his own gnawing sense of failure at transforming India, as he'd once hoped it might be transformed, soon after freedom came. "Has success itself loosened the fibre which gave strength to the Congress in the past?" asked the one Indian who best knew how hollow most official reports of economic growth and development were, how slow, in fact, the process of change remained. "Our discipline is weakening and without discipline no organization can function effectively," Nehru warned.

A year later he asked in a lecture in New Delhi:

> What is India? . . . We have the growth of nuclear science and atomic energy in India, and we also have the cow-dung age. In the tumult and confusion of our time, we stand facing both ways, forward to the future and backwards to the past, being pulled in both directions. How can we resolve this conflict and evolve a structure for living that fulfills our material needs and, at the same time, sustains our mind and spirit?

He offered no facile solutions, but argued, seeking as much to convince himself perhaps as those who heard him:

> We have accepted socialism as our goal not only because it seems to us right and beneficial but because there is no other way for the solution of our economic problems. It is sometimes said that rapid progress cannot take place by peaceful and democratic methods. I do not accept this proposition. Indeed, in India today any attempt to discard democratic methods would lead to disruption and would thus put an end to any immediate prospect of progress. The mighty tasks that we have undertaken demand the fullest co-operation from the masses of our people. . . . The problem before us is ultimately to change the thinking and activities of hundreds of millions of people, and to do this democratically by their consent.

Nehru's last years in office were darkened by the Chinese invasion and his own increasing fragility, a combination of kidney and circulatory weakness that ended with a ruptured aorta and death on May 27, 1964. Indira was with him to the end, and there is good reason to believe that Nehru hoped she would succeed him immediately to the office of prime minister. Indira was only forty-seven at the time, however, and had neither Lok Sabha nor cabinet experience, although she had presided over the Congress party. She was, moreover, a widow, and her two most powerful competitors for her father's mantle, Lal Bahadur Shastri (1904–1966) and Morarji Desai (b. 1897), refused to offer her support. Morarji later reported that Nehru had, in his last days, sent a "message" inviting Desai to serve as Indira's deputy prime minister, if he would support her as Premier. Morarji was negative, however, and Shastri was apparently never approached with a similar request.

Although less officious than Morarji, Lal Bahadur was at least as ambitious. A loyal, hard-working Congress leader all his life, Shastri clearly considered himself best qualified to follow in Nehru's footsteps. Born to a Kayastha jati in Varanasi, tiny, frugal Lal Bahadur looked a bit like Gandhi and modeled himself on the Mahatma. He was jailed early and often during India's freedom struggle, like Nehru spending seven years behind British bars. As Congress general secretary from U. P., Lal Bahadur proved his mettle at the self-effacing hard labor of party organization work. He asked for little and took nothing for himself. His honesty and integrity were as rare in Indian politics as was his diligence. His memory for names, faces, facts, and human weaknesses was also remarkable. In virtually every respect he was the ideal number-two man, and Nehru found him most useful in dealing with Congress deputies during the 1951/52 campaign. He was India's first cabinet minister to resign his post at the head of transportation after a tragic rail crash in 1956. He subsequently returned to more powerful positions, including the Home Ministry, where he commanded India's more than half million police. Nehru trusted him, although Indira had her doubts for many years as to just how "selfless" Lal Bahadur actually was.

Shastri's brief premiership was probably the most democratic interval in recent India's history, since he lacked Nehru's charisma and sought fairly to arbitrate among factions within his own cabinet as well as various regional interests representing diverse states. He even invited Indira Gandhi into his cabinet as Minister for Information and Broadcasting, a relatively minor position that she endowed with much more prestige and glamor than it ever enjoyed before or since. In many ways Shastri epitomized India more than either Nehru or his daughter did. He looked, spoke, and behaved, after all, like the "average" Indian, and even spun and wove some of his own cloth. He believed devoutly in the Mahatma Gandhian tradition of useful hand labor. "I am a small man and believe in small projects with small expenditure so that we get quick results," Shastri informed his first cabinet, shifting development priorities to hand-loom and cottage industries, away from steel and heavy manufactured goods. No general election was held during Shastri's interlude of "collective Syndicate leadership," but his popularity seemed to be quite high when he died of heart failure in Tashkent, after reaching agreement with Pakistan in the aftermath of the second undeclared Indo–Pak War of 1965.

Indira Gandhi might not have been elected prime minister following the ten days of national mourning after Shastri died had it not been for the powerful support she received from Congress President K. Kamaraj Nadar of South India. Kamaraj had been a loyal lieutenant of Nehru's and knew of Panditji's dreams for his talented daughter. He also believed that she would be far more friendly and manageable than her arch-rival, Morarji Desai, who was hardly the sort of man anyone except his own son could manipulate. Indira seemed so much sweeter and easier. He knew, of course, that she was not the "dumb doll" some old Socialist party "friends" called her. But Kamaraj hoped she would prove more malleable and grateful for the way he "managed" her election as Lok Sabha leader. Morarji refused to back down from an open succession struggle. The Congress Parliamentary party met in New Delhi and elected Indira by more than twice the votes cast for Morarji. On January 24, 1966, Mrs. Gandhi took her first oath as India's prime minister. She was forty-nine. Her elder son, Rajiv, was twenty-one; his brother Sanjay, eighteen.

Asked how she felt as a "woman" prime minister, Mrs. Gandhi replied: "I'm no feminist, I'm a human being. I don't think of myself as a woman when I do my job. According to the Indian Constitution, all citizens are equal. . . . I'm just an Indian citizen and the first servant of the country." She proved, in fact, to be stronger and shrewder than any man in her cabinet or party. Kamaraj soon learned, as Morarji had, that he could not boss her around, intimidate, or defeat her, once she made up her mind. She was singularly tenacious, as much the "born" leader as her father had been. She was less talkative than Nehru, less profligate with her time. She suffered few fools, had little small talk. Nor was she really ideological, although she could speak Socialist rhetoric as well as her father had. Her fatal weakness was her passion for power and her unbridled ambition for herself and her sons.

Famine and internal conflict in the northeast impelled Indira to fly to Washington two months after she took office, seeking desperately needed food grains and financial assistance. She received both from President Johnson in return for her promise to devalue the much-inflated rupee, agreeing also to more intimate Indo-U.S. educational and cultural ties. Indira and LBJ responded to each other warmly during that March visit. Before Prime

Minister Gandhi flew out of Washington she said: "I trust there will always be a touch of spring in Indo-American relations." But devaluation cut so deep that India's ensuing inflation almost toppled Mrs. Gandhi's government. Then Vietnam became such a disastrous bog of blood that Indira's India soon turned away from Washington toward Moscow for superpower friendship and support. Kamaraj and other Congress bosses started to lose confidence in Indira's judgment after the devaluation debacle, and urged her to invite Morarji into her cabinet as Deputy Prime Minister and Finance Minister. Morarji enjoyed the confidence of Indian financiers, bankers, and industrialists, many of whom were his fellow Gujaratis. Indira feared and hated her rival, however, and fought her first general election in 1967 without him.

The result was a narrow victory for Congress in Lok Sabha, its majority reduced from over a hundred to a bare minimal twenty seats. The loss of eight state assemblies, moreover, made that election seem like a national vote of no-confidence in Congress. Kamaraj himself was ousted from Parliament, as were other Syndicate mughals. The party was disheartened, the nation fragmenting politically into regional power bases that had no coherence, little relation to one another, and the economy continued to deteriorate. Kamaraj and several other old-guard bosses of Congress convinced Indira to take Morarji into her cabinet as Deputy Prime Minister and Minister of Finance. But Morarji had no magic panacea for the near-fatal stag-flation that crippled India's economy far more than it did stronger western European and American economies. What Morarji advised was to end inhibiting government regulations and controls over Indian banks and industries and personal incomes, stimulating the private sector of India's mixed economy. Indira, however, opted for a more vigorous larger public-sector economy, favoring nationalization of more banks and insurance companies and imposing stricter limits on landholdings and personal incomes as well as corporate profits, and terminating former princely purse-pensions. In 1969, Mrs. Gandhi thus decided to turn "left" rather than "right," cutting the silver cord that had tied her to the Congress old guard. She forced Morarji to resign by personally taking control of the finance ministry. Indira pushed her own candidate, V. V. Giri, for election as President of India, against the Congress party's candidate Sanjiva Reddy, leading to her expulsion from Congress for "indiscipline." Instead of meekly accepting that blow, Indira fought back.

Before the end of 1969, Congress split into its "Indira" and "Morarji" wings. Mrs. Gandhi knew that to retain power she had to appeal to the enfranchised mass of Indians over the heads of those who so jealously guarded Congress' machine. She forged a new left-wing coalition with other parties, including several small Socialist and Communist factions with members in the Lok Sabha, and with powerful state parties demanding greater autonomy, especially in Tamil Nadu in the South, among Sikhs in Punjab, and with Muslims in Kashmir. It was stormy petrel, but Prime Minister Gandhi was politician enough to know that she had no other way of retaining power, since most of her father's former comrades, and all the Maharajas whose pensions she cut off in 1969, turned against her. She had her own "natural" constituency of India's women, and courted ex-Untouchables as well as minority Muslims, Sikhs, and Tamils. She also appealed to India's growing landless and impoverished peasant mass. She was a progressive person, sensitive to the mass suffering and poverty she saw wherever she went in India. In good measure her "ruthlessness" was a product of her impatience with incompetence, venality, and stupidity of lesser officials in every branch of government. She had traveled the world over with her father, after all, and knew how things could and should be done to stimulate change. Only in India, nothing changed fast enough to keep up with the new mouths to be fed.

Indira took her single platform campaign of "Abolish Poverty" to the people in 1971, dissolving the Lok Sabha early to seek a new mandate, and won with a comfortable majority of 352. It was her peak year of power in foreign policy as well, for by mid-December the Indian Army easily defeated Pakistan in the east and Bangladesh emerged as an independent republic. For the next year or two Indira was hailed by many of her followers as the Mother Goddess incarnate. Soon the slogan "Indira is India, and India is Indira!" became popular. By 1973, however, as inflation ran rampant, fueled by rising OPEC (Organization of Petroleum Exporting Countries) oil prices, Indira's popularity waned, especially among fixed-income middle-level bureaucrats and college students. Peasants also felt the economic pinch, and throughout much of India poverty appeared to be winning rather than facing imminent elimination.

From Bihar to Gujarat, riots and strikes spread from early 1973 to mid-1975. A surprising coalition of Indian capitalists, banking interests, poor peasants, landless laborers, and Socialist students joined forces as tides of disaffection from "Indira's Raj" mounted across the land, led by Morarji Desai and Jaya Prakash (J.P.) Narayan (1902–1979). The new *Janata* ("People's") movement had a single slogan and purpose, "Oust Indira!" She was viewed by many of India's elder statesmen and venerable leaders of the nationalist struggle as a "dangerous dictator," alternately called a "Communist" and a "Fascist." Charges of electoral malpractice had been brought against her in Allahabad's High Court by her defeated opponent, Raj Narain, and although most of them were dismissed as too trivial, or for insufficient evidence, two were sustained in June 1975. That very week, Indira's Congress candidate lost an important by-election in Gujarat, and Mrs. Gandhi's political fortune seemed bankrupt. If her Allahabad conviction was confirmed by India's Supreme Court, she would be required by law to resign her office and hold no future elective position in government for six years. Indira's senior cabinet colleagues advised her to "step down" until her appeal was decided, turning over her portfolios of power to a "temporary troika" among them.

Indira Gandhi's ambitious younger son, Sanjay, however, urged his mother to fight her "enemies" rather than surrendering to them. Whether his advice echoed or anticipated her own position, Indira chose to act upon it, opting to call on her President to proclaim a national state of emergency, thus suspending India's Constitution rather than her own career. Morarji and J.P. had called for nationwide protests against Mrs. Gandhi's Raj, indeed, announcing a Gandhian Satyagraha campaign to be launched on June 26, 1975. The night before that, however, Indira's special police force struck, arresting all Janata leaders, pulling circuit-breakers on all power lines in the region of Delhi where every newspaper was published so that none could appear the next day, then convening her cabinet to tell them what she had decided, after instructing her President as to what he should do. It was a busy night for her and Sanjay.

"The decision to have emergency was not one that could be taken lightly," Mrs. Gandhi later told her listeners, "but there comes a time in the life of the nation when hard decisions have to be taken. When there is an atmosphere of violence and indiscipline and one can visibly see the nation going down." True enough, perhaps, yet it had also been true before her own conviction of "malpractice." As it had been true before her party lost an election. Why had she waited so long? "I do admit that had I taken action earlier it would have been less drastic action."

Not since the days of British rule had Indian jails filled so fast with venerable leaders of the old Congress and the Nationalist movement. Many were quite ill, among them J. P. Narayan, who kept a *Prison Diary*, published in 1977 by Bombay's Popular Prakashan under that title. "Here was I trying to widen the horizons of our democracy," J. P. wrote from his prison cell that wretched July in 1975. "I went wrong in assuming that a Prime Minister in a democracy would use all the normal and abnormal laws to defeat a peaceful democratic movement, but would not *destroy* democracy itself and substitute for it a totalitarian system. . . . Events have shown that my mistake was in assuming that, whatever Mrs. Gandhi's personal inclination, it would not be possible for her to become a dictator. First, I thought that the people would not allow it and she would have no courage to go ahead. . . . Well, events have proved me wrong."[1]

More than 100,000 Indians were jailed without trial, held without due process for more than a year, kept behind bars in their own independent nation, by their own government. Every opposition party was banned. All newspapers and radio broadcasts were totally censored. Sanjay personally read the editorials and lead articles of many major papers before they could be run. Nothing negative was ever written or implied about Indira or her son or their Emergency Raj. For twenty-one months India's trains ran on time! There were fewer strikes, less absentee "illness," less smuggling, hoarding, blackmarketeering, fewer complaints against government officials. Fear motivated millions of Indians to greater efficiency. Police were free to do as they liked, especially with young prisoners, "troublemaker" students, and political "activists." A chill climate of silent terror gripped many Indian homes, for no one knew who might be listening, recording, reporting "treasonous" remarks. Sanjay's "eyes and ears," his hoodlum friends in power, were everywhere. "We all have ideas about our children," Mrs. Gandhi once wrote. "Some parents do all they can to force their children to develop in a particular way. But they cannot. Each child has his own personality. . . . This also applies to one's country. No matter what one wants and what one does for it, it develops in its own way."

"I had always believed that Mrs. Gandhi had no faith in democracy, that she was by inclination and conviction a dictator," wrote J. P. from prison. "My belief has tragically turned out to be true." But then, in January 1977, she relented, ordering the release of aged Morarji and ailing J. P. and many of their followers, finally calling for new elections—only a year late. But Janata rallied, and that March India's voters flocked to polling booths in response to J. P.'s cry to vote now or possibly never again. Janata promised "Bread and Freedom!" with the warning that the alternative might be "Slavery!" Most Indians chose "freedom," and Morarji Desai rode to power with a handsome majority in the Lok Sabha, where Congress was reduced to a mere 154 members, neither Indira nor Sanjay among them. What an opportunity for progressive change! Indians could speak their minds again, unafraid of police bullying or detention. Janata wasted its golden mandate, however, using precious months in petty haggling among elderly party chiefs over the loaves and fishes of power each of them labored to preempt for himself. The only true "freedom" restored by Janata was laissez-faire. Prices and profits rose dramatically again as inflation ran away. A year of useless sweeping with Morarji's old broom made Indira's Emergency Raj look better and better. At least Mrs. Gandhi's government had "worked." Fear of prison and police had compelled people to arrive at their factories and offices promptly. Fear obviously had its advantages. Ancient warnings of Manu and punishments prescribed by Chanakya may have been wiser and more appropriate than all this imported democracy and freedom in a land of so many languages, castes, creeds, and classes, so long ruled by Maharajas, Shahs, and Padishahs!

Little more than two years after the Janata tide washed Mrs. Gandhi from her pinnacle of New Delhi power, a new "Indira Wave" rolled back, and in mid-1979 Morarji resigned his high office on the eve of a no-confidence vote that would have forced him out. Ailing J. P. died as his coalition of hope collapsed, while interim P. M. Charan Singh (1902–1987) desperately clung to its fast sinking hull until Janata actually went down in December 1979. If any of her opponents still doubted Mrs. Gandhi's stamina or determination to rule India, the elections of 1980 taught them otherwise. By briefly jailing her in the wake of their victory, Morarji's government had only added a wreath of martyrdom to her white crown. She easily won both seats she contested in the Lok Sabha, her Congress (I) party enjoying a comfortable majority, which included Sanjay Gandhi. Janata won fewer seats than the Communist party—Marxist, which with thirty-five members of Parliament posed no serious challenge to Indira's central government, yet managed to gain control of three state governments: West Bengal, Kerala, and Tripura. Tamil Nadu remained in Dravidian party hands, under ex-Tamil movie star Chief Minister M. G. Ramachandran. Punjab was nominally returned to Congress control. But Punjab remained Mrs. Gandhi's most intractable problem, clouding the four remaining years of her life, which was shrouded after June 1980 when Sanjay's rocketing career went down in the flames of his stunt plane over New Delhi's flying club.

Sikh *Akali Dal* ("Eternal Party") demands for a separate state, "Punjabi Suba" as they called it, had been grudgingly granted by Delhi's Center (Central Government) in 1966, when the former Punjab was further partitioned, into three states: a Sikh-majority Punjabi-speaking Punjab, a new Hindu-majority Hindi Haryana buffer between itself and New Delhi, and a larger *Himachal Pradesh* ("Mountain Province") to which former Sikh princely territories were added in the high altitudes around Simla. Sikh demands that the expensive Le Corbusier-designed capital of Chandigarh should remain sole capital of their new Punjab were rejected by Mrs. Gandhi's first government, which insisted that since Chandigarh bordered Punjab and Haryana it should serve both states as joint capital, with a single governor, high court, and university, and the actual Union Territory of Chandigarh should be centrally administered. That "solution" satisfied no one. Legislation designed to solve Hindu–Sikh conflicts within Punjab, passionate conflicts compounded by emotional, linguistic, and religious differences as well as real economic and political interests, thus served only to intensify communal disputes. Secular-minded Indians joined forces with fundamentalist Hindus in opposing increasingly shrill and violent Sikh demands not only for Chandigarh but also for official recognition of Sikhism as a separate religion from Hinduism, rather than a mere "sect" of Hinduism, as India's Constitution called it.

The Punjabi "Suba" demand was viewed by New Delhi as little less than another Pakistan movement, hence a fundamental threat to India's unity. Since Punjab itself bordered Pakistan and Sikhs held a disproportionately high number of senior officer and command posts in India's Army, any Sikh agitation, especially violent agitation, was viewed by India's cabinet with alarm. The loyal, important role played by Sikh soldiers in the War of 1965 against Pakistan over Kashmir helped convince Mrs. Gandhi of the need to grant more of the Punjabi Suba demand. Therefore, in 1970 she conceded that Chandigarh should become sole capital of Punjab to avoid potentially drastic repercussions from a self-immolation threat by Akali Dal "Saint" (*Sant*) Fateh Singh. Haryana was at the time promised enough money to build its own capital and a further grant of land inside Punjab that it claimed by virtue of Hindu majorities.

But that 1970 agreement was never implemented. Political rivals of Akali Dal leadership within the Sikh community, primarily Giani Zail Singh, Congress Chief Minister of Punjab from 1972 to 1977, and in 1980 Mrs. Gandhi's Home Minister and then President of India (1982–1987), fought against Akali power. Hindus complained that "greedy" Sikhs were already too rich, too powerful, too pampered by New Delhi. With only 2 percent of India's population, hard-working Sikhs enjoyed over 10 percent of its wealth, and Punjab per capita income was more than double the average income in the nation. What more did "those people" want? Why were Sikhs never satisfied? They had more tractors, more tubewells, more water, producing more wheat, than any other Indian state! They came to be viewed through green eyes for having availed themselves so successfully of India's "Green Revolution" on land that yielded more grain per acre than any other portion of South Asia. Besides everything else, they considered themselves "God's chosen people"!

Akali Sikhs fought vigorously against Mrs. Gandhi's Emergency Raj and nearly 50,000 filled Punjabi jails. In 1977, therefore, an Akali-Janata landslide victory turned Zail Singh out of power and brought Sardar Prakash Singh Badal's Akali coalition ministry to Chandigarh. Ousted Congress Sikh politicians then sponsored a hitherto unknown young fundamentalist Sikh "Saint" (*Sant*) Jarnail Singh Bhindranwale (1947–1984) as a counter to older Akali leadership. Bhindranwale soon proved himself more popular, violent, and independent than his Congress patrons expected him to be. Congress leaders soon reaped the whirlwind. After her reelection in January 1980, Mrs. Gandhi dissolved the Akali-Janata government of Punjab and called for new elections that May, which Congress won. Mrs. Gandhi then chose Darbara Singh to serve as Chief Minister of Punjab. Akali Dal opposition in the state assembly was led by Prakash Singh Badal, but a new Akali party president was elected in 1980, Sant Harchand Singh Longowal (1928–1985). Giani Zail Singh remained at Mrs. Gandhi's side in New Delhi, and after 1982 as President of India, the first Sikh to hold that high office.

The moderate opposition of Badal and Longowal to Congress Raj in Punjab was put to "shame" in the eyes of extremist Sikhs by the violent tactics of Bhindranwale and his armed band of youthful supporters. Terror became their major tactic, motor-scooters and rapid-fire guns their favorite weapons. Bhindranwale, ignoring all appeals for restraint from his former sponsors, led a growing network of violence that claimed the lives of moderate Sikhs and Hindus alike. Yet Bhindranwale remained "immune" to punishment. Zail Singh once informed the Lok Sabha that his Home Ministery had insufficient "proof" of the "Sant's" role in several prominent murders. By the time sufficient evidence was collected, however, Bhindranwale and his disciples were inside Amritsar's Golden Temple, heavily armed, well stocked with food and ammunition, fanatically determined to remain at the heart of their Sikh faith until every one of their demands for a separate Sikh "Land of the Pure" (*Khalistan*) had been met, or death brought them martyrdom.

On June 2, 1984, Mrs. Gandhi approved the launching of her army command's "Operation Bluestar" plan to remove Bhindranwale and his terrorists from the Golden Temple. She was obviously convinced that Bluestar was the only feasible way of dealing with the armed "sit-down" inside Amritsar's holiest of holies, although why a blockade or light commando raid was not tried first remains a mystery. Perhaps she simply knew that a dramatic martial show of overwhelming force against Sikhs, no matter how bloody the cost, would prove politically popular. Elections had to be held by year's end, after all. So the army was given permission to do whatever it considered necessary, and on June 3, 1984, tanks rolled into the temple's compound, cannon blazing, as helicopters buzzed overhead and heavy mortars fired deadly missiles from neighboring Jallianwala Bagh, garden birthplace of Congress' own freedom-struggle revolution sixty-five years earlier. In the ensuing days and nights of heavy fighting, Bhindranwale and close to one thousand of his followers were killed, another thousand taken prisoner, at the cost of nearly 200 Indian soldiers' lives. "Khalistan" had its first martyrs, and seeds of silently sworn Sikh vengeance were sown that would lead before year's end to Mrs. Gandhi's assassination. Most Hindus in Haryana and New Delhi and elsewhere across the country were, however, pleased that their Prime Minister and Army had "finally" put "those people" in their "place." Mrs. Gandhi's political ratings climbed dramatically in the immediate aftermath of Operation Bluestar, and chances for a Congress victory in forthcoming elections appeared much brighter. By late October, however, Mrs. Gandhi still had not announced the actual date for elections, although she sounded like a candidate whenever addressing large crowds across the land, and assured her party faithful in Orissa before returning to New Delhi at month's end, "If I die today, every drop of my blood will invigorate the country."

In the morning of October 31, 1984, Prime Minister Indira Gandhi left her home at One Safdarjung Road in New Delhi to walk up the garden path toward her office at One Akbar Road. Two treacherous Sikh guards emptied their guns into the frail orange-sari-clad body they had been hired to defend with their own lives as she reached the garden gate. Self-proclaimed Sikh leaders of "Khalistan" in London toasted reports of Mrs. Gandhi's assassination with champagne, shouting, "We have taken revenge!" One assassin was killed almost immediately by other guards; the second stood trial and was subsequently sentenced to hang. As word of Mrs. Gandhi's death spread across Delhi's dark plain that harrowing evening, rampaging mobs of hate-filled Hindus led by Congress thugs set fire to every Sikh they could find and to every Sikh home, business, car, taxi, or pedicab. An orgy of unrestrained murder and arson turned India's sprawling cosmopolitan capital into her most dangerous field of battle for three harrowing days and nights following Indira's assassination. Thousands of innocent Sikhs were murdered in Delhi alone, and communal retaliation spread across all of North India, where easily identifiable Sikhs suddenly found themselves targets of lifelong Hindu neighbors and former friends. India's Army had to be called out with orders to shoot vandals or looters "on sight" before the horrible mob violence ended. But the karmic legacy of that dreadful aftermath to Mrs. Gandhi's death was that Hindu–Sikh communalism displaced Hindu–Muslim communal conflict as India's most incendiary internal problem. Few Hindu officers commanding Sikh regiments slept soundly in the wake of that dreadful new crack in the heart of India's body politic.

President Zail Singh flew home to New Delhi the day his Prime Minister died to administer the oath of premier office to her forty-year-old son, Rajiv, who had shunned politics until the death of his younger brother in 1980. Rajiv Gandhi, an Indian Airlines pilot, was a graduate of India's posh Doon School and had studied engineering at Trinity College, Cambridge, where he met his Italian-born bride, Sonia Maino. Unlike Sanjay, Rajiv was quiet, unaggressive, and seemingly without ambition. He took up the "burdens" of Sanjay's Lok Sabha seat and leadership of the Youth Congress, however, at his mother's insistence, thus positioning himself someday to inherit her premier power. But no one expected him to be called upon so soon. Rajiv was unrattled, however, never shrinking from the job that was "thrust" upon him.

Constitutionally, the senior-most member of India's cabinet should have been sworn in as interim prime minister, but advisers in the president's entourage did not worry about fine points of democratic procedure as clouds of hatred and cries of "Blood for blood!" darkened Delhi's raging plain. "She was mother not only to me but to the whole nation," Rajiv told his people in his first broadcast, urging them to shun "violence" and "remain calm." With no police or soldiers to stop them, the blood-thirsty mobs ran wild for another two days and nights. On November 3, order was restored and Indira Gandhi's remains were cremated along the Yamuna River bank, where Mahatma Gandhi's pyre and Jawaharlal Nehru's, as well as Lal Bahadur Shastri's, had all been lit and left to burn until only ashes remained of independent India's leaders.

Rajiv Gandhi wisely called general elections for December 1984. A tidal wave of sympathy for his martyred mother brought her son's Congress back to power with its largest majority of some 400 Lok Sabha seats. Rajiv proved himself a more popular campaigner than his mother, reminding many Indians of his handsome grandfather's "clean" and reassuring image. His charisma charmed millions on TV as well as in vast public meetings, and he soon emerged as India's most popular star. India's electorate thus stamped its democratic seal of approval on the choice of the handful of "Kingmakers" who had picked their *Raj*-iv before any votes could be cast or counted. It seemed, of course, appropriate for India's Congress party government to celebrate the centenary of the Indian National Congress in Bombay in December 1985 with a scion of *the* "Nehru family" at its head as prime minister. Nor did Rajiv spare the rod of rebuke to the huge audience assembled under Bombay's sultry sky to hear him say:

"We talk of the high principles and lofty ideals needed to build a strong and prosperous India. . . . But we obey no discipline . . . follow no principle of public morality, display no sense of social awareness, show no concern for the public weal. Corruption is not only tolerated but even regarded as the hallmark of our leadership." Many old party stalwarts were shocked at so stinging a rebuke from the chief, yet others agreed, adding: "He surely knows of what he speaks."

Rajiv gave highest priority to seeking a way of restoring calm and democratic rule to martially governed Punjab. He met with released Akali Dal moderate leader Sant Harchand Singh Longowal and they reached agreement in July 1985, an agreement that seemed to augur the dawn of an era of peace for Punjab. Chandigarh was again promised to become the state's exclusive capital after January 26, 1986. Other Sikh demands, for more water, for religious autonomy, and for greater control of taxation, were to be resolved by "impartial commissions." State elections were to be held in September 1985. But on August 20, Sant Longowal was assassinated by Sikh terrorists. Punjab elections held nonetheless, returned an Akali Dal government, led by moderate Surjeet Singh Barnala, but the violence continued. Armed disciples of Bhindranwale again filled the Golden Temple at Amritsar and recaptured its Akal Takht headquarters. The center balked at fulfilling its promise on Chandigarh in the aftermath of vociferous protests by Haryana Hindus, who threatened to surround the Lok Sabha unless their demands for "justice" were heeded. The tragic loss of so many lives since Operation Bluestar thus seemed to have achieved nothing, except to reelect a Congress party government, which now washed its hands of Punjabi Akali Dal in-fighting, leaving Chief Minister Barnala to deal with extremist Sikhs in the Golden Temple, reverting to the pre-Rajiv–Longowal agreement status quo. Prospects for permanent peace in Punjab appeared no closer by 1987 than they had been forty years earlier. Terrorist violence intensified, and that May New Delhi decided to displace Barnala's ministry with President's Rule, which gave all power to Punjab's heavily augmented police, under its Goan Chief Julio Ribeiro, and centrally appointed Bengali Governor, S. S. Ray. Predictably, however, autocratic rule only added to that tortured state's annual death toll, rather than diminishing it. In 1988 the toll of Punjab dead climbed to over 2,000, and although the crudeness of Operation Bluestar's tank-led assault on the Golden Temple was replaced by precision shooting during Operation Black Thunder, no peace could return to Punjab as long as Rajiv ruled Delhi.

Punjab was the most violent internal problem during the closing years of Rajiv's tenure, but corruption proved at least as damaging to his once pristine reputation and image. Millions of dollars in kick-back commissions appear to have been paid by the Swedish firm of Bofors to secret Swiss accounts owned by close friends of the Indian prime minister. As Rajiv's Minister of Finance, V. P. Singh had tried to expose the fraudulent tax evasion and peculation of some of India's leading business houses, including several very supportive of the prime minister, but just as he started making public what he'd found in long-buried files, he was shifted by Rajiv to the Ministry of Defense. There, of course, he uncovered the Bofors bombshell, which led to his dismissal from Rajiv's cabinet. V. P. was not, however, easily intimidated, nor would he remain silent, despite every form of official coercion, including charges of virtual "treason" hurled against him from high places. V. P. carried his Janata campaign directly to India's millions, telling the story of just how much was rotten in Delhi at mass rallies from Bombay to Calcutta over the two long years he was forced to wander in India's political wilderness before his lonely voice elicited the roaring echo of elective victory. When the hundreds of millions of votes were all counted by late November 1989, Rajiv's majority of 400 had faded to 190 seats in the Lok Sabha, most of whose new members supported V. P. Singh's deceptively small Janata Dal party, which in itself had only 145 seats but commanded allegiance from parties to its right and left.

"If power is a sword, it will be wielded on behalf of the poor and the toiling masses," the new prime minister promised his nation that December, the day after he was sworn in by President Ramaswamy Venkataraman in Delhi. Four days later, V. P. flew to Amritsar, his first official trip out of the capital, and walked into the Golden Temple to express "my regrets for whatever happened in the past," wisely adding that "problems cannot be solved with bullets, but they can be solved with love." That one fearless visit to Punjab helped restore alienated Sikh faith in the equity of Delhi's new leadership, although it would not put an end to violence in Amritsar overnight. Thanks to V. P. and his wise Punjabi Cabinet colleague, Inder Gujral, however, the political process, by which alone an ultimately peaceful solution to Punjab's long trauma and pain would someday evolve, had at least been started. State elections still remained to be held, and the transfer of Chandigarh affected, as well as the trial and punishment of those guilty of heinous crimes against Sikhs in the blood-strewn streets of Delhi during the Massacre of early November 1984.

Since 1971, when Bangladesh was formed, millions of landless Muslims from that impoverished nation in the heart of India's eastern wing had fled starvation, illegally crossing over into sparsely populated lush Assam and other Indian border states. Violent Assamese nativist attacks against those Muslim migrants cost many thousands of them their lives as entire villages were put to the torch by angry Assam "students" who wanted all "aliens" to leave their state. In mid-1985 Rajiv reached an Accord with Assam's populist young leader, Prafulla Kumar Mahanta, whose Asom Gana Parishad party enlisted the support of the most active nativist students. Delhi promised to withdraw its troops and hold state elections, which Mahanta's party easily won, after the disenfranchisement and deportation of illegal Muslim aliens from Assam to other parts of India. Mahanta promised to call off his "boys," urging them to leave their killing fields and return to their colleges. For almost two years the Accord held, and peace returned to Assam, but more desperate Bangladeshis continued to cross the jungle border, and new gangs of young Assamese chauvinists soon emerged around Gauhati to attack and murder them, defying remote Delhi as well as their own Chief Minister Mahanta, now viewed by some nativists as a "turncoat" softened by establishment power. Rajiv's final "solution" to the growing Assamese Liberation Army and its violent activists was to start erecting a barbed-wire fence through India's jungle border with Bangladesh. Heavy monsoons and thick forests have made so futile an enterprise profitable only to the owners of fence-making companies.

Economic Planning and Development

For at least four millennia India's economy has been in some measure planned by its government. The standard-sized burned bricks of Harappa and the elaborate hypocaust and drainage system of Mohenjo-daro bear mute but eloquent testimony to the success of India's earliest "planning commission." By the fourth century B.C., Mauryan bureaucrats paid as much attention to economic matters, from the taxation of remote villages to the management of Pataliputra's arsenal and mint, as the *Arthashastra* attests they did to the education of Indian monarchs in realpolitik.

Modern Indian economic planning, while part of a deep-rooted tradition, is primarily the product of India's National Congress commitment since 1931 to the "eradication of poverty" through the growth and development of India's natural resources and the more equitable distribution of her wealth. Mahatma Gandhi favored rural revitalization and the "Uplift of All" (*Sarvodaya*) by daily hand-spinning and weaving in village ashrams, communes of shared labor and wealth, where all would work, eat, and live in loving harmony. The Mahatma and his followers viewed urban industrial development more as a polluting blight than a liberating force of modern society. Hand labor and locomotion by foot were encouraged as the healthiest sources of economic strength, and India's rural masses were taught to take pride in the simplicity of their daily lives and to use their idle time in productive handicraftsmanship. Jawaharlal Nehru and most of the leadership of Congress, however, believed it essential for India to develop industrial self-sufficiency in order to protect and retain her hard-won national independence.

Nehru first visited Soviet Russia in 1927 and was so impressed by the planned economic development he observed there that he became India's foremost advocate of Five Year Plans as the key to "resolving" her premier problem of poverty. One of the major goals of the 1931 Karachi Congress Resolution that Nehru drafted was "real economic freedom" for India's "starving millions." As chairman of free India's first planning commission, Prime Minister Nehru insisted on launching his nation's first Five Year Plan in 1950, saying, "If there is economic inequality in the country, all the political democracy and all the adult suffrage in the world cannot bring about real democracy." That initial plan was, however, a modest infusion of capital designed to repair and replace most of India's sadly depleted wartime railnet and rolling stock, and to bring enough fresh irrigation water to India's soil to raise food-grain production by 11 percent, barely enough to keep pace with population growth.

India's second Plan was more ambitious, heavy industry receiving enough development funds almost to triple annual iron ore output, while doubling coal production and electric-power capacity. Food-grain yields were 60 percent more than they had been in 1950, but population jumped from 360 to 440 million. Thanks to U.S., Russian, British, and German aid and technological assistance, India leap-frogged to the seventh most advanced steel-producing nation in the world by the end of her third Five Year Plan, with production totaling over 7 million tons of finished steel in 1966. The rest of India's economy remained so backward, however, that most finished steel was exported to Europe or Japan during those early years of accelerated industrial production. India would start building her own locomotives and steel ships as well as bicycles during her third Plan. Foreign cars were assembled in India, but the production of her own *Maruti* (the Vedic "Wind" god), first attempted by Sanjay Gandhi in the late 1970s, proved a most expensive failure, reborn only in the mid-1980s with major Japanese technological and financial aid.

Nehru stressed the development of an indigenous iron and steel industry as essential for India's continued freedom from foreign intervention or imperial domination. He even insisted on launching an Indian program of nuclear development, which was to rock the sands under Rajasthan with India's first plutonium test exactly a decade after his death. The top priority Nehru gave to economic planning and industrial development has advanced India to somewhere around the tenth most advanced industrial nation of the world. During much of Nehru's era, real industrial growth was more than 5 percent per annum. As a result of U.S. military aid following the Chinese invasion of 1962, and Russian military support since the eve of the Bangladesh War of 1971, India now has a well-equipped modern army of more than a million men, and produces her own submarines, surface warships, and domestically assembled modern fighter-bombers as well as helicopters.

With her Tarapur nuclear facility and well-trained pool of Tata research nuclear scientists, India is capable of building and launching her own nuclear missiles whenever she opts to do so. Oil resources now tapped off Bombay, together with oil produced in Assam, are sufficient to fuel India's modern economy well into the twenty-first century. Urban and industrial India boasts many modern electronics as well as petrochemical plants, whose products enrich India's economy by boosting exports and directly enhancing agricultural yields, which have more than tripled since Independence. The tragic cost in lives and health of rapid industrial development within India's still mostly peasant economy, however, may prove much higher than her early planners imagined, as Union Carbide's horrible Bhopal disaster of late 1984 indicated.

"We stand for democracy and for socialism," Prime Minister Nehru affirmed less than a year before he died. "Obviously, everybody will agree, almost everybody, that we have to provide a good life to all our citizens . . . a good life means certain basic material things that everybody should have, like enough food and clothing, a house to live in, education, health services and work. . . . How do we do that?" How, indeed! For India's 150 million or so affluent and certainly comfortable members of her new "middle class" those problems have been solved since Independence. But as India's population climbs well above 800 million it has become painfully obvious that poverty, for many hundreds of millions of Indians, tends to increase more rapidly than affluence. Population pressures and inequitable economic distribution of goods and resources have increased the unbridgeable distance between independent India's insular "haves" and her ocean of "have-nots." Government reports have never admitted to more than 15 or 20 million unemployed Indians, but when underemployment is taken into consideration, at least half of India's population must be added. There is hardly an office in any modern Indian city, including Bombay and New Delhi, that would not be run more efficiently if half its personnel were removed. The same is true of most Indian fields, except for the Punjab, perhaps, and parts of Haryana.

India's overall rate of economic growth from 1950 averaged 3.25 percent, and, since until 1985 population growth rates averaged about 2.2 percent, it was clear that economic progress was being made, in real terms, despite grossly unequal distribution. Population, however, has jumped since 1986 to a growth rate now closer to 2.5 percent, which, if sustained, would almost totally absorb developmental advances and actually reverse the trend for those at the brink of starvation among the lower half of India's populace. With the current annual addition to its population equal to that of Canada's, pressure for radical change of every variety has intensified. The one program, however, that has become political anathema is birth control. Although Hinduism has no doctrinal objection to limiting family size, most Indians prefer to have as many children as possible, not only because most Indian children are loved and useful, but also as old-age security for parents who might otherwise have no source of financial support.

Sons are specially desired, since they generally live at home after marriage and can perform vital religious practices, from lighting parents' pyres to praying for their souls after death. India's one concerted effort to reduce population growth by sterilization, vigorously pursued during Indira's Emergency Raj at the initiative of Sanjay Gandhi, proved most unpopular at the polls, helping mother and younger son both to lose their seats in the 1977 elections. Closer analysis of the antisterilization wave revealed that many men forced by police to undergo sterilization had never been married. The operations were supposed to have been performed only on fathers of two or more children. Many Muslims and ex-Untouchables, moreover, believed they were specially selected "guinea pigs" by a government seeking systematically to "eliminate" their kind from India's future. More judicious administration of such a birth-control program might have made considerable difference to India's future. Widespread backlash to sterilization turned birth control into political suicide, however, for New Delhi since 1977. Other than sterilization there is no easy way as yet to limit India's population, since all other methods require more privacy, running water, education, or hygienic sophistication than is generally available in most of rural and much of urban India.

Lal Bahadur Shastri, like Nehru, insisted that "economic issues are most vital for us and it is of the highest importance that we should fight our biggest enemies—poverty and unemployment. . . . Socialism is our objective," the newly elected Prime Minister informed Parliament in June 1964. Shastri addressed India's National Development Council that October, urging more "self-help" along the lines of Mahatma Gandhian village coöperation and handicrafts labor. "All of us know that our achievements in the agricultural sector have not been up to the mark," Shastri told his planning colleagues. He added:

> What we need now is . . . action. . . . We are planning many major irrigation projects. But . . . are we doing all we can in the field of minor irrigation? Cannot more wells be dug, cannot ponds be deepened, cannot the available waters of irrigation projects already completed be more fully utilised? Surely these are within our reach if we go about our task in a spirit of self-help. . . . What should be the main objective of the Fourth Plan? It must ensure that . . . the move towards a better life for the common people maintains its momentum.

In less than a year, however, India was at war again with Pakistan, and all of Shastri's energy would be consumed by foreign affairs, his precarious heart soon sacrificed to the arduous struggle for finding a peaceful solution to South Asia's festering conflicts. The fourth Plan, nonetheless, focused on seeking to reduce the blight of poverty, which Prime Minister Indira Gandhi made her most frequently stated goal.

By 1970 India's "Green Revolution" was launched, with U.S.- and U.N.-developed high-yield wheat and rice seeds to double and quadruple grain harvests per acre for those farmers sufficiently enterprising and affluent to try and buy the new seeds. The upper tenth of India's peasant population prospered as they reaped enough harvests to feed much of India, but the lower half lacked purchasing power to buy enough food to sustain their growing families. Revolutionary Communist agitation grew among the lower half of India's landless and unemployed and among the growing army of college and university students who could find no jobs and were fast losing hope in a system whose leaders grew rich on corruption and "black money."

"The important thing for Mrs. Gandhi is to find out why university students burn buses and commit similar other acts," wrote J. P. Narayan in his *Prison Diary* during Indira's Emergency Raj:

> I am afraid the middle classes, from whom most politicians, bureaucrats, teachers, businessmen, professionals . . . come, will, on one specious pretext or another, block any revolutionary change either in the educational system or the socioeconomic, political, cultural sphere. . . . Under the Emergency there may be no buses being burnt today and Mrs. Gandhi might think she has solved the problem of student unrest, indiscipline and violence. But if the Emergency lasts longer, Mrs. Gandhi may be faced with a most unexpected explosion.

It was a cautionary warning she ultimately took to heart. But Janata proved itself no braver or wiser at coping with the inequities of India's class system and the ever-widening gulf between India's rich and poor, the overfed and starving at opposite ends of India's expanding economic spectrum. Nor did J. P. outlive his own party's failure to achieve any meaningful changes in India's lumbering elephantine peasant economy, which carried the burden of its princely few in a bejeweled, golden howdah of plenty and pleasure at the top.

Mrs. Gandhi's autocratic Emergency Raj managed temporarily to curb inflation and diminish blackmarketeering and hoarding. The Twenty Point Program of reforms she introduced was clearly needed and basically designed to distribute India's wealth more equitably and to assist the weakest, most impoverished half of society. Point one promised to "bring down prices" and that hitherto elusive goal was, in fact, achieved. She also promised to end "tax evasion" and confiscate "smugglers' property" and managed considerable progress in both laudable goals by arresting cheats and thieves and keeping them behind bars. She called for the "liquidation of rural indebtedness" and the "abolition of bonded labour," more ambitious goals that could hardly be realized in only two years. Still, much positive good was begun, and had it not been for the dark cloud of personal motivation that obfuscated everything accomplished during the Emergency Raj, more that was started then might have survived its demise. For Mrs. Gandhi rightly reminded her nation in July 1975, "There is only one magic which can remove poverty, and that is hard work sustained by clear vision, iron will and the strictest discipline."

Austerity measures that she introduced into public enterprises were obviously long overdue. Just as fear of losing her elective power had galvanized Indira to act, fear of prison and confiscation of property motivated millions of weaker Indians to abandon tax evasion, smuggling, blackmarketeering, and price gouging. Mrs. Gandhi told the Commonwealth Parliamentary Conference in October 1975, seeking to justify the undemocratic means of her Emergency Raj:

> Democracy is not just an ideal or an objective. Any system can prevail only so long as it keeps pace with changing conditions and proves its ability to solve the problems of its people. When the majority are struggling for survival, will they tolerate luxury for a few, either material or in the form of licence to do what they wish? The essential is: to what extent a part of its alternatives can truly reflect the wishes and aspirations of the people. . . . Welcome to India, a strange land, strange not only to those who have come from abroad but even to many who have lived here all their lives. . . . We wish not merely to satisfy the creature comforts of our people but to liberate them for creative and contemplative pursuits. We believe, as Mahatma Gandhi taught, that rights flow from duty well done. . . . In our world-view all turbulence ends in order, all conflict ends in resolution, all travail ends in tranquility.

India's sixth Five Year Plan was launched in 1980, calling for "A progressive reduction in the incidence of poverty and unemployment." It also urged "Improving the quality of life of the people in general with special reference to the economically and socially handicapped population" and "Strengthening the redistributive bias of public policies and services in favour of the poor, contributing to a reduction in inequalities of income and wealth."

Only 5 percent of public-sector funding devoted to that sixth Plan actually went to schemes designed to provide jobs for the jobless and minimal food grains for the starving. World Bank Reports of the early 1980s indicated that the lowest fifth of India's population received less than 7 percent of her annual income, while the highest 20 percent consumed some 50 percent of all goods and services. Less than 30 percent of India's landowners controlled almost 75 percent of India's productive 450 million acres of rural land. More than a quarter of India's peasant population was landless by 1986, and that percentage was annually increasing, rather than diminishing. Although modern methods of agriculture, better seeds, and greater irrigation yielded over 150 million tons of food grains annually by the mid-1980s, that did not quite suffice to guarantee minimal nutrition for all. Unless gross inequities in purchasing power and distribution were rectified, India could again face mass disasters of famine and pandemic disease.

The "solution" of Rajiv Gandhi's seventh Five Year Plan, started in 1985, was to stimulate economic growth by relieving the rich of inheritance taxes, reducing income taxes, and removing onerous licensing regulations from industry in order to stimulate Indian investment and attract more foreign capital. Such "trickle-down" economies certainly work at the top, and helped spur record stock rises and prime new enterprises in Bombay and around New Delhi. "We share the conviction that democracy is the best guarantor of enduring development," Rajiv told a joint session of the U.S. Congress in June 1985, during his first official visit to Washington. With half a billion dollars' worth of high-technology equipment being sent to India from the United States in 1986 alone, a new level of Indo-U.S. cooperation in scientific, developmental, and military aid had begun, which would, it was hoped, help India's economy grow richer while assisting India to remain strong.

"To your scientists and technologists," Prime Minister Rajiv Gandhi added, "the people of India will always be grateful." High-tech computers and NASA-launched weather satellites would provide early storm and drought warnings to Indian farmers across the subcontinent, and could help further to increase Indian yields of every variety. Indian agriculture and industry might thus be on the brink of a new leap forward in overall productivity, if monsoon rains always came on time! The critical problem, however, was how to ensure the latter contingency, and if a monsoon or two failed, how to keep the lower half of India's submerged populace, close to half a billion human beings, from starving. Rajiv and his computer-minded managerial elite paid much less attention to the problem of poverty than had any previous independent government of India. Rajiv's rhetoric, unlike his mother's, included no promises about "abolishing poverty." Everyone's hope, of course, was that a buoyant economy, accelerating productivity in all sectors, and increased foreign trade as well as investments from abroad might eventually solve India's oldest and most intractable problem, or at least diminish its ocean of want. Delhi's glittering package of investment "incentives"—tax-free income, high-interest yields, and so on—codified as a new policy in the 1980s, had indeed attracted close to a billion dollars from nonresident Indians (NRIs) by mid-1987, helping to prime the pump of Indian development. Impressive as that NRI infusion of capital could prove to be, however, much more "black money" was leaving India for "investment" in secret Swiss bank accounts. The illicit flight of currency from Bombay's major industrial and commercial houses became so scandalous by 1985 that V. P., as finance minister, had launched several major investigations, resulting first in his own expulsion from the cabinet by Rajiv, then in his emergence as prime minister.

The last years of Rajiv's rule were plagued with inflation in (and in some instances, almost doubling of) prices of every vital consumer food—grains, sugar, milk, vegetable oil. Such inflation was credited by some analysts as the leading cause of Rajiv's defeat in 1989. V. P.'s economic policy was to bring down inflation as quickly as possible. But the "right to work" was also promised to every Indian adult seeking a job. The new Planning Commission, chaired by the prime minister, with former Karnataka Chief Minister Ramakrishna Hegde as vice-chairman, was charged with seeing to it that at least half of all resources invested during the eighth Plan (started in 1990) were expended in rural areas. Less than 30 percent of Rajiv's plan funds had been used for village uplift work. The previous plan, of course, had focused on high-tech investments in big cities. Now Delhi was reversing gears, returning to priorities stressed by Mahatma Gandhi and Lal Bahadur Shastri, decentralization, rural rehabilitation, and the "uplift of all" by creating more jobs and making more food, shelter, and other essential goods available to India's poverty-stricken peasantry. "In some ways it's more easily said than done," Rajni Kothari, a new member of the Planning Commission, confessed, explaining how Rajiv had "left the coffers empty," by going on "a spending spree to buy people over for votes," at the very end of his era. Delhi's foreign exchange reserves were all but gone early in 1990, and its debt-servicing costs had climbed above 25 percent. But V. P.'s new broom was braced to clean up the mess he'd been left, and if enough states could be encouraged to take greater responsibilities for regional and local planning, Delhi's idealistic new team hoped at least that more people would soon be able to work harder and reap the reward of enough food each day to keep themselves from starving.

Environmental concerns have also emerged as a high priority of V. P.'s government. Minister of State Maneka Gandhi was swiftly immersed in swirling waters of controversy over the recently projected Narmada River and Tehri Dams. The Narmada Dam was designed to submerge over 100,000 hectares of Madhya Pradesh ("Middle Province"; M.P.) land around the river Narmada, in order to provide water and power for about 120,000 hectares in neighboring Gujarat State. "Which means robbing Peter to pay Paul," Minister Maneka explained, noting that there were, in fact, many less environmentally costly alternatives. The young minister charged with protecting India's dwindling forests as well as her precious air and water was most concerned about the estimated 300,000 people of the region, who would have to be displaced. "Where do you plant 300,000 people?" she asked. More volatile still was the struggle building over the proposed Tehri Dam that is supposed to be erected on seismic rock in the Garhwal Hills of U.P. Since the dam, if built, might be ruptured by an earthquake, inestimable damage could be done to every villager living in its shadow. India's oldest conservationist hero, saintly Sunderlal Bahuguna, who models himself on the Mahatma, undertook a "fast unto death" to stop the Tehri project, but called it off when Maneka invited him to speak to her cabinet colleagues in Delhi. Less costly run-of-the-river turbines have been proposed as an environmentally safer alternative to the dangerous high dam, although many industrial builders are keen to embark on that more lucrative project. What did Maneka Gandhi expect the outcome of this latest of India's monumental struggles to be? As a member of the cabinet that would collectively have to resolve those problems, and so many others, Minister Maneka refused to venture a guess at that, but the "other Mrs. Gandhi," as she is sometimes called, responded with quiet intensity, "I just want to keep this India safe for our children."

With the largest rail net and second largest fleet in Asia, as fifth largest producer of power as well as coal in the world, self-sufficient in oil, steel production, and food grains, India is now one of the mightiest nations on earth, and has one of the largest, best-trained pools of scientific and technical school graduates. India's economic achievements since Independence have been remarkable, her future prospects for growth and economic "take-off" even more impressive. Still the past clings. Floods, drought, famine, and poverty continue to drag her down each time she seems ready to spread wings of prosperity and fly toward a brighter field full of richer harvests. Now that the Demon Corruption has suffered ignominious defeat, perhaps the new

Team with its new Plan will prove capable of overcoming the bogs of inertia and despair, generating enough hope and strength in enough hearts and hands to lift India's continental economy, half modern and half medieval, out of its stagnating rural swamps toward a future of progress and more rapid development.

Foreign Policy

Indo-Pak Relations

India's foreign policy has long been plagued by the bitter legacy of Partition, triggering no fewer than three undeclared wars with Pakistan in less than a quarter century of independence. Serving as his own Foreign Minister, Jawaharlal Nehru articulated goals of "nonalignment" and "peaceful coexistence" as pole stars of Indian policy, but was unable to adhere to either ideal. A widely traveled liberal Socialist intellectual, Nehru was India's most outspoken advocate of "World Peace" and called for an end to Cold War conflicts between the superpowers, yet found it impossible to reach agreement with Pakistan over Kashmir, or with China over their common border.

On the eve of Partition in August 1947 all except three princely states of British India—Kashmir, Hyderabad, Junagadh—had opted to join either India or Pakistan. Kashmir, the largest, most strategically important, and most valuable of those states, sits like a crown atop both new nations, hence by the test of geographic contiguity could have gone to either. Most of its populace was, however, and remains Muslim, demographically tilting the choice of integration to Pakistan on grounds of majority religious affiliation. But Kashmir's Maharaja was Hindu, and the prince alone was legally empowered to decide which Dominion his state would join. Maharaja Hari Singh could not make up his mind as the day of decision passed, hoping Kashmir might remain independent, the Switzerland of Asia. Only two months of such standstill procrastination was vouchsafed to him.

In October 1947 Pathan Muslims from Pakistan's North-West Frontier Province were driven in British-Pakistani Army trucks into Kashmir and started looting and raping as they headed toward the capital of Srinagar. Shortly before those Muslim "volunteer" raiders reached Srinagar, however,

Lord Mountbatten and Nehru agreed to order Indian aircraft carrying the First Sikh Battalion from New Delhi into Kashmir's Vale. Hari Singh then signed a document ceding Kashmir to India, Nehru promising Mountbatten that India would accept whatever decision was reached by the people of Kashmir themselves as to their state's ultimate disposition, through "impartial plebiscite." Undeclared war in Kashmir continued to preoccupy forces of India and Pakistan for more than a year, until a UN cease-fire was agreed upon early in 1949. That de facto battleline of partition has since remained the border between Pakistan's western quarter of *Azad* ("Free") Kashmir and India's Jammu and Kashmir State.

Nehru kept more than 100,000 Indian troops regularly garrisoned inside Kashmir on full alert throughout the remaining years of his tenure as prime minister. Every UN attempt to arrange for an internationally supervised plebiscite was rejected by India on grounds that Pakistan must "first vacate its aggression" by withdrawing all Pakistani forces from every inch of Kashmiri territory. Pakistan refused, however, insisting it would only order its troops out of Kashmir if and when India flew its army out. India claims that Hari Singh's accession legally endorsed her right to "keep the peace" in Kashmir by whatever means might be deemed necessary. Hence the stalemate and de facto partition continue. For several years Nehru repeated his pledge to hold an impartial plebiscite on the principle of self-determination, which he had always supported and advocated for oppressed peoples the world over. After some time, however, he argued that Indian elections in Jammu and Kashmir served, in fact, as such a "plebiscite." The most popular leader of Kashmir, Sheikh Muhammad Abdullah, founder of the democratic Muslim Conference party, was, however, jailed throughout most of Nehru's era, despite Nehru's often-expressed admiration for the Sheikh, whom he called his "friend."

India fought a second war with Pakistan over Kashmir in 1965, little more than a year after Nehru's death. Pakistan's ruler at the time, Field Marshal Ayub Khan, personally planned Operation Grand Slam, which he hoped would totally cut Kashmir off at its narrow southern neck from India's Punjab. Ayub was a giant of a man, as tall and sturdy as India's Prime Minister Lal Bahadur Shastri was small and physically frail. But India's army was four times larger than Pakistan's, and quickly dispelled the popular Pakistani myth that one Muslim soldier was "worth ten Hindus." Operation Grand Slam ground to a halt as soon as India's tanks rolled west across the

Punjab border to the environs of Lahore. In three weeks the second Indo–Pak War ended in what appeared to be a draw when the embargo placed by Washington on U.S. ammunition and replacements for both armies forced cessation of conflict before either side won a clear victory. India, however, was in a position to inflict grave damage to, if not capture, Pakistan's capital of the Punjab when the cease-fire was called, and controlled Kashmir's strategic Uri-Poonch bulge, much to Ayub's chagrin.

Russian Premier Aleksei Kosygin invited Shastri and Ayub to Tashkent for talks that ended in agreement to withdraw both armies to their prewar positions. The Tashkent Accord, signed on January 10, 1966, committed the leaders of India and Pakistan to restoring "peaceful relations" and "to promote understanding and friendly relations between their peoples." They resolved in future "to settle their disputes through peaceful means," and promised to work to restore all forms of trade and exchange. Lal Bahadur Shastri never awoke to help implement that hopeful Accord, however, dying of heart failure before the dawn. In Kashmir the "cease-fire" line continued to serve as a target range, despite the presence at several checkposts of UN observers. Constant "infiltration" across that porous high-altitude border led to skirmishes every month, always followed by diplomatic protests that were usually ignored by the Foreign Offices of both sides. Yet the third Indo–Pak War started and was for the most part fought in the East, in the mango groves and mud of Bengal.

Although Bangladesh was not born until 1971, most Bengali Muslim politicians believed that its "autonomous and sovereign" existence as an "Independent State" was intended by the Muslim League drafters of the famous Lahore Resolution since at least 1940. The heat of pressured history, however, led to the Partition of British India and the emergence of a single Pakistan, divided into East and West, instead of two nations, Pakistan and Bangladesh. With some 95 percent of its population speaking only Bengali, that crowded impoverished "half" of Pakistan was separated from the Western Urdu-speaking Punjabi and Pathan generals and bureaucrats who ruled them from remote Karachi and Islamabad by almost 1,000 miles of India. East Pakistanis thus came to feel more like colonial "subjects" of the West than fellow citizens. The only bridge that united them was Islam, and even that was weakened by regional sectarian and cultural variations. By 1970, therefore, when Pakistan's first general elections were finally held, Sheikh Mujibur Rahman's (1920–1975) autonomy-demanding *Awami* ("People's")

League swept every poll in the East, winning 160 out of 162 seats, a clear majority, in what was to have been Pakistan's newly representative Parliament. Zulfikar Ali Bhutto's (1928–1979) popular Pakistan People's Party won a solid majority in the West, but less than half the total seats won by Mujib's party; hence the latter should have become Pakistan's prime minister early in 1971. Martial Law Administrator General Yahya Khan, who apparently never expected Mujib to win the elections he'd called, opted for massacre in Dakha in the last week of March, however, rather than agreeing to the "humiliation" of serving peacefully under a Bengali, who was considered an "Indian agent" and "traitor" to Pakistan by many Westerners.

Ten million Hindu refugees from the East poured across India's border into West Bengal, ringing Calcutta in crowded camps reminiscent of the early days of Partition. Mujib and his leading lieutenants were arrested, but Bangladesh was proclaimed independent by underground freedom-fighters, who received Indian encouragement and armed support, setting up their new "nation in exile" on the border of West Bengal. Indira Gandhi urgently appealed to Washington for assistance in seeking a just solution to what had become an intolerable situation by mid-1971, but with Richard Nixon in the White House, nothing useful was done, no word of democratic hope or plea for justice was uttered by the "leader" of the "free" world. Nixon and Kissinger supposedly "needed" Yahya Khan to serve as their China-connection middleman, hence decided to turn blind eyes toward Bangladesh and their own State Department cables pleading desperately for some humane action to stop the Dakha massacre of helpless civilians.

Nixon's personal dislike of Mrs. Gandhi was well known, but official silence on the Bangladesh massacre and ensuing tragedy was unforgivable, in both human and diplomatic terms. For not only did Nixon ignore the virtual genocide being carried out with U.S. tanks, planes, and guns by West Pakistan's army, he also drove the prime minister of India into the open diplomatic arms of Soviet Russia. In August 1971, following months of chilling White House hostility, Mrs. Gandhi signed a twenty-year Treaty of Peace, Friendship and Cooperation with Russia. Premier Kosygin warmly welcomed Prime Minister Gandhi to Moscow the following month, affirming that "Never before has there been such solidarity between the peoples of India and the Soviet Union." Russian planes, tanks, and heavy artillery poured into New Delhi's airport, thence flown and driven directly to the border of Bangladesh. Before the end of November, a massive convoy of

Russian and Indian arms moved East with Bengali troops led by Parsi and Sikh commanders to liberate Dakha. Pakistan's general surrendered his entire army on December 15, 1971, a few days after vowing to "fight to the last man." Nixon ordered the nuclear armed USS *Enterprise* to the Bay of Bengal to "assist with evacuation" of Pakistani forces, but it arrived too late. Indians viewed the nuclear carrier steaming so close to their coastline only as Washington's missile-rattling, helping further to undermine Indo-U.S. relations. Watergate and the rape of Vietnam were thus not the only high crimes perpetrated by Nixon in the White House.

The liberation of Bangladesh proved the high point of Indira Gandhi's popularity at home and power abroad. Pakistan futilely attempted to bomb Agra, New Delhi, and other Indian airports, hoping to launch a second "front" in Kashmir, but no serious damage was done. India emerged from that third Indo–Pak War by the end of 1971 as South Asia's foremost power. Mujibur Rahman was released from prison in Pakistan and flew home to a hero's welcome in Dakha to become prime minister of the People's Republic of Bangladesh, whose 10 million refugees were also shipped home by India. Millions of other Bangladeshis would soon leave their country in different directions, heading North and East to seek land to feed them in India's Assam, Manipur, Tripura, and Mizoram States, causing problems of a different sort for Indira. But in 1972 India was supreme in South Asia, and it seemed then that what remained of Pakistan in the West would never be strong enough to pose any future challenge to Indian sovereignty in Kashmir, or anywhere else for that matter. Yet after so humiliating a defeat to Pakistani arms, Yahya stepped down and Zulfikar Ali Bhutto "picked up the pieces," which appeared painfully small at the time, of Pakistan's residual polity, first as president, later as prime minister, of his Islamic Republic. With his remarkable charisma and oratory, Bhutto managed to lift his defeated compatriots' shattered spirits from the dust of defeat to new heights of hope and pride in themselves and their Islamic homeland. Even Indira Gandhi found it impossible to resist Mr. Bhutto's political charm, meeting him at Simla for a South Asian Summit in 1972 that helped mark Pakistan's return to more rarefied altitudes of potential power as well as political negotiation.

Mr. Bhutto's political genius and amazing energy led Pakistan to the unanimous adoption of a new Constitution in 1973 and won external support for its martial as well as economic revival from China, Libya, Iran, Saudi Arabia, and other Islamic states that looked toward Pakistan as the potential "sword arm" of Islam in the region around the Persian Gulf and the Arabian Sea. Under Mr. Bhutto's leadership Pakistan started secretly to gather materials to build a thermonuclear bomb, which was sometimes called an "Islamic Bomb," constructed with the aid of Libyan fuel and money. Just before General Zia ul-Haq's (1917–1988) coup in 1977, leading to Mr. Bhutto's trial and execution, he had, in fact, won French support for his nuclear project, much to Washington's displeasure and chagrin.

Zia's martial dictatorship appeared close to collapse on the eve of the Russian invasion of Afghanistan in late 1979. Owing to Russia's massive martial presence in Kabul, however, billions of dollars worth of U.S. military and economic support were rushed to bolster our new "front-line" friend. When Zia first seized power in 1977 he promised "early elections" to restore democratic government to Pakistan, but with the Russian menace next door and American aid and equipment flooding into Karachi and flying into Islamabad-Rawalpindi, he quickly forgot about his promises to restore democracy in his eager enthusiasm to strengthen Islam by arming Afghan refugees to fight the Russians. For more than a decade then, martial dictatorship returned to Pakistan, until Zia's sudden death in a plane crash in August 1988. Soon after that, free elections were held again in Pakistan and Mr. Bhutto's brilliant daughter, Benazir Bhutto (b. 1954), emerged as the victorious popular leader of the reborn Pakistan People's party, to serve eighteen months as prime minister before she was unexpectedly "dismissed" by President Ghulam Ishaq Khan in August 1990.

With the restoration of democracy in Pakistan under such attractive youthful leadership, relations with India had at first improved, early 1989 being a most cordial and promising interlude for what was South Asia's mildest, happiest Spring. By Summer 1989, however, a new wave of violence swept over Kashmir, launched by daring young Muslim activists, and by late 1990 heavy firing was exchanged by Indian and Pakistan artillery. The Jammu and Kashmir Liberation Front was the most visible of a growing number of well-armed Kashmiri "independence" groups, who were ready to fight to the death, it seemed, to "free" Kashmir from Indian "occupation." Most Pakistanis, of course, continued to believe that India had "robbed" them of Kashmir at the birth of their nation. Azad Kashmir's leaders had no qualms, therefore, in encouraging their people to do whatever possible to help Islamic brothers across the "line" win "Freedom." Young Kashmiris who came over the border to Muzaffarabad, the capital of Azad Kashmir, were thus welcomed as heroes, receiving arms as well as alms before heading back with renewed vigor and fervor. In Peshawar and Pindi, Islamabad, Karachi, and Lahore crowds marched and chanted, demanding that a "Plebiscite" be held in Kashmir, or simply calling for "Freedom" there. With the Russians withdrawn from Afghanistan, Pakistan's military could more easily turn their attention toward and focus their dreams on Srinagar again. Not that any responsible leaders of Pakistan's army or central government were eager to launch another round of martial conflict with India, for all of them were old enough to recall how much Pakistan had lost from earlier ventures of that sort. And India's army was much stronger now. Pakistan's "Combined Opposition" to Benazir, one of whose most powerful leaders was chief minister of Punjab, Mian Nawaz Sharif, himself a Kashmiri by birth, viewed the Kashmir issue as an important political weapon. Benazir's dismissal was seen as clear evidence of reassertion of primary power by the Pak Army, despite President Khan's promise to hold "free and fair" elections in October. Similarly in New Delhi, Rajiv Gandhi, now leader of Congress' opposition to V. P.'s government in the Lok Sabha, was quick to accuse V. P. of being "soft" on Kashmir, which by 1990 had become as emotionally volatile an issue in India as it was in Pakistan. As cries for freedom spread across Kashmir's Vale, India flew more troops into the state, imposing strict curfews in all major cities together with President's Rule, under Delhi's tough martial administration. Farooq Abdullah, who had been reelected chief minister in 1986, resigned to "watch from the sidelines" as the fighting escalated. All foreign correspondents were flown out of Srinagar, and all tourists stopped flying into that beautiful city on Lake Dal, destined to witness many more young deaths, it seemed, before the fighting would stop, or even be diminished. India and Pakistan's oldest conflict was now very much ablaze, with anxious friends the world over fearing that this most explosive South Asian problem might once again lure India and Pakistan to war.

Sino-Indian Relations

Nehru hoped that India's foreign relations with China might become a model for world peace and good neighborly conduct. China, after all, had emerged as India had from Western colonial domination, and like Indians, Chinese were "Asians." The popular Hindi slogan "*Hindu-Chin bhai bhai!*" ("Indians and Chinese are brothers!") seemed to sum up Indian and Chinese relations, at least for Nehru. There were also "Five Principles" (*Panch Shila*) that defined more specifically how Indian and Chinese "brothers" should behave toward one another. Those noble principles were adopted in a Sino-Indian Treaty of Trade with Tibet in 1954. They began with "mutual respect for each other's territorial integrity and sovereignty" and ended with "peaceful coexistence."

The following year at an Afro-Asian conference held in Bandung, Indonesia, Nehru was challenged by China's Premier Chou En-lai for leadership of the emerging "Third World." Nonetheless, in reporting on Bandung in the Lok Sabha, Nehru sounded optimistic about the "universal application" of the Five Principles, saying: "In the Bandung Declaration we find the full embodiment of these Five Principles. . . . We have reason to feel happy that this Conference, representative of more than half the population of the world, has declared its adherence to the tenets that should guide . . . relations of the nations of the world if world peace and cooperation are to be achieved."

Chinese construction of a road across India's northern tier in remote Aksai Chin two years later presaged a rude awakening in New Delhi that turned the Sino-Indian slogan of brotherhood into "Hindu-Chin bye-bye!" Had Nehru studied Chinese maps more carefully, he would have realized earlier that Chou En-lai and his Chinese predecessors never accepted the McMahon Line northern "border" that had been adopted by the British Raj in 1914 and inherited by India's foreign office at Independence. Feeble Indian efforts to oust the Chinese from their new road linking Sinkiang with Tibet only backfired. Indian border police were killed by better-trained, better-armed Chinese troops.

China's "cartographic aggression" continued to frustrate and infuriate Delhi's foreign office, until a full-scale Chinese invasion over India's northeastern passes in 1962 buried most of India's flimsy force in Himalayan ice and snow, threatening the very capital of Assam before the Chinese opted unilaterally to withdraw that November. Perhaps they had caught wind of the sound of engines as wing after wing of U.S. cargo planes carrying high-altitude martial equipment flew into Calcutta in the immediate aftermath of China's India War. Thanks to Ambassador John K. Galbraith's prompt and vigorous support, enough supplies and equipment were sent from Washington over the next few months to outfit no fewer than ten high-altitude Indian Army divisions along her northern tier. India would never again be left so vulnerable to Chinese attack. Nehru's policy of "nonalignment," together with his dream of Panch Shila were, however, shattered and abandoned:

> "We are men and women of peace in this country," Nehru informed his people that Fall of 1962. "We are unused to the necessities of war. . . . But all our efforts have been in vain in so far as our own frontier is concerned, where a powerful and unscrupulous opponent, not caring for peace . . . has continuously threatened us and even carried the threats into action. . . . Everything else is secondary to the freedom of our people and of our Motherland. If necessary, everything else has to be sacrificed in this great crisis. . . . We must change our procedures from slow-moving methods of peacetime to those that produce results quickly. We must build up our military strength by all means at our disposal. . . . Freedom can never be taken for granted."

That traumatic Chinese invasion was a blow from which Nehru never recovered. A year and a half later he was dead, his dreams for world peace and Asian brotherhood destroyed, India's weakness and vulnerability exposed as never before. "It is sad to think that we in India, who have pleaded for peace all over the world, sought the friendship of China, and treated them with courtesy and consideration and pleaded their cause in the councils of the world, should now ourselves be victims of a new imperialism and expansion. . . . History has taken a new turn in Asia," Nehru told his Lok Sabha that dark November. As Sino-Indian friendship collapsed, Sino-Pak relations brightened and were viewed from New Delhi as a potential Northern and Western pincer's threat to Indian security. In direct response to those fears, India turned not only to Washington for martial aid, but to Moscow as well, especially since the United States and Pakistan were militarily linked through CENTO and SEATO (Central Treaty Organization and Southeast Asia Treaty Organization).

Russia began to play a more important diplomatic role in South Asia from the Ayub-Shastri summit in Tashkent at the dawn of 1966, and Indira Gandhi was careful to visit Moscow on her way home from her first and most successful meeting that March with President Lyndon Johnson in Washington. Indira's interest in Russian arms and support was no more based on her ideological preference for the Soviet Union than Nehru's willingness to accept offered U.S. military aid in 1962 had been based on any sudden tilt toward Washington. For Nehru and his daughter, as indeed for all of India's prime ministers, Indian sovereign and strategic interests have always come first and dictated what might otherwise seem New Delhi's "inconsistent" swings in foreign policy. By never exclusively aligning herself with either superpower, India has benefited from support, both economic and military, sent to New Delhi from Washington as well as Moscow. India's highly principled foreign policy might, therefore, almost seem to have been designed with Chanakyan shrewdness.

Indo-Sri Lankan Relations

India's relations with the island republic to her south, Sri Lanka, have long been strained by a virtual civil war between Sri Lanka's Sinhala Buddhist majority, governed from Colombo, and its alienated minority of mostly northern Hindu Tamils settled around Jaffna. Although there are only four million Tamils in Sri Lanka, whose Sinhalese majority outnumber them by over three to one, India's Tamil population just across Palk Strait from Jaffna total more than 50 million. Most of those Tamil Nadu Indians share strong bonds of kinship with their linguistic brethren, and Indian Tamils have long supported Sri Lanka Tamil aspirations for independent statehood with money and arms. Since 1972, when Sri Lanka's Constitution made Sinhala the *only* official language of that "Buddhist" republic, militant Tamil agitation increased, and several well-armed terrorist bands, the most powerful of which were the "Tamil Tigers," soon emerged around Jaffna.

In 1976 most Tamil political parties united to form the "Tamil United Liberation Front" (TULF), which resolved to work toward the creation of a "free, sovereign, secular, socialist state of *Tamil Eelam*." That demand for a Tamil Nation and the partition of Sri Lanka received strong support from many Tamils in the north, but was totally rejected by President Junius Jayewardene's government in Colombo. Neighboring beaches and villages of India's Tamil Nadu were used by Tamil Tigers and *Eelam* activists to train and arm guerrilla fighters from Sri Lanka in what soon became a deadly conflict. New Delhi then found itself in a highly ambivalent position, since no central government of India could afford to support any linguistic separatist movement so close to its own multilingual borders, yet no Indian leader dared to alienate 50 million Indian Tamils! Rajiv Gandhi initially hoped to settle the conflict by inviting both sides to a "peace" conference in

Bhutan in 1985. Those Thimpu talks soon broke down and fighting resumed throughout Sri Lanka. Thwarted by Colombo's uncompromising position, New Delhi stopped trying to mediate any solution, leaving South India's Tamils to do virtually as they liked about helping their *Eelam*-bent neighbors, till December of 1986, when Rajiv flew Tamil Tiger leader Prabhakaran to Bangalore for Summit talks with himself and President Jayewardene.

Sri Lanka's president was then ready to concede virtual Tamil autonomy over Jaffna's northern province, but still refused to grant Tamils power over Sri Lanka's eastern province as well, since they then had an actual majority in only one-third of the eastern districts.

For six months following the breakdown of those December 1986 talks, Colombo's Army repeatedly attacked Jaffna, inflicting heavy casualties from air raids and exacting an even heavier toll on Tamil life by cutting off all fuel and food supplies to Sri Lanka's northern region with its dense population. Mounting pressure from Tamil Nadu finally brought New Delhi's air force into the Sri Lanka War by mid-1987, air-dropping vital food and medical supplies over Jaffna, after Colombo's navy intercepted a mercy fleet of unarmed boats from Madras.

On July 29, 1987 the Sri Lanka Accord, a peace accord signed by Rajiv Gandhi and Junius Jayewardene in Colombo, brought a temporary halt to Sri Lanka's Civil War. India sent enough troops to her island neighbor to oversee the disarmament of Tamil militants and ensure the brief cessation of hostilities. Tamils were promised control over both northern and eastern provinces, at least until free elections to Provincial Councils could determine the will of Sri Lanka's majority in both regions. Tiger leader Prabhakaran complained about the imposed terms but was convinced by New Delhi to accept the Accord in apparent hopes of becoming the first Chief Minister over autonomous Tamil provinces. Extremist Sinhalese Buddhists violently opposed the agreement, however, bitterly attacking it as little more than "surrender" to Indian "Imperial bullying." Most impartial observers recognized the Sri Lanka Accord as the best hope for restoring peace to that sadly torn island of great natural beauty, marking what appeared to be a new stage for India's peace-keeping capacity in South Asia and the Indian Ocean. But the Sri Lanka Accord quickly broke down as the Tigers balked at surrendering their arms, and no pressure from Delhi seemed capable of persuading them. President Jayawardene was replaced by his former prime minister, Ranasinghe Premadasa, in Colombo, but the bloodbath continued around

Jaffna in the north and Batticaloa in the east, soon spreading to the south as well. Premadasa insisted that Indian troops be withdrawn from his nation, seeing the Indian Peace Keeping Force (IPKF) as more of a stimulus to violence among his own people than a force for moderation and restoring calm. By the end of 1989 Sri Lanka was an island torn apart by terror in every major city, and as Indian troops pulled out, Delhi withdrawing the last of them in early April 1990, the Island hovered on the brink of resumed civil war. Tamil refugees fled north in boats, seeking havens once again along the coast of Tamil Nadu, but their South Indian brothers were by now so sick of the violence and pain they invariably caused that for the first time such refugee boats were forbidden permission to land around Madras, turned back toward Jaffna, and what would be almost certain death, unless Sri Lanka's sorely divided small land could learn to harmonize its deep ethnic differences, or reconcile itself to partition.

Afghanistan

Since December 1979 the Russian invasion of Afghanistan had posed the greatest external danger to South Asia as a whole, a threat to which the United States responded by heavily arming Pakistan openly and Afghan *Mujaheedin* ("Freedom-fighter") guerrillas covertly. The thirty-year Indo-Soviet Treaty of Peace, Friendship and Cooperation, signed in 1971, muted New Delhi's response to the unexpected advance of more than 100,000 Russian troops across the River Amu Darya (formerly Oxus) into Kabul and Qandahar. Mrs. Gandhi remained loyal to Comrade Brezhnev, despite warnings from Delhi Foreign Office advisers that if Russian tanks rolled over the Khyber into Pakistan's Peshawar there would really be nothing to stop them from rolling right on into New Delhi's diplomatic quarter. In Chanakyan "Mandala" realpolitik terms, Pakistan, as India's immediate neighbor, remained its traditional "enemy," while Afghanistan, as the neighbor's neighbor, would be viewed as India's "friend." Yet even if Mrs. Gandhi was thinking only in *Arthashastra*-circles, Russia, as the friend's neighbor, should surely be perceived as India's "enemy." The actual presence of so many Russian troops so close to the Khyber Pass was as unsettling to most Indians in high Delhi places as was the rapid upgrading of Pakistan's air force and armor by the U.S. Pentagon. More than 100 UN nations lined up with Pakistan and the United States in repeatedly voting to condemn Russia's invasion of Afghanistan, urging Moscow to withdraw all its troops from that barren and tormented land. India, however, merely abstained in such votes.

By the late 1980s Indian strategists worried, as their British imperial predecessors had a century earlier, about Russian armies coming over the Khyber, which must have seemed a strange irony to them. British India's 1947 Partition and subsequent Indo–Pak conflicts had kept most troops of both South Asian nations pinned down confronting each other rather than facing northwest toward the Afghan Frontier, which had thus become increasingly vulnerable to possible invasion. In mid-1985 Prime Minister Rajiv Gandhi, taking a more outspoken stand against Russia's martial presence in Afghanistan than his mother had ever expressed, called upon all "foreign forces" to leave South Asia. Rajiv also tried to reintegrate, at least in small measure, the national South Asian pieces that fell out in the shattering aftermath of the British imperial demise. In December 1985 the leaders of South Asia's nation-states met in Dakha for the birth of a new South Asian Association for Regional Cooperation (SAARC). It was but the first of many regularly planned meetings that would open a continuing dialogue on regional problems, conflicts, and mutual interests in economic and socioreligious as well as military affairs. Rajiv took the lead in founding the new Association, as seemed fitting in view of India's size and premier power among the seven nations that included not only Pakistan and Bangladesh but also Sri Lanka, Bhutan, Nepal, and the Maldives. The most important twosome in SAARC, President General Zia ul-Haq of Pakistan and Prime Minister Rajiv Gandhi, met in New Delhi a week after the new Association was born, and reached a "mutual understanding" not to attack each other's "nuclear facilities." Zia spent only one day in India, but his visit presaged an era of diminishing tensions between the two powers whose traumatic birth four decades earlier had left a legacy of violent distrust, fear, and hatred that had threatened a South Asian nuclear war in the early 1980s.

India's first nuclear explosion in Rajasthan on May 18, 1974 had not been followed up with any further bomb tests or actual stockpiling of nuclear weapons. In announcing the awesome underground blast at the time, Mrs. Gandhi insisted that it was merely part of India's "peaceful atomic energy" program and that India had "no intention" of becoming a "nuclear weapons country." There are, indeed, several nuclear-fueled electric-power plants operating in India, but the multimegaton plutonium explosion of 1974 could only have served the purpose of testing the capability of nuclear weapons or of warning India's neighbors, China as well as Pakistan, that India was on the threshold of becoming a nuclear power, and could do so whenever she wished. The latter message was clearly communicated, for in the wake of that fateful blast, felt in Sind as well as Rajasthan, Prime Minister Zulfikar Bhutto's government launched its top-priority secret drive for the development of a Pakistani Bomb, which some called an "Islamic Bomb," since its uranium fuel may have come from Libya or Iraq or have been purchased elsewhere with funds from a consortium of Muslim nations, as a possible counter to Israeli nuclear capability.

Many centrifuges and other vital equipment required for processing nuclear fuel and building a bomb were secretly procured by Pakistani scientists and agents the world over and assembled at Pakistan's nuclear development center at Kahuta. Although Mr. Bhutto himself was hanged in 1979, before his Bomb could be finished, General Zia continued to support, while officially denying, Pakistan's nuclear bomb-building effort, which his erstwhile patron had so vigorously sponsored. Throughout the 1980s Pakistan was rumored to be on the verge of triggering a nuclear explosion, and a site for it had supposedly been set up in Pakistan's Azad Kashmir. Other rumors claimed that China's "New Province" or Tibet provided the site and that an "explosion" had actually occurred in 1984.

Indian strategists argued that India could wait no longer to launch her own nuclear weapons program, which should not require more than six months or so, since India had, in fact, been processing plutonium since 1964. Some Indian officers favored even more extreme action, advising Mrs. Gandhi and Rajiv to "take out" Pakistan's Kahuta plant the way Israel had bombed Iraq's half-finished nuclear facility. There were rumors that Israel might be "willing to do the job" if India requested such help and provided refueling facilities. With her own Muslim population almost as large as Pakistan's, however, India had as yet not even dared to fully recognize Israel by exchanging ambassadors, keeping official Indian exchanges with Tel-Aviv and Jerusalem minimal.

The Rajiv-Zia understanding of December 1985 thus dramatically lowered prospects of any South Asian nuclear war to be launched from either side of the Indo-Pak border. That initial step toward defusing the most explosive problem dividing India and Pakistan would be followed by many other agreements, economic and cultural, as well as diplomatic and military. Discussion of a possible future "No War" or positive "Peace Pact" had been mooted. With settlement reached at the U.S.-Soviet summit on Afghanistan, and the Russians finally withdrawing all their troops from Kabul just a decade after they invaded, as President Mikhail Gorbachev promised they would, the diplomatic future for South Asia as a whole seemed to become much brighter in early 1989. By 1990, however, there were still close to 4 million Afghan refugees in Pakistan and many squabbling bands of armed Mujaheedin, who fought one another more vigorously than they fought President Najibullah's Kabul Army. Although the Cold War had ended for Moscow and Washington, fighting remained very hot in Jalalabad and around Kabul, and was unfortunately starting to boil again in Srinagar.

Indo-U.S. Relations

Relations between India and the United States have been alternately cordial and suspicious, friendly and hostile, warm and cool in frustratingly ambivalent sequence since the birth of India's Republic, reflecting in part misunderstandings of each other's worldviews, but also basic differing realities animating and motivating both distant nations in a complex world. As the world's largest democracy, whose leaders have all been educated to speak and read English and have either fought for or are descended from families that struggled for independence from British rule, India naturally has much in common with the United States. As individuals, Indians and Americans generally like each other at first sight and sound, and often become close friends. As a rule Indians respond positively to American openness in social relations, warmth, helpfulness, good nature, generosity, and readiness to criticize themselves as well as others in what is often a fearless—some might say foolhardy—search for truth. Conversely, Americans appreciate Indian intelligence, sensitivity, seeming humility, warmth, loyalty to friends and family, kindness, and open-minded curiosity about most things.

Indo-American differences were for some time extensive, however, especially concerning the Soviet Union. American "Cold War" fears of Russian imperialism led to our frenzied search for global security behind a steel fence of allies on the perimeter of continental Russia committed to its "containment." Several military pacts (NATO, CENTO, SEATO) were thus forged by Western powers in the decade following the end of World War II. Pakistan eagerly joined our alliances, providing bases near Peshawar for U-2 spy flights in return for massive martial aid. India, of course, viewed such U.S. support for Pakistan with the greatest trepidation, justifiably fearing that American arms would be used against Indian rather than Russian troops. John Foster Dulles, however, self-righteously believed that any nation in the world that was not "with" us must be "against" us. Nehru's nonalignment came to be viewed in Washington, therefore, as a "pro-Russian plot" rather than the purely pro-Indian policy it was. The legacy of such Cold War mistrust, compounded by the more bitter poison of Partition and the birth of Pakistan, generated dark clouds of karmic fallout that have polluted Indo-U.S. relations for over forty years. New Delhi continues to fear the flow of U.S. arms to Pakistan as much as Washington once feared waves of Russian imperial expansion crashing over the North-West Frontier of South Asia. Such global differences in strategic perspectives were enhanced, moreover, by deep-rooted Indo-U.S. psychocultural differences in behavior.

Whether as missionaries or Peace Corps workers, engineers, Ford fellows, or business executives, Americans like to "get things done." Indians usually seem content to wait until some future lifetime. Change is perhaps the first "law" of modern American life, but remains one of the lowest priorities for most Indians, where traditional continuity counts highest. Most Americans treasure personal freedoms strongly enough to be willing to die for their preservation. To Indians, familial and jati duties or responsibilities are far more important than freedom, even in such personal matters as marriage, work, and general life-style. Indians will often become most violently passionate, however, about the preservation and purity of religious customs or shrines, responding to any threat or attack upon their faith or its institutions much the way Americans might react to an attack on their liberty or country. Sikh reactions to Operation Bluestar are a recent case in point. Violent Muslim explosions in response to any interference with their religious marital laws or customs by India's "secular" state can also erupt overnight, as they did late in 1985 as a result of the Shah Bano case.

Shah Bano, a sixty-five-year-old penurious Indian Muslim woman, divorced by her wealthy husband, who paid her only the rupee equivalent of two dollars and fifty cents a month, sued him for some $20 in monthly alimony. That modest enough demand was granted by the High Court of Madhya Pradesh, but Shah Bano's outraged husband appealed its judgment to India's Supreme Court, which affirmed the High Court's decision. That was when the communal rioting started in Rajasthan, Bihar, Maharashtra, Uttar Pradesh, and Kashmir. Muslim fundamentalists charged that Indian courts were deliberately "misinterpreting" the *Qur'an* and Shariat Law, by which a Muslim husband who divorced his wife owed her no support, in order to "convert" good Muslims into apostates. The shouting reached the floor of the Lok Sabha and the inner recesses of Rajiv's cabinet. The Prime Minister himself actually felt obliged to apologize to angry Muslims for having said in Parliament that he hoped by the twenty-first century that "all Indians" would come to think of themselves first as "Indians," not as Hindus, Muslims, Sikhs, or Parsis. So the same petrol that had given birth to Pakistan in 1947 remained potentially explosive in the Muslim quarters of thousands of crowded cities throughout India. One such, of course, was Ayodhya, where the communal controversy over whether Babri Mosque should be permitted to remain above "Lord Rama's Birthplace" would doubtless claim many more lives before being resolved.

The Future

All of the above is but to say that India's present and future continue to reflect her past. The River flows on, gathering new streams, absorbing new currents of thought, new technologies, new peoples and beliefs, yet in the process of such absorption each and all of them become *Indian*. Even as Mother Ganga absorbs countless ashes of expired bodies, assimilating each within the depths of her thick and turbulent flow, ever changelessly changing. While Sikhs and Muslims assert their individual faiths more insistently and demand greater autonomy, reaffirming special identities that they fear might otherwise be "lost" forever, dissolved in the swift-flowing currents of today and tomorrow, India's Hindu majority becomes, or remains, more *Hindu*. State elections in March 1990 brought more power to L. K. Advani's Hindu–first Bharatiya Janata Party (BJP) than to any other political group. Although Advani chose to remain outside V. P.'s cabinet, his party's growing strength throughout the Hindi-speaking Hindu heartland of North India have catapulted him and the BJP over which he presides to a position of power second only to that of V. P. himself in modern India. Without Advani's support the National Front would fall, yet the price of his support is continued militance in Kashmir, a tougher stand in support of Lord Rama's Temple in Ayodhya, and a slower pace of secularization.

So India keeps changing, but Indian faith in cyclical change makes every return to past norms or traditional values and beliefs seem somehow natural, more proper than what might be viewed as "backsliding" in the West. And as the Wheel turns, India sheds her peeling patina of Victorian mannerisms and dress, even as she has come out from behind the abandoned shield of British arms and British martial leadership successfully to fend for herself in strongly defending the continent she controls, as much her legacy from indigenous Mauryan and Guptan Imperial rulers as from foreign Mughal or British conquerors. Perhaps that is why, more in India than anywhere else on earth, her past remains prologue; or in Hindu terms, her Karma continues to ripen and bear fruit. As Jawaharlal Nehru wrote in his final testament:

> Though I have discarded much of past tradition and customs, and am anxious that India should rid herself of all shackles that bind and constrain and divide her people. . . . I am conscious that I too, like all of us, am a link in that unbroken chain which goes back to the dawn of history in the immemorial past of India. . . . I do not want any religious ceremonies performed for me after my death. I do not believe in any such ceremonies. . . . My desire to have a handful of my ashes thrown into the Ganga at Allahabad has no religious significance, so far as I am concerned. . . . I have been attached to the Ganga and Yamuna Rivers in Allahabad ever since my childhood. . . . The Ganga, especially, is the river of India . . . symbol of India's agelong culture and civilization, ever-changing, ever-flowing, and yet ever the same.

Secular socialist though he was, therefore, Nehru's mortal remains were cremated at *Shanti Ghat*, the "Steps of Peace," along the Yamuna at Delhi, near the *Raj Ghat*, where Mahatma Gandhi had been cremated sixteen years earlier. Then a portion of that most modern of India's Westernized leader's ashes were carried by his equally modern daughter, Indira, to the most sacred confluence of the three most worshiped Rivers of Hindu India, Goddesses Ganga, Yamuna, and (invisible) Saraswati for immersion at that *Triveni* at Allahabad, while hundreds of Brahmans chanted ancient Vedic mantras. Yet that was no religious ceremony! Ah, India.

Lord Shiva's dance of life continues, even as the Buddha's Wheel of the Law turns on, each double-*Kalpa*-cycle of Time transforming a world of purest goodness, bliss, and gold into a dark age of wretched violence, hatred, and suffering, only to roll on, back to light, beauty, and truth, as this world of illusion, this sporting-game of Shiva plays on, until the gods themselves grow old and die, each day in the life of Brahma witnessing all the joy and glory together with all the misery and pain of human existence on this planet of ours, in the cosmos called India. For in India, as elsewhere, entropy tends to increase, karma to ripen, so the past clings and its problems proliferate, fester, explode, before they finally dissipate and dissolve in the acid of tears and the ocean of Time. Thus the bloodthirsty legacy of a Mahmud of Ghazni remains to haunt Hindu–Muslim harmonies, as does the memory of what Aurangzeb did. So the anguished cries of Amritsar's Jallianwala Bagh and Golden Temple during the blazing darkness of Operation Bluestar resound and reverberate down long decades, agonized years, echoing dissonance and death. Yet from that same soil sprang a Guru Nanak, from the very genetic line that bred Aurangzeb came an Akbar before him, even as the Buddha, Ashoka, and Mahatma Gandhi were all children of Indian Civilization, contributing so much of enduring value to the wisdom of the World.

Ah, India, who can fathom your depths or reconcile your complexities? "India has not ever been an easy country to understand," Prime Minister Indira Gandhi once noted, speculating that "perhaps it is too deep, contradictory and diverse, and few people in the contemporary world have the time or inclination to look beyond the obvious." As modern India's most powerful leader and one of history's most powerful women, Indira was surely uniquely equipped to "understand" her Nation and its deepest currents, yet she so sadly misunderstood Sikh feelings as to trigger the Amritsar action that brought her own violent death in New Delhi. Perhaps like India, Indira was too contradictory herself, too complex and emotional a being to be ruled by reason and logic, but rather falling victim to passions too powerful to elude or resist, a victim to all the coexisting opposites that are India. Even as "Great-Souled" *Mahatma* Gandhi, father of his nation, fell victim to the violent hatred of one of his "devout," "patriotic" Brahman Hindu sons! Nothing Indian is quite as simple as it seems. Many maya-veils of History hide her modern "reality," and each general "truth" about that Continent-country named "River" is in some ways false.

Perhaps only poetry can capture the essence of India's Civilization, her fragile strength, her mighty weakness, the beauty of her poverty, the pleasures of her pain-filled heart, the eternal youthfulness of her age, the mystic identity of her individual Atman with universal Brahman, the suffering born of her love, the moksha-release brought at the end of any search for understanding her true genius. Paradoxically, considering the growing pressures of India's population and the communal character of so much of Indian life, in urban as well as village settings, the poem that I think best captures the essence that epitomizes India is Gurudev Rabindranath Tagore's *Ekla Chalore* ("Walk Alone"):

If they answer not to thy call,
Walk Alone.
If they tremble and cower mutely
Facing the Wall,
O thou of evil luck,
Open thy mind and speak out alone.
If, when crossing the wilderness,
They turn away and desert you,
O thou of evil luck,
Trample the thorns under thy tread,
And along the blood-strewn path,
Walk alone.
If, when the night is troubled
With storm,
They do not hold up the light,
O thou of evil luck,
With the thunder flame of pain,
Ignite thine own heart,
And let it burn alone.

Om

The End

Notes

Historic Prologue

1. Quoted in Stanley A. Wolpert, *Tilak and Gokhale: Revolution and Reform in the Making of Modern India* (Berkeley and Los Angeles: University of California Press, 1961), p. 191.
2. Quoted in Stanley A. Wolpert, "The Indian National Congress in Nationalist Perspective," in *Congress and Indian Nationalism: The Pre-Independence Phase*, by Richard Sisson and Stanley Wolpert, eds. chap. 2 (Berkeley, Los Angeles, London: University of California Press, 1988), p. 22.
3. Quoted in Stanley A. Wolpert, *Jinnah of Pakistan* (New York: Oxford University Press, 1984), p. 62.

Religion and Philosophy

1. E. M. Forster, *A Passage to India* (New York: Harcourt Brace, 1924), pp. 285–288.
2. McKim Marriott, "The Feast of Love," in *Krishna: Myths, Rites and Attitudes*, Milton Singer, ed. (Honolulu: East-West Center Press, 1966), pp. 200–212.
3. *The Thirteen Principal Upanishads*, trans. from Sanskrit by Robert Ernest Hume; 2d rev. ed. from the *Chandogya Upanishad* (London: Oxford University Press, 1931), pp. 246–248.
4. See Ramakrishna's "Parables and Sayings," quoted in W. Theodore de Bary, ed., *Sources of Indian Tradition* (New York: Columbia University Press, 1958), pp. 643–646.
5. Swami Vivekananda, "Man is God," in de Bary, ed., *Sources of Indian Tradition*, p. 648.
6. Swami Vivekananda, "Indian Thought to Conquer the World," in de Bary, ed., Sources of Indian Tradition, p. 652.
7. Sir Francis Tuker, *While Memory Serves* (London: Cassell, 1950), p. 160.
8. Khushwant Singh, *Ranjit Singh: Maharajah of Punjab, 1780–1839* (New Delhi: Orient Longman, 1985).

9. Mahatma Gandhi, *Young India, 1919–1922* (New York: B. W. Huebsch, Inc., 1924), pp. 12–14.
10. Jawaharlal Nehru, *Toward Freedom* (New York: The John Day Co., 1941), p. 49.
11. Motilal Nehru, "Responsible Self-Government," Presidential Address to the Indian National Congress, Amritsar, December 27, 1919, pp. 7–8 in *The Voice of Freedom, Selected Speeches*, K. M. Panikkar and A. Pershad, eds. (London: Asia Publishing House, 1961).

Society

1. William H. Wiser and Charlotte Viall Wiser, *Behind Mud Walls, 1930–1960*, with a sequel: *The Village in 1970* (Berkeley, Los Angeles, London: University of California Press, 1971), pp. 41–42, 143–144, 189–190.
2. B. R. Ambedkar, *What Congress and Gandhi Have Done to the Untouchables* (Bombay: Thacker & Co. Ltd., 1945), p. 302.
3. Indira Gandhi, *My Truth*, presented by Emmanuel Pouchpadass (Delhi: Vision Books, 1981), p. 54.
4. Mohandas K. Gandhi, *An Autobiography: The Story of My Experiments with Truth* (Boston: Beacon Press, 1957), p. 9.
5. Lakshmibai Tilak, *I Follow After*, E. Josephine Inkster, trans. (Madras, New York: Oxford University Press, 1950), p. 12.
6. Anandibai Karve's "Autobiography," in *The New Brahmans: Five Maharashtrian Families*, D. D. Karve, trans. (Berkeley and Los Angeles: University of California Press, 1963), pp. 58–79. Irawati Karve's memoir of "Grandfather" follows in ibid., pp. 80–104.
7. Krishna (Nehru) Hutheesing, *With No Regrets: Recollections* (London: L. Drummond Ltd., 1946), p. 27.
8. Vijaya Lakshmi Pandit, *The Scope of Happiness: A Personal Memoir* (New York: Crown Publishers, 1979), p. 56.
9. Milton Singer, *When A Great Tradition Modernizes: An Anthropological Approach to Indian Civilization* (New York: Praeger Publishers, 1972). M. N. Srinivas, *Caste in Modern India and Other Essays* (Bombay: Asia Publishing House, 1962).
10. *Who Are The Guilty?* Report of an Inquiry into the Delhi Riots of October 31–November 4, 1984 by the Indian People's Union for Demo-

cratic Rights and Indian People's Union for Civil Liberties, published jointly by Gobinda Mukhoty and Rajni Kothari (Delhi: Sunny Graphics, 1984). *Report of the Citizens' Commission*, headed by former Chief Justice of India S. M. Sikri, "Delhi, 31 October to 4 November 1984" (Delhi: Citizens' Commission, Tata Press Ltd., January 1985).

Arts and Sciences

1. Poem 57 of *Gitanjali* ("Garland of Songs") from Sir Rabindranath Tagore, *Gitanjali and Fruit-Gathering* (New York: Macmillan, 1919), pp. 52–53.
2. Jayadeva's *Gita Govinda*, quoted in Barbara Stoler Miller, ed., trans., *Love Song of the Dark Lord: Jayadeva's Gītagovinda* (New York: Columbia University Press, 1977), pp. 76–77.
3. *The Kama Sutra* of Vatsyayana, Sir Richard F. Burton, trans. (New York: E. P. Dutton, 1962).
4. Ananda K. Coomaraswamy, *The Dance of Shiva*, rev. ed. (New York: The Noonday Press, 1957), pp. 66–78.
5. R. K. Narayan, *The Ramayana: A Shortened Modern Prose Version of the Indian Epic* (New York: The Viking Press, 1972). Also by the same author, *The Mahabharata: A Shortened Modern Prose Version of the Indian Epic* (New York: The Viking Press, 1978).
6. Kalidasa's "The Cloud-Messenger," in *Shakuntala and Other Writings by Kalidasa*, Arthur W. Ryder, trans. (New York: E. P. Dutton & Co., 1959), pp. 185–208.
7. Ibid., pp. 3–94.
8. Nirad C. Chaudhuri, *The Autobiography of an Unknown Indian* (Berkeley and Los Angeles: University of California Press, 1968), p. 222.
9. "The Language of the Masses," quoted in de Bary, ed., *Sources of Indian Tradition*, p. 709; see also Sunil Kumar Banerjee, *Bankim Chandra* (Calcutta: Firma K. L. Mukhopadhyay, 1968).
10. "The White Man's Burden," 1899, in *Rudyard Kipling's Verse: Inclusive Edition, 1885–1918* (Garden City, N.Y.: Doubleday, Page & Co., 1922), pp. 371–372.
11. E. M. Forster, *The Hill of Devi* (New York: Harcourt Brace, 1953).
12. Forster, *A Passage to India*, p. 322.

13. Mulk Raj Anand, *Untouchable* (New Delhi: Orient Paperbacks, 1970).
14. Mulk Raj Anand, *Coolie* (Delhi: Hind Pocket Books, 1972).
15. R. K. Narayan, *Swami and Friends* (East Lansing: Michigan State College Press, 1954); idem., *Bachelor of Arts* (Mysore: Indian Thought Publications, 1965); idem., *My Days* (New York: Viking Press, 1974); idem., *The Financial Expert* (East Lansing: Michigan State College Press, 1953); idem., *The Guide* (New York: Viking Press, 1958).
16. Ved Mehta, *Face to Face* (Oxford: Oxford University Press, 1957), p. 15.
17. V. S. Naipaul, *India: A Wounded Civilization* (New York: Vintage Books, 1978), pp. x–xi.
18. Salmon Rushdie, *Midnight's Children* (New York: Knopf, 1981).
19. Paul Scott, *The Jewel in the Crown* (London: William Heinemann Ltd., 1966); idem., *The Day of the Scorpion* (New York: William Morrow & Co., Inc., 1968); idem., *The Towers of Silence* (London: William Heinemann Ltd., 1971); idem., *A Division of the Spoils* (London: William Heinemann Ltd., 1975).

Polity and Foreign Policy

1. J. P. Narayan, July 21, 1975 entry in his *Prison Diary*, A. B. Shah, ed. (Bombay: Popular Prakashan, 1977), p. 1.

Suggested Additional Reading

1: The Environment

Bhardwaj, O. P. *Studies in the Historical Geography of Ancient India*. Delhi, 1986.

Brown, W. Norman, ed. *India, Pakistan, Ceylon*. Rev. ed. Philadelphia, 1960.

Chatterjee, S. P., ed. *National Atlas of India*. Calcutta, 1957.

Kuriyan, George. *India: A General Survey*. New Delhi, 1969.

Law, B. C. *Historical Geography of Ancient India*. 2d ed. Delhi, 1976.

Schwartzberg, Joseph E., Shiva Bajpai, et al., eds. *A Historical Atlas of South Asia*. Chicago, 1978.

Spate, O. H. K., and A. T. A. Learmonth. *India and Pakistan*. 3d ed. London, 1967.

2: Historic Prologue

Basham, A. L. *The Wonder That Was India*. 3d ed. New York, 1967.

Broomfield, J. H. *Elite Conflict in a Plural Society*. Berkeley and Los Angeles, 1968.

Brown, W. Norman. *The United States and India, Pakistan, Bangladesh*. 3d ed. Cambridge, 1972.

Embree, Ainslie T., ed. *Sources of Indian Tradition*. 2d ed. New York, 1988.

Furber, Holden. *John Company at Work*. Cambridge, 1948.

Ikram, S. M. *Muslim Civilization in India*. Edited by A. T. Embree. New York and London, 1964.

Kautilya. *Arthashastra*. Translated by R. Shamasastry. 5th ed. Mysore, 1956.

Kopf, David. *British Orientalism and the Bengal Renaissance: The Dynamics of Indian Modernization, 1773–1834*. Berkeley and Los Angeles, 1969.

Majumdar, R. C., ed. *History and Culture of the Indian People*. Vol. 1, *The Vedic Age*. London, 1951. Vol. 2, *The Age of Imperial Unity*. Bombay, 1951. Vol. 3, *The Classical Age*. Bombay, 1954. Vol. 4, *The Age of Imperial Kanauj*. Bombay, 1955. Vol. 5, *The Struggle for Empire*. Bombay, 1957. Vol. 6, *The Delhi Sultanate*. Bombay, 1967. Vol. 7, *The Mughal Empire*. Bombay, 1969.

Philips, Cyril Henry. *The East India Company, 1784–1834*. 2d ed. Manchester, 1961.
Singh, Khushwant. *A History of the Sikhs*, 2 vols. Princeton, 1963.
Sisson, Richard, and Stanley Wolpert, eds. *Congress and Indian Nationalism: The Pre-Independence Phase*. Berkeley, Los Angeles, London, 1988.
Spear, Percival. *A History of India*. Vol. 2. Harmondsworth, 1970.
Stokes, Eric. *The English Utilitarians and India*. Oxford, 1959.
Thapar, Romila. A History of India. Vol. 1. Harmondsworth, 1966.
Trautmann, Thomas R. *Kautilya and the Arthashastra*. Leiden, 1971.
Wheeler, Sir Mortimer. *Civilizations of the Indus Valley and Beyond*. New York, 1966.
Woodcock, George. *The Greeks in India*. London, 1966.
Wolpert, Stanley A. *Tilak and Gokhale: Revolution and Reform in the Making of Modern India*. Berkeley and Los Angeles, 1962.
———. *Morley and India, 1906–1910*. Berkeley and Los Angeles, 1967.
———. *Jinnah of Pakistan*. New York and Oxford, 1984.
———. *A New History of India*. 3d ed. New York and Oxford, 1989.

3: Religion and Philosophy

Ahmad, Aziz. *An Intellectual History of Islam in India*. Edinburgh, 1969.
Bloomfield, Maurice. *The Religion of the Veda*. New York, 1908.
Bolle, Kees, trans. *The Bhagavadgītā: A New Translation*. Berkeley, Los Angeles, London, 1979.
Edgerton, Franklin, trans. *The Bhagavad Gita*. Cambridge, 1972.
Embree, Ainslie T., ed. *The Hindu Tradition*. New York, 1966.
Hawley, John Stratton, and Mark Juergensmeyer, eds. *Songs of the Saints of India*. New York and Oxford, 1988.
Hume, Robert E., trans. *The Thirteen Principal Upanishads*. 2d rev. ed. London, 1931.
Ions, Veronica. *Indian Mythology*. London, 1967.
Kramrisch, Stella. *Manifestations of Shiva*. Philadelphia, 1981.
Macdonell, A. A. *History of Sanskrit Literature*. 5th impression. Delhi, 1962.
Müller, F. Max. *Heritage of India*. Calcutta, 1951.
O'Flaherty, Wendy Doniger. *Śiva: The Erotic Ascetic*. Oxford, 1973.
———, trans. *The Rig Veda: An Anthology*. Harmondsworth, 1981.
Radhakrishnan, S. *The Hindu View of Life*. London, 1954.

Rahman, Fazlur. *Islam*. Garden City, N.Y., 1968.
Singer, Milton, ed. *Krishna: Myths, Rites and Attitudes*. Honolulu, 1966.
Warren, Henry C. *Buddhism in Translations*, 3 vols. Cambridge, 1922.
Zimmer, Heinrich. *Myths and Symbols in Indian Art and Civilization*. Joseph Campbell, ed. Princeton, 1972.

4: Society

Ambedkar, B. R. *What Congress and Gandhi Have Done to the Untouchables*. Bombay, 1945.
Bailey, F. G. *Tribe, Caste, and Nation*. Manchester, 1960.
Ballhatchet, Kenneth. *Race, Sex and Class Under The Raj*. New York, 1980.
Béteille, André. *Caste, Class, and Power*. Berkeley and Los Angeles, 1969.
Ghurye, G. S. *Caste and Class in India*. Bombay, 1957.
Karve, D. D., trans. *The New Brahmans: Five Maharashtrian Families*. Berkeley and Los Angeles, 1963.
Lannoy, Richard. *The Speaking Tree: A Study of Indian Culture and Society*. New York, 1971.
Mandelbaum, David G. *Society in India*. Vol. 1, *Continuity and Change*. Vol. 2, *Change and Continuity*. Berkeley, Los Angeles, London, 1970.
Mannoni, O. *Prospero and Caliban: The Psychology of Colonization*. Translated by P. Powesland. New York, 1964.
Mayer, Adrian C. *Caste and Kinship in Central India: A Village and Its Region*. London, 1960.
Moon, Penderel. *Strangers in India*. New York, 1945.
Rudolph, Lloyd I., and Susanne H. Rudolph. *The Modernity of Tradition*. Chicago, 1967.
Singer, Milton. *When A Great Tradition Modernizes: An Anthropological Approach to Indian Civilization*. New York, 1972.
Srinivas, M. N. *Caste in Modern India and Other Essays*. Bombay, 1962.
———, et al., eds. *Dimensions of Social Change in India*. New Delhi, 1978.
Wiser, William H., and Charlotte Viall Wiser. *Behind Mud Walls, 1930–1960*, with a sequel: *The Village in 1970*. Berkeley, Los Angeles, London, 1971.

5: Arts and Sciences

Anand, Mulk Raj. *Untouchable*. New Delhi, 1970.
———. *Coolie*. Delhi, 1972.
Basham, A. L., ed. *A Cultural History of India*. Oxford, 1975.
Chaudhuri, Nirad C. *The Autobiography of an Unknown Indian*. Berkeley and Los Angeles, 1968.
Coomaraswamy, Ananda K. *The Dance of Shiva*. Rev. ed. New York, 1957.
Dimock, Edward C. *The Literatures of India*. Chicago, 1974.
———. *In Praise of Krishna: Songs from the Bengali*. Garden City, N.Y., 1967.
Edgerton, Franklin, trans. *The Panchatantra*. London, 1965.
Forster, E. M. *A Passage to India*. New York, 1924.
———. *The Hill of Devi*. New York, 1953.
Kalidasa's *Shakuntala and Other Writings*. Translated by Arthur W. Ryder. New York, 1959.
Kipling, Rudyard. *Kim*. Harmondsworth, 1987.
Rudyard Kipling's Verse: Inclusive Edition, 1885–1918. Garden City, N.Y., 1922.
McDermott, Robert A., and V. S. Naravane, eds. *The Spirit of Modern India*. New York, 1974.
Mehta, Ved. *Face to Face*. Oxford, 1957.
———. *The New India*. New York, 1978.
Miller, Barbara Stoler, ed., trans. *Love Song of the Dark Lord: Jayadeva's Gītagovinda*. New York, 1977.
Miller, Barbara Stoler, Edwin Gerow, and David Gitomer, eds., trans. *Theater of Memory: The Plays of Kalidasa*. New York, 1984.
Naipaul, V. S. *India: A Wounded Civilization*. New York, 1978.
Narayan, R. K. *The Financial Expert*. East Lansing, Mich., 1953.
———. *Swami and Friends*. East Lansing, Mich., 1954.
———. *The Guide*. New York, 1958.
———. *Bachelor of Arts*. Mysore, 1965.
———. *My Days*. New York, 1974.

6: Polity and Foreign Policy

Azad, Maulana Abul Kalem. *India Wins Freedom*. Bombay, 1988.

Bhutto, Benazir. *Daughter of the East*. London, 1988.

Bouton, Marshall M., ed. *India Briefing, 1987*. Boulder, 1987.

Brecher, Michael. *Nehru. A Political Biography*. London, 1959.

Brown, W. Norman. *The United States and India, Pakistan, Bangladesh*. Cambridge, 1972.

Galbraith, John Kenneth. *Ambassador's Journal*. Boston, 1969.

Gandhi, Indira. *My Truth*. Delhi, 1981.

Gandhi, Mohandas K. *An Autobiography: The Story of My Experiments with Truth*. Boston, 1957.

Hutheesing, Krishna (Nehru). *With No Regrets*. London, 1946.

Iyer, Raghavan N. *The Moral and Political Thought of Mahatma Gandhi*. New York, 1973.

Johnson, B. L. C. *Development in South Asia*. Harmondsworth, 1983.

Kalia, Ravi. *Chandigarh: In Search of an Identity*. Carbondale, Ill., 1987.

Kaminsky, Arnold P. *The India Office, 1880–1910*. Westport, Conn., 1986.

Lapierre, Dominique. *City of Joy*. London, 1986.

Mehta, Ved. *The New India*. New York, 1978.

Myrdal, Jan. *India Waits*. Chicago, 1986.

Nayar, Kuldip, and Khushwant Singh, eds. *Tragedy of Punjab: Operation Bluestar & After*. New Delhi, 1984.

Neale, C. *Developing Rural India*. Riverdale, Md., 1988.

Nehru, Jawaharlal. *Toward Freedom*. New York, 1941.

Nehru, Motilal. *The Voice of Freedom*. Edited by K. M. Panikkar and A. Pershad. London, 1961.

Palmer, Norman D. *The Indian Political System*. 2d ed. Boston, 1971.

Pandit, Vijaya Lakshmi. *The Scope of Happiness: A Personal Memoir*. New York, 1979.

Roach, James R., ed. *India 2000: The Next Fifteen Years*. Riverdale, Md., 1986.

Singh, Patwant, and Harji Malik, eds. *Punjab: The Fatal Miscalculation*. New Delhi, 1985.

Wallace, Paul, and Surendra Chopra, eds. *Political Dynamics and Crisis in Punjab*. Amritsar, 1988.

Weiner, Myron. *Sons of the Soil: Migration and Ethnic Conflict in India*. Princeton, 1979.

Wolpert, Stanley. *A New History of India*. 3d ed. New York, 1989.

Ziring, Lawrence, Ralph Braibanti, and W. H. Wriggins, eds. *Pakistan: The Long View*. Durham, N.C., 1977.

Index